THE SKILLFULNESS OF VIRTUE

D0998952

The Skillfulness of Virtue provides a new framework for understanding virtue as a skill, based on psychological research on self-regulation and expertise. Matt Stichter lays the foundations of his argument by bringing together theories of self-regulation and skill acquisition, which he then uses as grounds to discuss virtue development as a process of skill acquisition. This account of virtue as skill has important implications for debates about virtue in both virtue ethics and virtue epistemology. Furthermore, it engages seriously with criticisms of virtue theory that arise in moral psychology, as psychological experiments reveal that there are many obstacles to acting and thinking well, even for those with the best of intentions. Stichter draws on self-regulation strategies and examples of deliberate practice in skill acquisition to show how we can overcome some of these obstacles and become more skillful in our moral and epistemic virtues.

MATT STICHTER is an associate professor of philosophy at the School of Politics, Philosophy, and Public Affairs at Washington State University. He is the author of numerous journal articles and book chapters in ethical theory.

THE SKILLFULNESS OF VIRTUE

Improving Our Moral and Epistemic Lives

MATT STICHTER

Washington State University

CAMBRIDGE
UNIVERSITY PRESS

CAMBRIDGE
UNIVERSITY PRESS

University Printing House, Cambridge CB2 8BS, United Kingdom

One Liberty Plaza, 20th Floor, New York, NY 10006, USA

477 Williamstown Road, Port Melbourne, VIC 3207, Australia

314-321, 3rd Floor, Plot 3, Splendor Forum, Jasola District Centre, New Delhi - 110025, India

79 Anson Road, #06-04/06, Singapore 079906

Cambridge University Press is part of the University of Cambridge.

It furthers the University's mission by disseminating knowledge in the pursuit of education, learning and research at the highest international levels of excellence.

www.cambridge.org
Information on this title: www.cambridge.org/9781108459389
DOI: 10.1017/9781108691970

First published 2018
First paperback edition 2021

A catalogue record for this publication is available from the British Library

ISBN 978-1-108-47237-1 Hardback
ISBN 978-1-108-45938-9 Paperback

Cambridge University Press has no responsibility for the persistence or accuracy of URLs for external or third-party internet websites referred to in this publication, and does not guarantee that any content on such websites is, or will remain, accurate or appropriate.

To my parents, for a lifetime of love and support, for which
I am truly thankful.
To Claudia, for encouraging me to develop my ideas, and
providing invaluable advice along the way.

Contents

Introduction

In the past forty years, the concept of virtue has risen to prominence within ethics, and with that has come a renewed interest in moral development. The reason for the connection between virtue and moral development is that acquiring a virtue is thought to shape a person's thoughts, emotions, intentions, and behavior. That is, coming to possess a virtue is supposed to alter how we perceive and react to situations of moral import, for we are cultivating new habits or dispositions. A similar trend has occurred within epistemology over the last thirty years, with the rise of virtue epistemology. The interest in virtue there has led to a focus on the characteristics that are important for achieving knowledge, understanding, and other epistemic goods.

However, in the past two decades, there has also been much skepticism about what virtue theorists tend to envision that we are acquiring when we acquire a virtue, namely a well-entrenched global character trait. Research from the field of social psychology has cast doubt on the plausibility of acquiring cross-situationally consistent character traits that will lead us to act appropriately across a variety of contexts. Virtue theorists have since been put on the defensive, and this has brought the experimental results of moral psychology to the forefront of discussions of virtue, both for critics and defenders. However, the topic of virtue in general (in contrast to specific applications of it to virtue ethics or virtue epistemology) has always been connected with psychology, because acquiring a virtue is understood as a process of psychological development. So figuring out what virtue is and how to acquire it is then inseparable from views about human psychology and questions about how people can alter patterns of behavior.

This book contributes to virtue theory and the ongoing exchange between philosophers and psychologists by defending the idea that the acquisition of a virtue is a process of acquiring a skill.[1] Expertise in a skill enables us to be reliably responsive to reasons and to act well in demanding situations, and acquiring expertise requires the motivation to hold oneself to high standards – all of which are elements we typically associate with possessing a virtue. This 'virtue as skill' thesis has an ancient pedigree, though it has really only been developed in detail within the last twenty years.[2] The idea originates in ancient Greek discussions of virtue.[3] Aristotle, for example, in his account of virtue frequently invoked comparisons to skills, in an effort to illuminate the process by which virtue would be acquired. In a well-known discussion of virtue, Aristotle claims that:

> we acquire them as a result of prior activities; and this is like the case of the arts, for that which we are to perform by art after learning, we first learn by performing, e.g., we become builders by building and lyre-players by playing the lyre. Similarly, we become just by doing what is just, temperate by doing what is temperate, and brave by doing brave deeds.[4]

Acquiring virtue for Aristotle involves a process of learning by doing, which should be familiar to us from our own experiences of acquiring skills. Learning a skill is a process of acquiring practical knowledge, that is, the knowledge of how to do something, like building a house or driving a car. With virtue, the practical knowledge is the knowledge of how to act well, like acting honestly or kindly. Virtues, like skills, require experience and practice to acquire. You cannot learn how to surf merely by reading a book about it, and likewise, you cannot acquire the virtue of kindness just by reading one of the current books on virtue. You need to learn by doing – to get good at surfing you need to surf, and acquiring kindness requires doing kind acts.

Such structural similarities between virtues and skills have been noted by others in the virtue literature, both in virtue ethics and virtue epistemology, but often it is taken to be merely a helpful analogy. Rarely is it

---

[1] This is to be distinguished from a weaker claim that virtues are merely associated with skills, such that people who have certain virtues tend to have related skills as well (for example, if self-control were merely a skill we would expect a virtuous person to have acquired).

[2] I should note that sometimes I refer to the 'virtue as skill' thesis as the 'skill model of virtue'.

[3] Despite the influence of the ancient Greeks on contemporary discussions of virtue as skill, I will not be giving an historical reconstruction of their views. But for differing perspectives on the virtue as skill thesis in Ancient Greek thought, see Angier, Tom, *Techne in Aristotle's Ethics: Crafting the Moral Life* (New York: Continuum, 2010); Annas, Julia, *Intelligent Virtue* (Oxford: Oxford University Press, 2011); Hutchinson, D.S., "Doctrines of the Mean and the Debate Concerning Skills in Fourth-Century Medicine, Rhetoric, and Ethics," *Apeiron*, 21 (1988), 17–52; Stichter, Matt, "Ethical Expertise," *Ethical Theory and Moral Practice*, 10 (2007), 183–194.

[4] Aristotle, *Nicomachean Ethics* (Grinnell: The Peripatetic Press, 1984), 1103a32–1103b3.

thought that the reason why people find so many similarities is simply because *virtues are skills*, which is the position this book defends. Certainly one of the advantages of the 'virtue as skill' thesis is that given the vast research done on skills and expertise by psychologists, there is no psychological skepticism about the ability of people to acquire skills (in contrast to being able to acquire global character traits). Of course, it will still take the rest of this book to argue that we should not be skeptical of people being able to acquire virtues as skills, but I suspect that some of the resistance to conceiving of virtues as skills is due to an underappreciation of the complexity of skill acquisition and skillful performances.

If the thesis that a virtue is a skill is correct, then it will have a significant impact on our conceptions of virtue development. Determining whether this is plausible requires answering several questions. First, what is the nature of skills and expertise? Second, what characteristics would virtues and the virtuous person have if they are modeled on skills and expertise? Third, do we have evidence that virtue development tracks skill acquisition? There are two related difficulties in answering these questions. First, the comparison of the virtuous person to experts in a skill is what matters most for the 'virtue as skill' thesis. However, although most of us have acquired several skills, few of us have achieved the level of expertise with regard to those skills. Since research shows that those with expertise approach problems in a qualitatively different way than those less skilled, our own experiences may thus mislead us about the nature of skill.

Second, this potential for misleading characterizations of skills and expertise leads to philosophers implicitly working with different conceptions of skills. Furthermore, if there are different conceptions of skills, then there can also be different conceptions of the 'virtue as skill' thesis. Thus, an apparent agreement between philosophers that virtues are skills can mask serious underlying disagreement, if they are operating with fundamentally different conceptions of skills. Progress on this issue will be next to impossible without some general agreement amongst philosophers as to the nature of skills. Furthermore, the usefulness of any comparison of virtues to skills depends upon the accuracy of the account of skills being referenced.

This book addresses these questions by grounding an account of skill in the recent psychological research on self-regulation and expertise, as well as in recent advances in cognitive science. I then explore the philosophical implications of that research for the 'virtue as skill' thesis. While I am constructing a general account of virtue, I tend to focus on cases of moral virtues, given that my primary area of interest and background is in ethics.[5] But I also devote some time to discussing epistemic virtues, especially since there is starting to be more work done in virtue epistemology on the connection between virtues and skills than in virtue ethics.[6] However, I do not attempt to provide a full taxonomy of these categories of virtues, as that requires further empirical work (rather than mere philosophical reflection) to be carried out.

Chapter Outline

The explication of the 'virtue as skill' thesis, and a look at its implications in different fields of virtue theory, is divided into five chapters. Chapter 1 provides an extensive overview of the psychological theories relevant to developing my virtue as skill thesis. Instead of diving straight away into the literature on skills and expertise, I begin with theories of self-regulation. The reason for this is that they provide the foundation for understanding how we set goals and standards for ourselves, along with strategies for reaching those goals and upholding those standards. In order to reach more complicated goals you will often need to acquire skills, as skill development allows us to handle that complexity in stages. The chapter then covers the essential elements of skill acquisition and expert performance, which provides the building blocks for the development of a skill-based account of virtue in the next chapter. In addition, these elements are further explained by reference to 'dual-process' theories in cognitive science. After detailing the process of skill acquisition and expert performance, I then show some of the problems with two prominent philosophical accounts of skill that have been used recently to build skill models of virtue. These two accounts give a very incomplete picture of skillfulness, and are not based in the framework of self-regulation.

Chapter 2 begins the process of building my virtue as skill account, based on the framework from the previous chapter. I say 'begins the process', as this chapter provides the bare bones of the account, which

---

[5] In brief, virtues can be broadly grouped together by the kind of ends at which they aim. So moral virtues aim at moral ends (usually determined in reference to living a flourishing life), epistemic virtues aim at epistemic goods (like truth, knowledge, understanding, etc.), aesthetic virtues aim at securing aesthetic goods like beauty, and prudential virtues are generally useful to securing any kind of good (which could encompass virtues such as courage, patience, or integrity), etc. I will be concerned in this book only with moral, epistemic, and prudential virtues.

[6] This is due to the influence of Ernest Sosa's approach to virtue epistemology, which I discuss in Chapter 3, which likens cognitive performances to skilled performances.

then continues to be fleshed out throughout the rest of the chapters. I begin this chapter with a discussion of self-regulation with respect to moral goals and standards, before moving on to discuss how virtue development can be understood as a process of skill acquisition. I address topics familiar to the virtue literature, such as the role of experience in acquiring moral knowledge, moral judgments being arrived at in an intuitive way, debates as whether we should expect those with virtue to be able to articulate their knowledge, etc. Finally, I begin the work of individuating the moral virtues, as a skill model of virtue will require rethinking some of the traditional virtue categories. As I build this account, I also respond to various objections that have been posed to conceptualizing virtues as skills. Overall my account turns out to have many affinities with a neo-Aristotelian approach to virtue, as neo-Aristotelian accounts of the virtuous person often bear a striking resemblance to descriptions of experts.

Chapter 3 tackles the most prominent objection to virtue as skill, namely that virtues involve an essential element of motivation that is lacking in skill. This objection surfaces both in the context of virtue ethics and virtue epistemology. I try to tease out the core of the objection through a discussion of several cases, before arguing in reply that we can capture concerns about people's motivations even in the context of skill. Given the substantial effort that goes into acquiring skills and expertise, one needs to be strongly motivated to act well in order to improve one's skillfulness. Furthermore, we frequently make evaluations of skilled performers based on their motivations, and in ways that mirror the evaluations we make with virtue. Having established this line of response, I look more in depth at this issue as it arises in virtue epistemology, as it divides the two main camps of virtue epistemologists – reliabilists and responsibilists. I defend a reliabilist account of epistemic virtue as skill from some objections from responsibilists. In so doing, I continue the work of individuating the virtues, both in separating those virtues aimed at achieving moral versus epistemic goals, and also from those prudential virtues that are broadly supportive of the achievement of any kind of goal.

Chapter 4 finally brings out an element of virtue that I think is not found in skill development – practical wisdom. Getting clear, though, on what practical wisdom amounts to is not easy. There are competing conceptions of practical wisdom, which makes it difficult to determine whether practical wisdom has an analogue in expertise, or whether it is unique to virtue. I argue that while several important aspects of practical wisdom are already captured by the notion of expertise, the core idea of being knowledgeable about which ends are worth pursuing is unique to virtue. Practical wisdom requires thinking about your goals and actions relative to an overall conception of what it is to live well as a person, such that you are considering what makes people's lives go better or worse. Acquiring a skill never requires this kind of reflection, but virtue does. However, although I think this kind of reflection involves skillfulness, I express skepticism that the work of practical wisdom can be reduced to the work of a single reflective skill. Nevertheless, I claim that part of the role of practical wisdom in an account of virtue is that it brings some unity to (at least) the moral virtues. I end the chapter with the suggestion that our conception of practical wisdom has to also incorporate reflections on relations of power in society, for there is a need to be aware of the dynamics of power as it shapes our views about what ends are worth pursuing in life.

Chapter 5 address the most significant challenge to emerge recently to virtue theory both in virtue ethics and virtue epistemology – the 'situationist' challenge that arises from experimental results in social psychology. In short, the experiments show that our actions are far more influenced by situational variables than we previously thought, thus throwing into question how much personal characteristics can explain or predict what we do. My account of virtue as skill has the advantage of being able to draw on numerous resources from the framework of self-regulation and skill acquisition to show how we can counter some of these situational influences. In turn, this bolsters the argument for seeing virtue development as requiring the kind of practice and training that goes into skill acquisition. Beyond the situationist critique, I address the troubling moral phenomenon of 'moral disengagement', which receives little to no attention in virtue theory let alone ethical theory more broadly, which is all the more surprising given its substantial negative influence on moral behavior. Disengagement from our moral standards is something that can become a habit, and it can threaten the exercise of any moral virtue. A discussion of the causes of moral disengagement, as well as ways to resist it, highlights the ways that social discourse and power structures can impact the cultivation of virtue and vice.

CHAPTER I

Self-Regulation and Expertise

Virtue theory has been around for about twenty-five hundred years, but in the last twenty-five years the role of virtue has come into serious dispute. Owen Flanagan (1991) was among the first to note that current psychological research was calling the possession of traditional conceptions of virtue into question. This turned into serious skepticism about virtue with Gilbert Harman (1999) and John Doris's (2002) "situationist" critiques on the instantiation of virtue presumed by contemporary virtue ethical theories, due to experimental results in social psychology that seemingly showed moral behavior to often be largely a result of situational variables rather than personality traits or moral reasoning.[1] This initiated a vast new literature within virtue theory, with adherents and opponents scouring the psychological literature to see whether virtue could be given an empirically adequate grounding. The most important realization of this debate has been that for those who are concerned with moral development, as are most virtue theorists, attention must be paid to the psychological research on personality, situational influence, and behavior. Recommendations for moral development cannot be done merely from the philosophical armchair anymore, as theorists need to be aware of the psychological mechanisms that affect how people actually behave. This idea is neatly summarized by Flanagan's "Principle of Minimal Psychological Realism," which states that any prescription of a moral ideal should involve only those processes or behaviors that we have reason to believe are possible for humans.

In recognition of the importance of this principle, this chapter provides an overview of the general psychological mechanisms underlying human agency in the form of self-regulation, and the more specific mechanisms involved with skill acquisition, before I move on in the following chapters

---

[1] Also, this critique has been recently extended to virtue theory in other areas of philosophy, such as virtue epistemology. I will take up this issue at length in Chapter 5.

to explore how we might reconceive of virtue given the psychological mechanisms for improving our behavior that we know are available to us. In the process of summarizing these various mechanisms, I will also be synthesizing numerous psychological theories that are usually discussed in isolation from each other, in order to provide a broader psychological framework.[2] I caution the reader that there is a fair amount of ground to cover before I start discussing the philosophical implications of this research, but it will prove important to present an overall framework at the outset.

I begin with social cognitive theories of human agency, which understand the exercise of agency primarily in terms of self-regulation. In understanding self-regulation, I divide the discussion into two sections that explain the connected activities of goal setting and goal striving. This will provide a starting foundation for understanding skill acquisition more specifically, as skill acquisition is a complex form of self-regulation. The next two sections discuss key elements in skill acquisition. The first covers the role of deliberate practice in improving one's level of skillfulness, while the second draws on dual-process theories of cognition to explain how, in practicing, we can make initially effortful tasks in skilled performance become effortless. In the two sections that follow, I discuss important aspects of the knowledge that people gain when acquiring a skill, first in terms of schemas and mental models, and second in terms of the limitations in articulating and codifying that skillful knowledge.

Finally, having presented the overall framework, I am then in a position to critique the two main philosophical accounts of expertise that appear in the virtue as skill literature. The work of both Julia Annas and Hubert Dreyfus have made significant contributions to the 'virtue as skill' thesis. However, each has also made some unwarranted assumptions about skills and expertise, and neither of their accounts is grounded in an understanding of self-regulation more broadly.

Self-Regulation: Goal Setting

According to social cognitive theories of agency, human functioning is the result of a triadic interaction between the environment, the intrapersonal

---

[2] While my goal is not to provide new psychological theories for either self-regulation or skill, as the main aim of this chapter is to provide an accurate and in-depth account of skill to provide the foundation for virtue as a skill in the next chapter, nevertheless the integration of these psychological theories is new.

(cognitive and affective) features of a person, and the behavior of that person.[3] First, human behavior is not a product solely of one's intrapersonal features, independent of the environment in which one acts. Second, behavior is also not a product solely of one's environment. Instead, behavior is the result of the interaction between the environment and the person, where it matters how someone construes their situation in determining their response to it. Third, behavior is not merely a passive by-product of the interaction between environment and person, as behavior can lead to changes in both environmental and intrapersonal factors. The current social environment, for example, is the product of previous human behavior, as is the current natural environment, say, with respect to global climate change. With regard to one's own intrapersonal features, behaving in a way that successfully achieves a goal, for example, is likely to produce a feeling of self-satisfaction, and encourages the actions that brought about the achievement. Failure, on the other hand, often prompts feelings of disappointment, which could go along with either thinking about how to do better in the future or giving up on the goal altogether.

As another kind of example of this triadic relationship, you can also take steps to mediate the potentially negative effects that an external environment or your own intrapersonal features may be having on your behavior. If you are trying to study in a noisy environment, you may not be able to stop that noise from distracting you from focusing on your studies. In response, you can try to block out the noise via headphones, or move to some quieter location, in effect changing the environment so that you can effectively study.[4] With regard to our own intrapersonal features, if a

---

[3] Virtue theorists may already be familiar with some aspects of social cognitive theory through the work of Mischel and Shoda, which Daniel Russell and Nancy Snow have recently incorporated into their accounts of virtue. Bandura's work on social cognitive theory is both earlier and broader than Mischel and Shoda's work that followed on the cognitive-affective personality system (where they basically go into more detail on the personality aspect of the triad). However, it should also be noted that their approach has been critiqued as being unable to account for some broad personality regularities, such as the Big Five personality traits (DeYoung and Weisberg), as well as being unable to account for virtues (Miller). See Mischel, W. and Shoda, Y., "A Cognitive-Affective System Theory of Personality: Reconceptualizing Situations, Dispositions, Dynamics, and Invariance in Personality Structure," *Psychological Review*, 102: (1995), 246–268; Russell, Daniel C., *Practical Intelligence and the Virtues* (New York: Oxford University Press, 2009); Snow, Nancy E., *Virtue as Social Intelligence: An Empirically Grounded Theory* (New York: Routledge, 2010); DeYoung, Colin G. and Weisberg, Yanna J., "Cybernetic Approaches to Personality and Social Behavior," in Snyder, M. and Deaux, K. (eds.), *Oxford Handbook of Personality and Social Psychology*, Second Edition, in press (New York: Oxford University Press); Miller, Christian, *Character and Moral Psychology* (Oxford: Oxford University Press, 2014).

[4] Zimmerman gives an example of a golfer having trouble with her swing because the sun is blinding her. By putting on sunglasses, she is changing the effect her current environment has on her, and this will enable her to have a better swing. Zimmerman, Barry J., "Development and Adaptation of

basketball player feels that she is in a high-pressure situation, it may produce internal stress that negatively affects her behavior – 'choking'. She can then attempt to change her construal of the situation, thinking about just playing well in general and not obsessing about the details of a maneuver, so that it prompts different behavior. Because of the interactive framework, in order to pursue our goals, we may first need to alter our intrapersonal processes or the environment, before we can act effectively.

Social cognitive theory locates agency in our attempts to self-regulate, where self-regulation is a matter of having a goal that one is trying to achieve. Control theory, or cybernetics, has long studied the processes involved with goal-oriented systems, both in machines and in animals. The basic stages to any form of regulation involve having: (1) a goal (or desired state of affairs); (2) a representation of the current state affairs; (3) a way to compare (1) and (2) to see if the goal is currently being met; and (4) if the goal is not being met, an action available within the system that can change the current state of affairs to meet the goal (and the system must then go through stages [2] and [3] again in order to know when the goal has been achieved).[5] A simple example of this is a thermostat that is set to keep a room at a minimum level of warmth. The thermostat has: (1) a set temperature goal; (2) a way to check the current status of the ambient temperature; and (3) the ability to compare the goal temperature with the current temperature. What it does in response to the comparison depends on whether there is a discrepancy between the goal and current temperatures. If there is no discrepancy, it does nothing. If instead the status of the temperature is below the goal, then the thermostat has (4) a method for triggering the heater to turn on. Furthermore, the thermostat keeps checking the current temperature, so that it can turn off the heater when the goal temperature is reached.

Of course, that is just the most basic picture of a goal-directed system, and more complex systems will add additional layers of processes to this initial picture. For example, if the system has multiple means of achieving the goal, then there needs to be an additional process for selecting a particular means. In addition, if a system has multiple goals, and a situation affords opportunities to pursue multiple mutually exclusive goals,

Expertise: The Role of Self-Regulatory Processes and Beliefs," in Ericsson, K. Anders (ed.), *The Cambridge Handbook of Expertise and Expert Performance* (Cambridge: Cambridge University Press, 2006), 705–722.
[5] It is important to note that these stages need not be strictly speaking sequential, as these processes might be going on in parallel. DeYoung, Colin G., "Cybernetic Big Five Theory," *Journal of Research in Personality*, 56 (2015), 33–58.

then there needs to be a process for selecting which goal will be pursued on that occasion. Furthermore, when thinking of humans, we also need to account for additional processes of coming up with new goals, as well as new strategies for achieving preexisting goals.

The basic model of control is just one of discrepancy reduction between the goal and the existing state of affairs (e.g. the thermometer reducing the discrepancy in temperature), but in giving ourselves goals to strive for, we instead produce new discrepancies between the current state of affairs and what we desire them to be.[6] In other words, thermometers do not get bored, but people do. Boredom and, more positively, curiosity seem to motivate the adoption of new goals.[7] Finally, when there is a discrepancy between a goal state and the existing state of affairs, we can also choose to give up the goal instead of continually trying to achieve it (unlike the case of the thermometer), thus involving another set of processes.

Given the complexity of human behavior, I will be touching on all of the aforementioned aspects of goal-directed behavior at various times throughout the book. However, it is well beyond the scope of this book to try to provide a comprehensive view of all the possible processes and factors that bear on self-regulation. So, I will be focusing instead on those processes that are most relevant to understanding humans pursuing important goals related to skill acquisition, as well as internalized moral and epistemic norms as goals. To handle the overall complexity, it helps to divide self-regulation into the related activities of setting goals and striving to reach them.[8]

Self-regulation begins with commitment to a goal, which implies adopting a certain standard of behavior by which one judges oneself. With humans, unlike the thermometer, this also has an affective dimension, as Albert Bandura relates:

> The self-regulatory control is achieved by creating incentives for one's own actions and by anticipative affective reactions to one's own behavior

[6] Bandura, Albert, "Self-Regulation of Motivation and Action through Internal Standards and Goal Systems," in Pervin, Lawrence A. (ed.), *Goal Concepts in Personality and Social Psychology* (London: Lawrence Erlbaum Associates, 1989), 19–85, 38.

[7] Haase, Claudia Maria, Poulin, Michael, and Heckhausen, Jutta, "Engagement and Disengagement across the Life Span: An Analysis of Two-Process Models of Developmental Regulation," in Greve, W., Rothermund, K., and Wentura, D. (eds.), *The Adaptive Self: Personal Continuity and Intentional Self-Development* (New York: Hogrefe, 2005), 117–135.

[8] This is adapted from the Rubicon model of action phases, a more specific theory regarding goal-oriented behavior in humans. Gollwitzer, Peter M., "Action Phases and Mind-Sets," in Higgins, E. Tory and Sorrentino, Richard M. (eds.), *Motivation and Cognition: Foundations of Social Behavior*, Vol. 2 (New York: The Guilford Press, 1990), 53–92.

depending on how it measures up to personal standards. Thus, people pursue courses of action that give them self-satisfaction and a sense of self-worth, but they refrain from behaving in ways that result in self-censure.[9]

Achieving a goal is of course a source of self-satisfaction, while failing to do so can lead to self-censure. Furthermore, the strength of the self-reaction, in terms of the motivation it provides for self-regulation, depends on how the goal is valued. Goals that are highly valued by a person provide more self-satisfaction from achievement, and likewise more self-censure from failing to achieve them, than goals that are only minimally valued. A highly valued goal will make you feel really bad for violating it or really good for conforming to it.[10] So motivations arise from self-evaluative reactions (anticipated feelings of self-satisfaction or self-censure), the strength of which depends on the degree of value placed on the goal.

The value that a goal has, however, is not the only factor to affect motivation. The above assumes a situation where the person believes that the desired outcome can be achieved, or the undesirable outcome can be avoided, by acting. If instead someone believes that she is not capable of achieving the desired outcome, she will have little motivation to self-regulate. The term "perceived self-efficacy" refers to people's beliefs about what they are capable of achieving, and self-efficacy beliefs can strengthen or undermine one's motivation to engage in self-regulation. As Bandura points out, "[a]mong the self-referent thoughts that influence human motivation, affect and action, none is more central or pervasive than people's judgments of the personal efficacy ... Unless people believe that they can produce desired results by their actions, they have little incentive to act or to persevere in the face of difficulties."[11] Both goal setting and striving are affected by these self-efficacy beliefs.

Psychologists have also shown that our goals are hierarchically organized, as a highly valued (or superordinate) goal gives rise to more context-specific subsidiary (or subordinate) goals. As Carver and Scheier point out,

---

[9] Bandura, Albert, "Social Cogntive Theory of Personality," in Pervin, Lawrence A. and John, Oliver P. (eds.), *Handbook of Personality: Theory and Research* (New York: The Guilford Press, 1990), 154–196.

[10] Though as will be pointed out in Chapter 5, there can be failures of monitoring that circumvent this self-sanctioning process – with respect to moral standards, this is referred to as "moral disengagement."

[11] Bandura, Albert, "Social Cognitive Theory of Personality," in Pervin, Lawrence A. and John, Oliver P. (eds.), *Handbook of Personality: Theory and Research* (New York: The Guilford Press, 1999), 154–196, 180–181.

In a hierarchical organization of feedback systems, the output of a high-level system consists of the resetting of reference values at the next-lower level of abstraction. To put it differently, higher order systems "behave" by providing goals to the systems just below them. The reference values are more concrete and restricted as one moves from higher to lower levels. Each level regulates a quality that contributes to (though not entirely defining) the quality controlled at the next-higher level. Each level monitors input at the level of abstraction of its own functioning, and each level adjusts output to minimize its discrepancies.[12]

Take, for example, the traditional New Year's resolution of 'getting fit' or 'being healthy'. A goal like that is fairly abstract and vague. How will you know when you have reached your goal? It would help to break that abstract goal into more concrete goals – like 'eat less' and 'exercise more' – each of which could contribute to better health and fitness (even though they do not entirely define what it means to be healthy or fit). Subgoals like these can provide better benchmarks by which to measure your progress towards more distant superordinate goals. But these subgoals can also benefit from more specificity.[13] To eat less you could adopt a specific diet plan, and to exercise more you could take fitness classes (though there might be other ways to achieve those goals), and so on.[14] Goals like these might be ongoing, while other more specific goals might be something you only need to do once (e.g. joining a gym that offers fitness classes). So, the goal hierarchy might look like this:

- Superordinate goal (be fit)
  - Subgoal 1 (exercise more)
    - Subgoal 2 (take fitness classes)
      - Subgoal 3 (join gym)

This hierarchical structure is due in part to the fact that a goal can usually be achieved by a variety of different strategies, and so choosing to go about achieving a goal with a particular strategy produces a lower-level

---

[12] Carver, Charles S. and Scheier, Michael F., "Self-Regulatory Perspectives on Personality," in Millon, Theodore and Lerner, Melvin J. (eds.), *Handbook of Psychology, Vol. 5: Personality and Social Psychology* (Hoboken, NJ: John Wiley & Sons, Inc., 2003), 185–208, 189.

[13] Bandura, Albert, "Self-Regulation of Motivation through Anticipatory and Self-Reactive Mechanisms," in Dienstbier, R. A. (ed.), *Perspectives on Motivation: Nebraska Symposium on Motivation*, Vol. 38 (Lincoln: University of Nebraska Press, 1991), 69–164, 102.

[14] Similarly, having more specific strategies to achieve the goal (like restricting oneself from eating during specific times of the day), will make it easier to self-regulate than vague strategies (like 'snack less often'). See Gollwitzer, Peter. M., "Implementation Intentions: Strong Effects of Simple Plans," *American Psychologist*, 54 (1999), 493–503. I will discuss implementation intentions in more depth in this and later chapters.

goal that is more specific about how the higher-level goal is to be achieved.
As Angela Duckworth puts it: "Lower-order goals are more numerous,
context specific, short-term, and substitutable, whereas higher-order goals
are typically fewer in number, more abstract, more enduring, and more
important to the individual."[15] The higher-order goals represent the goals
that are most intrinsically valued, and those most tied to our sense of self.
These are goals we do not give up lightly.[16] Contrast that to lower level
goals, which can be given up more easily. For example, if you find that
your normal route home from work is blocked by construction, you can
easily substitute that with another route. Presumably, getting home by a
particular route will not be strongly tied to your identity.

The relationship between the differing levels of the goals need not be
merely means-end reasoning, though, as sometimes the lower order goals
provide the constitutive elements of a higher order goal.[17] Or sometimes a
goal involves multiple contextual elements, such that those goals need
a more concrete specification of what it means to achieve that goal in a
particular context. For example, the goal of firefighting does not involve just
the extinguishing of the fire, as firefighters have to be concerned about
saving lives threatened by the fire, as well as trying to avoid extensive
property damage. So in any particular context of a fire, firefighters need to
have a more concrete idea of what the goal ought to be of their practice (say
by prioritizing the innocent lives first, and containing the fire second).[18]
Once you know what goal you are trying to achieve here and now, then you
need to figure out a particular strategy for trying to achieve it.

Self-Regulation: Goal Striving

Switching from the setting of a specific goal into striving to achieve it, takes
us from the vertical hierarchy of goal organization into a horizontal (or
temporal) perspective on action, which is represented by the Rubicon

---

[15] Duckworth, Angela and Gross, James J., "Self-Control and Grit: Related but Separable Determinants of Success," *Current Directions in Psychological Science*, 23:5 (2014), 319–325, 321.
[16] These are sometimes referred to as 'protected values'. Tanner, Carmen and Medin, Douglas L., "Protected Values: No Omission Bias and No Framing Effects," *Psychonomic Bulletin & Review*, 11:1 (2004), 185–191. There will be further discussion of this in Chapter 5.
[17] In fact, this is how many virtue theorists view the relationship between virtues and living well. Virtues are not merely means to the end of living well, but rather the virtues are constitutive of what it is to live well.
[18] This is also a relationship that is supposed to apply to virtue. You may have a goal of being honest, but you also need a specification of what honesty requires of you in this particular context (where what is required of you varies from one context to the next). Swartwood, Jason, "Wisdom as an Expert Skill," *Ethical Theory and Moral Practice*, 16 (2013), 511–528.

model of action phases.[19] Action phase theory separates goal setting and striving into four distinct phases: (1) choosing a goal to commit to; (2) planning how to achieve the goal; (3) taking action to implement the plan; and (4) evaluating the action in the light of the goal commitment.[20] The first phase involves what was discussed in the preceding paragraphs regarding the vertical hierarchical organization of goals, and it is the second phase which begins the horizontal (or temporal) movement towards achieving one of those goals.[21] On this model, a distinction is made between motivation (goal setting) and volition (goal striving). The reason for this distinction is that deciding whether to commit to a goal in the first place, or later whether to maintain commitment to that goal, requires a different kind of mindset from the activities associated with striving to achieve a goal (planning and acting).[22] In short, in phases of motivation you are undecided about your goal commitments, whereas phases of volition assume a decided goal commitment that you are now trying to realize.

[19] Achtziger, A., and Gollwitzer, Peter, M., "Motivation and Volition in the Course of Action," in Heckhausen, Jutta and Heckhausen, H. (eds.), *Motivation and Action* (New York: Cambridge University Press, 2007), 202–226; Heckhausen, Jutta, "The Motivation–Volition Divide and Its Resolution in Action-Phase Models of Developmental Regulation," *Research in Human Development*, 4:3–4 (2007), 163–180.

[20] While there is overlap here with the four fundamental stages in control/cybernetic theory discussed earlier, the action phases do not map on to those stages directly, in part because the Rubicon model is more specific in its focus than cybernetics. Action phases 1 and 2 represent having a goal and a means for achieving it, which any self-regulating system needs, though in cybernetics it is not required that the goal-oriented system deliberate about what goals to adopt or how to achieve them, as they may be fixed via programming in machines (e.g. the thermostat) or by instinct in living organisms. So, action phases 1 and 2 are more specific to processes of deliberating about ends and means. Though it should also be noted that the Rubicon model is not dealing directly with the processes by which one selects a specific goal to pursue among the many that a particular situation might afford, or for selecting amongst multiple means for achieving that goal. However, as will be detailed below, how strongly one commits to a goal and how detailed one's plans are for achieving the goal are both factors that influence which specific goal and means will be selected in a particular situation.

[21] It might be difficult to distinguish the relationship of superordinate–subordinate goal (vertically organized) from that of acting to achieve a subordinate goal (horizontally organized), as they can both admit of a means-end relationship (though again some of the relationships between goals are constitutive rather than instrumental). Subgoals are basically stages on the path to the superordinate goal, each of which requires figuring out how you are going to achieve it before you are in a position to start implementing a plan to achieve the next higher-ordered goal. So, you can think of the horizontal movement depicted by the action phase model as the steps one takes to achieve one of the subgoals, and part of the fourth phase is an evaluation of whether it is time to move on to tackling a higher-ordered goal.

[22] The two mindsets are usually referred to as 'deliberative' for motivation phases and 'implemental' for volition phases. I prefer, however, not to use this nomenclature at least for the 'deliberative' mindset, as it might suggest that conscious deliberation does not take place in the volitional phases – which would be untrue. It also evokes dual-processing theories of cognition, which often contrast 'deliberative' with 'automatic' processes, but that distinction does not map onto the difference in the two mindsets (as both types of cognitive processes can play a part in each mindset). I prefer to contrast the mindsets as 'commitment' versus 'implementation'.

1	2	3	4
Motivation Pre-decision	**Volition** Pre-action	**Volition** Action	**Motivation** Post-action
Deciding on a goal →	Planning how to achieve goal →	Acting to achieve goal →	Evaluating the action[23]

In the first phase, you are trying to decide what goals to set for yourself. It is a phase that involves "carefully weighing alternative goal intentions and deliberating the pros and cons regarding the goal's incentives (attractiveness of the activity itself, the outcome aimed for, and the consequences of the outcome) and expectancies about attaining those."[24] These two considerations are often referred to as 'desirability' and 'feasibility'. 'Desirability' can be thought of in terms of reflecting on why you might want to commit yourself to a goal, by thinking about what is valuable about achieving it. By contrast, 'feasibility' requires you to think about how likely it is that you can achieve that goal. Both considerations matter, though sufficient desirability can outweigh significant difficulties in feasibility, like for those setting out to become an Olympic athlete. Importantly, considerations of feasibility are affected by one's self-efficacy beliefs. As Bandura argues, "there are many activities that, if done well, produce valued outcomes, but they are not pursued by people who doubt they can do what it takes to succeed. Such exclusions of large classes of options are made rapidly on efficacy grounds with little thought of costs and

---

[23] Zimmerman claims that self-regulation takes place during three cyclical phases: forethought (before acting); performance control (while acting); and self-reflection (after acting). This maps onto phases 2–4 in action phase theory. For example, in forethought, one strategizes how to achieve some desired outcome. This is often done in terms of 'if-then' plans (or implementation intentions), figuring out in advance what you plan to do if you find yourself in a particular situation. While performing, you execute those strategies, perhaps even modifying them while acting. Following this, self-reflection allows one to evaluate the performance as to whether the desired outcome was achieved. This in turn can influence the next process of forethought (assuming the goal has not been fully achieved), and so can form a cyclical feedback system. However, this approach simply assumes a goal commitment already in place, so it misses distinctions within the initial phase 1 of goal setting, as well as the extent to which evaluations in phase 4 represent a different mindset from phases 2 and 3, for such evaluations might lead you to change your goal commitments. Zimmerman, Barry J., "Attaining Self-Regulation: A Social Cognitive Perspective," in Boekaerts, Monique, Pintrich, Paul R., and Zeidner, Moshe (eds.), *Handbook of Self-Regulation* (San Diego: Academic Press, 2000), 13–39, 16.

[24] Heckhausen, Jutta, "The Motivation–Volition Divide and Its Resolution in Action-Phase Models of Developmental Regulation," *Research in Human Development*, 4:3–4 (2007), 163–180, 166–167.

benefits."[25] One demonstrated strategy for improving decisions in this phase, which takes into account these considerations of desirability and feasibility, is 'mental contrasting':

> the strategy of mental contrasting entails conjoint mental elaboration of the desired future and the present reality, thereby making both simultaneously accessible and creating strong associations between them. In mental contrasting, the positive future is elaborated first, and the negative reality is framed as 'standing in the way' of realizing the positive future. The simultaneous activation of the desired future and present reality emphasises the necessity for action.[26]

This strategy works better with respect to eventual goal attainment than just focusing on either the positive future or the present obstacle, as it prevents one from being overly optimistic or pessimistic when considering the possible goal. It combines both the elements of desirability of the future goal, and feasibility in terms of what is the main obstacle to overcome. Ultimately phase 1 culminates in a commitment to realize a goal.[27]

Once you have committed yourself to realizing a goal, it is time to start figuring out how you are going to realize it, and this transitions from goal setting (motivation) to goal striving (volition). Phase 2 is

---

[25] Bandura, Albert, "Social Cognitive Theory of Personality," in Pervin, Lawrence A. and John, Oliver P. (eds.), *Handbook of Personality: Theory and Research* (New York: The Guilford Press, 1999), 154–196, 182.

[26] Duckworth, Angela Lee, Grant, Heidi, Loew, Benjamin, Oettingen, Gabriele, and Gollwitzer, Peter M., "Self-Regulation Strategies Improve Self-Discipline in Adolescents: Benefits of Mental Contrasting and Implementation Intentions," *Educational Psychology*, 31:1 (2010), 17–26, 18. Also, as I will note in the discussion of the second phase, this strategy works even better if combined with the strategy of 'implementation intentions' in the planning phase.

[27] It is worth highlighting Gollwitzer's claim that the:

> model of action phases does not ignore the fact that goal striving is hierarchically organized. This is most evident in the model's distinction between goal intentions and behavioral intentions. Behavioral intentions are supplements to goal intentions and serve to promote the implementation of goal intentions. Accordingly, the formation of a goal intention precedes the formation of behavioral intentions, and the latter are justified by the former. But not all of the intentions formed subordinately to some goal intention must be behavioral intentions. People frequently form goal intentions in the service of other (superordinate) goal intentions (e.g., when a person who has decided to become a psychologist makes up his or her mind to go to school abroad). In this case, the formation of the subordinate goal (i.e. going to school abroad) should be preceded by a concern not only for the feasibility of this goal, but also for its desirability.

Gollwitzer, Peter M., "Action Phases and Mind-Sets," in Higgins, E. Tory and Sorrentino, Richard M. (eds.), *Motivation and Cognition: Foundations of Social Behavior*, Vol. 2 (New York: The Guilford Press, 1990), 53–92, 61.

essentially a planning phase. Bandura notes this connection in self-regulation, stating that:

> people motivate themselves and guide their actions anticipatorily through the exercise of forethought. They anticipate likely outcomes of prospective actions, they set goals for themselves, and they plan courses of action designed to realize valued futures ... by cognitive representation in the present, conceived future events are converted into current motivators and regulators of behavior.[28]

Committing yourself to a goal in phase 1, with considerations of desirability and feasibility, is part of this process of forethought. It motivates the next phase of forethought in planning what steps to take to achieve that goal. So, in phase 2 you are likely trying to figure out what needs to be done, how you are going to do it, when and where you will take action, etc.

However, it is also common for people to spend little time on this phase, as they might think that committing themselves to a concrete goal, like 'snacking less often', is a specific enough intention to effectively act on. But a far more effective route to planning your goals is through the use of implementation intentions, which differ from the kinds of intentions we have when we decide to commit ourselves to goals (i.e. goal setting). Gollwitzer has been at the forefront of this research, and he explains the difference as follows:

> In contrast to goal intentions, implementation intentions specify a plan on the when, where, and how of acting on one's goal intentions. Implementation intentions are subordinate to goal intentions and have the format of "If situation x arises, then I will perform goal-directed behavior y!", thus linking an anticipated opportunity to a select goal-directed response. By forming implementation intentions, people plan out in advance (i.e. pre-select) which situations and behaviors they intend to use to achieve their goals (goal intentions).[29]

Basically, an implementation intention has an 'if-then' structure – if this situation arises, then I will respond in this particular way (in order to achieve the goal I have committed myself to). Perhaps this sounds rather obvious as a strategy to realize one's goals, but people frequently do not

[28] Bandura, Albert, "Self-Regulation of Motivation and Action through Internal Standards and Goal Systems," in Pervin, Lawrence A. (ed.), *Goal Concepts in Personality and Social Psychology* (London: Lawrence Erlbaum Associates, 1989), 19–85, 19.
[29] Trötschel, Roman and Gollwitzer, Peter M., "Implementation Intentions and the Willful Pursuit of Prosocial Goals in Negotiations," *Journal of Experimental Social Psychology*, 43 (2007), 579–598, 581.

form detailed implementation intentions at all and rely instead on having just a somewhat specific goal intention (e.g. I am going to snack less than I do now). Furthermore, there is significant evidence that forming a mere goal intention has a low correlation with actually acting on that intention.[30] Numerous studies have shown, however, that forming implementation intentions that detail when, where, and how a behavior will be performed significantly increase goal attainment.[31] For example, to achieve the goal of snacking less often, you might form the intention 'if I find myself filling up my plate at a buffet line in a restaurant, I will choose fruit instead of cake for dessert'. Forming such intentions requires you to anticipate the kinds of situations that might provide opportunities to advance your goal and decide on a course of action to take in response.

One of the reasons forming an implementation intention is beneficial is that it gives you direction as to what kind of situations you want to seek out, or avoid, in order to be in the best position to achieve your goal. Another advantage is that in having decided in advance of how you will respond to a particular situation, when that situation arises the effect of having made an implementation intention is that it automatically cues up the planned response, because you have formed a mental association between being in that situation and behaving in a particular way. Even better is combining implementation intentions with mental contrasting.[32] Since in mental contrasting you already identify a concrete obstacle to realizing your goal, you can then move in the planning phase to form implementation intentions regarding how you will overcome that obstacle.[33] So while people engage in some forethought during these initial two phases, mental contrasting and implementation intentions are examples of how you can do that well.

---

[30] Webb, Thomas L. and Sheeran, Paschal, "Does Changing Behavioral Intentions Engender Behavior Change? A Meta-Analysis of the Experimental Evidence," *Psychological Bulletin*, 132:2 (2006), 249–268.

[31] Trötschel, Roman and Gollwitzer, Peter M., "Implementation Intentions and the Willful Pursuit of Prosocial Goals in Negotiations," *Journal of Experimental Social Psychology*, 43 (2007), 579–598.

[32] Duckworth, Angela Lee, Grant, Heidi, Loew, Benjamin, Oettingen, Gabriele, and Gollwitzer, Peter M., "Self-Regulation Strategies Improve Self-Discipline in Adolescents: Benefits of Mental Contrasting and Implementation Intentions," *Educational Psychology*, 31:1 (2010), 17–26.

[33] This of course does not guarantee that you will act on that goal intention or with that particular method of implementing the goal when faced with that situation, but it does greatly increase the chances of both of those things happening. It is in this respect that what you do in phase 1 and 2 can have an influence on what specific goal and means you end up selecting in a particular situation – though of course there are other factors that influence the selection process as well (which is what the 'situationist' critique has highlighted, as I will cover in Chapter 5).

Once you are done with planning, the next phase is action. Phase 3 is where you can implement your plan and take action to achieve your goal. In this phase, "information processing should be narrowly focused on the action required to reach the goal and situational cues to prompt such action while blocking out any distractions or conflicts with other goal commitments."[34] If you have formed implementation intentions, then it will be easier to recognize the situational cues, and to block out other distractions.

But in this otherwise straightforward phase, you also have to deal with potential conflicts with other goal commitments that you have. Situations can afford opportunities to advance more than one of our goals, but often it will be the case that promotion of one goal requires bypassing opportunities to pursue another goal. Take, for example, the classic student dilemma between spending an evening studying and spending it partying. It is a conflict between two possible courses of action which serve different goals and is an occasion for exercising self-control to successfully resolve the conflict. The need for self-control stems frequently from a conflict like this between more highly valued goals and less valued goals, where the less valued goal is more appealing in the moment and perhaps more easily satisfied.[35] This can be due to more highly valued goals being abstract or whose realization would occur much further in the future (e.g. partying is fun now, while doing well in college or in a career might be still years off). Self-control is needed to maintain commitment to the more highly valued goal that you were originally trying to realize.[36]

Once you have taken an action to further a goal, it is time to reflect back on the action taken in the light of your goal commitment. In phase 4, you switch back to a mindset concerned with goal setting and motivation, as you will be asking questions regarding whether to maintain your goal commitment, based on whether you achieved it or not.[37] For example, if

---

[34] Heckhausen, Jutta, "The Motivation–Volition Divide and Its Resolution in Action-Phase Models of Developmental Regulation," *Research in Human Development*, 4:3–4 (2007), 163–180, 167.

[35] Note that this is a conflict between different goal hierarchies. It is not a conflict within a superordinate-subgoal hierarchy as outlined earlier in this chapter, as all the subgoals are constitutive of, or a means to, the superordinate goal – and thus do not generate this kind of conflict (though a poorly chosen means to an end might produce a result at odds with what one had as a goal).

[36] It is worth noting that self-control challenges are 'volitional' and not 'motivational' – as one is conflicted between multiple goals that one has already committed to, and thus it is a challenge to goal realization. See Duckworth, Angela and Gross, James J., "Self-Control and Grit: Related but Separable Determinants of Success," *Current Directions in Psychological Science*, 23:5 (2014), 319–325.

[37] This is of course a more complex process than with the feedback process of the thermometer, as the thermometer has only one fixed goal and so it keeps acting until the discrepancy in temperature is

your goal was achieved and was a low level subgoal (like getting a gym membership in order to exercise more frequently), then it may be appropriate to dismiss that subgoal so that you can focus on the next higher goal (like taking the fitness classes offered there). Or your goal may be more enduring and success at achieving it once will prompt you to maintain commitment to it (if you take a fitness class and like it, then you maintain your commitment to coming to class).

Part of what you are also assessing here is whether achieving your goal had the outcome you hoped. You might find that achieving your goal did not have the value or meaning you expected, in which case you might end up dismissing the goal commitment (like pursuing a major in college only to find out that you do not really find that discipline interesting after all). Concerns about 'desirability', which were present in the first stage, reappear here. On the other hand, if you find that you did not accomplish your goal, then your concerns are also going to include 'feasibility', as you have to assess whether you could do things differently to accomplish your goal in the future. Bandura highlights that it "is partly on the basis of self-beliefs of efficacy that people choose what challenges to undertake, how much effort to expend in the endeavor, how long to persevere in the face of difficulties, and affect their vulnerability to stress and despondency in the face of difficulties and failures."[38] If the goal seems too frustrating to achieve, you might cease your commitment to it entirely. But even if it is difficult to achieve, a really desirable goal can prompt you to maintain your commitment and renew your efforts at realizing it. While this phase certainly has potential implications for future planning (i.e. goal striving), as success supports taking the same strategy in the future while failure will require some re-planning, what is primary in this phase is a concern about motivation and goal setting, as having taken action to implement your goal provides you with new information to consider with respect to what goals you have set for yourself (both in terms of feedback on the desirability and feasibility of your goal).

The distinction between motivation and volition in the action phase model also shows up when discussing two different ways in which one might have to prevent highly valued goals from being sidetracked. As mentioned previously, in acting (phase 3), one might have to exert self-control

---

eliminated. There is no process for it to change its strategy for achieving this goal, to give up on this goal entirely, or to adopt a new goal.

[38] Bandura, Albert, "Self-Regulation of Motivation and Action through Internal Standards and Goal Systems," in Pervin, Lawrence A. (ed.), *Goal Concepts in Personality and Social Psychology* (London: Lawrence Erlbaum Associates, 1989), 19–85, 29.

to keep oneself from acting to further an overall less valued goal instead (because of short-term gratification). But in evaluating one's action (phase 4), there is a different danger of losing your commitment to a superordinate goal if you find achieving one of the subgoals too difficult. Angela Duckworth's distinction between self-control and grit can be understood in terms of the different challenges involved with phase 3 (volition) and phase 4 (motivation).[39] Both grit and self-control are ways in which we protect high level goals, but they do so with respect to different time frames. Whereas self-control is employed in the moment to resist some temptation to act in a way that prevents you from acting on a more highly valued goal, grit is a characteristic addressed to long-term commitment to goals that are highly valued. Grit refers both to the passion and determination with which one remains committed to long-term goals, over long periods of time and despite setbacks. So those with grit are more likely:

> when faced with setbacks, to find a way forward by "sprouting" new lower-order goals (or actions) when a current lower-order goal (or action) is blocked. For instance, if a grant proposal or manuscript is rejected, tears may be shed, but soon enough another funder or journal outlet is identified and pursued. In other words, in a gritty individual's domain of passionate interest, goals or actions deemed unfeasible are met with the response of an active search for—or even invention of—viable alternatives.[40]

Grit is a matter of whether one maintains commitment to a superordinate goal when it becomes difficult to achieve it, such that one might abandon it altogether to pursue some other superordinate goal. Thus, in evaluating your action (phase 4), if you did not meet your subgoal, you may: (1) decide that there is another means for achieving it and renew your commitment to that subgoal (and by extension to the superordinate goal it serves); (2) decide that one should drop commitment to this subgoal, but replace it with another subgoal that also supports the superordinate goal; or (3) drop your commitment to the superordinate goal altogether, and find some alternative superordinate goal to pursue. Those with higher levels of grit are more likely to end up finding alternative ways to pursue their superordinate goal (options (1) and (2)), and those with less grit are more likely to opt out (option (3)). Duckworth argues that self-control is more predictive of success in day-to-day life, in terms of resisting the temptations

---

[39] I will return to Duckworth on the domain-specificity of self-control in the next chapter.
[40] Duckworth, Angela and Gross, James J., "Self-Control and Grit: Related but Separable Determinants of Success," *Current Directions in Psychological Science*, 23:5 (2014), 319–325, 322.

that you will later regret; while grit is more predictive of success over long periods of time or even a lifetime. This is why grit is especially important for skill acquisition and expertise, given the long-term goals one is working towards.

In sum, self-regulation theory provides us a general account of goal-directed behavior. Goals provide us motivation to act, based in part on how valued those goals are, and often the pursuit of a superordinate goal is broken down into successive subgoals. It is important to separate out phases of goal setting and goal striving, as each involves different types of considerations. In goal setting, considerations of the desirability and feasibility of goals are important. There are helpful strategies such as mental contrasting when initially setting one's goal, as well as the potential need for grit in maintaining one's commitment to a goal in the long term. In goal striving, since a goal has been set, considerations turn to planning and acting to achieve the goal. There are effective strategies for planning, such as implementation intentions, as well as the potential need for self-control when acting in case there is a conflict amongst your goals. I will return to these elements of self-regulation not only in the next section with regard to skill acquisition, but throughout the book, as it will also help to clarify debates in virtue theory.

Skill Acquisition: Deliberate Practice

Skill acquisition is basically a sophisticated form of self-regulation, which we engage in so as to achieve a desired goal in a domain of high complexity.[41] It is important to note that a skill involves some flexibility in how one goes about achieving that outcome (to cope with changes in one's environment – which is part of what makes the domain complex), as well as a broad view of the outcome (such as in learning how to speak a language, rather than a single phrase). In committing yourself to acquiring a skill, you begin internalizing standards about what counts as a good performance, which will guide your efforts to learn the skill. Skill

---

[41] That is, not all acquired abilities are necessarily skills. Some tasks are so simple, such as tying one's shoelaces or opening doors, that once you have done it a few times there is nothing else to learn. The need to acquire sophisticated competences such as skills arises when dealing with complex issues, since the skills enable one to handle the complexity by progressively developing one's abilities. As such, my view is similar to that of Ellen Fridland, as she refers to "skills as the subclass of abilities, which are characterized by the fact that they are refined or developed as a result of effortful attention and control to the skill itself." Fridland, Ellen, "Skill Learning and Conceptual Thought: Making a Way through the Wilderness," in Bashour, B. and Muller, H. (eds.), *Philosophical Naturalism and Its Implications* (New York: Routledge, 2014).

acquisition requires a progression from tackling simple tasks to more
challenging tasks, no matter what level of skill you are aiming at, and of
course as one advances in skill development which tasks count as 'simple'
or 'challenging' will change. Learning how to be a competent and safe
driver on the road can be one's superordinate goal, and reaching that goal
requires successfully achieving many subgoals along the way (e.g. learning
how to start the car, how to change gears, how to back out of a driveway,
how to parallel park, etc.). Each of those subgoals requires planning how to
achieve them, and there is a progression of difficulty in the subgoals that
requires successful completion of the previous subgoal.

This progressive mastering of subgoals requires "practice, practice,
practice."[42] So how much practice is needed to acquire a skill at the level
of expertise? Frequent estimates place the amount of time necessary to
achieve expertise in any field at 10 years or 10,000 hours.[43] However, mere
experience is not sufficient for achieving expertise. People reach a certain
level of acceptable performance, after which further experience does not
lead to any improvement in performance. Additional experience may make
performing at that level of skillfulness easier, but that is not the same
as actually improving one's performance. Thus, the number of years
of experience one has is not a sufficient predictor of performance. While
having 10 years of experience may be necessary for expertise, it does not by
itself guarantee expertise.

What more is needed? Research indicates that a particular kind of
experience is necessary for expertise, as it turns out that the quality of
the practice matters just as much as the quantity. Improving your level of
skill requires not the mere repetition of things you already know how to
do, but continually striving to do things that you currently cannot do. This
kind of experience is referred to as 'deliberate practice', and it is roughly

---

[42] Though by no means is that the only factor that plays a role in skill acquisition. Also, hereafter when
I mention "research" I will be referring to the psychological research on expertise. Note that I will be
mainly summarizing the psychological literature at the outset for use in clarifying philosophical
debates later in this chapter and throughout the rest of the book. Fortunately, the psychological
research on expertise is fairly uniform in its findings across various different skill domains, and
general findings about expertise replicate across domains. In this respect it is far less contentious
than the research surrounding the person-situation debate within psychology, which requires careful
attention to the experimental details to determine precisely what is being shown, as well as some of
the famous experiments suffering from failures of replication.

[43] However, it should be noted, this number of hours can vary amongst different skill domains, and
for individuals working within the same domain due to natural talent. Horn, John and Masunaga,
Hiromi, "A Merging Theory of Expertise and Intelligence," in Ericsson, K. Anders (ed.), *The
Cambridge Handbook of Expertise and Expert Performance* (Cambridge: Cambridge University Press,
2006), 587–612, 601.

10,000 hours of deliberate practice that is needed for expertise. Deliberate practice requires having specific goals in mind for improvement, rather than the vaguer goal of 'getting better', as is true with self-regulation in general. There need to be specific aspects of your performance that you go about planning how to improve, which then structures the kind of deliberate practice you engage in.[44] As you engage in deliberate practice you seek out feedback about your performance, in the hopes of identifying and correcting errors. You keep monitoring your progress as you practice. If you do not seem to be progressing, you may need to redesign your practice sessions. If instead you keep up a steady progression, then at some point you achieve your current goal. At that point it is time to set out to strive to accomplish the next more difficult goal (i.e. you advance to planning how to achieve the next higher-ordered subgoal on the vertical hierarchy). This is how you improve upon your current level of performance.[45]

In this process of deliberate practice you can see the three action phases of self-regulation: planning (phase 2), when designing a deliberate practice session; engaging in practice (phase 3); and evaluation (phase 4), at the end of practice. Fortunately, coaches and teachers can help us with these phases, by helping us plan, monitoring our performance, and giving us feedback. However, it should be noted that feedback on your performance cannot come merely from others, as crucial as that is in the early stages of skill acquisition. As Barry Zimmerman points out, "[b]ecause high levels of skill must be practiced and adapted personally to dynamic contexts, aspiring experts need to develop a self-disciplined approach to learning and practice to gain consistency."[46] Often there will not be a coach around when you are exercising your skill, and so you need to learn how to provide yourself with feedback on your performance.

The point about adapting skill to dynamic context has another important implication. Not only does practice allow you to improve your level of skill, it can also function as a form of planning for actual performances (action phase 2) if the practice session attempts to simulate actual conditions under which someone will perform. K. Anders Ericsson provides an

---

[44] Horn, John and Masunaga, Hiromi, "A Merging Theory of Expertise and Intelligence," in Ericsson, K. Anders (ed.), *The Cambridge Handbook of Expertise and Expert Performance* (Cambridge: Cambridge University Press, 2006), 587–612, 601.

[45] This also helps to explain why Fridland takes "attention-governed, practice-related improvement as a criterion of skill," Fridland, Ellen, "They've Lost Control: Reflections on Skill," *Synthese*, 191 (2014), 2729–2750, 2740.

[46] Zimmerman, Barry J., "Development and Adaptation of Expertise: The Role of Self-Regulatory Processes and Beliefs," in Ericsson, K. Anders (ed.), *The Cambridge Handbook of Expertise and Expert Performance* (Cambridge: Cambridge University Press, 2006), 705–722, 706.

example of this with pilots who use simulators to engage in deliberate practice with regard to emergencies, and findings show that "if prior to the emergency event the expert pilots had practiced the same emergency situation in the simulator, they were reliably more successful in dealing with the actual event."[47] However, since skill acquisition is needed to deal with complex domains of action, where one has to be able to respond dynamically to the current situation, plans formed in the planning phase might specify a default approach to take that one also has to be prepared to modify while acting.[48] So, for example, a firefighter might go into a fire with a certain plan of how to keep it under control, but if the wind unexpectedly shifts, it will likely require a change in plans. Thus, to remain in control, one must be able to develop some flexible hierarchical structures to guide action in a dynamic context.[49]

Perhaps surprisingly, once expertise has been achieved in a skill, this same kind of deliberate practice is necessary to retain expert-level performance. While it might be thought that once you achieve expertise you never really lose it, Krampe and Charness' research on age and expertise shows that "maintaining skills is as effortful as acquiring them in the first place."[50] Expertise requires some level of routine practice to maintain it or the level of skill degrades over time. Given the overall difficulty of achieving expertise, one of the most important factors for determining whether someone can attain that level of performance is motivation. Any form of self-regulation is going to require motivation, but this is especially important with skill acquisition given the challenges involved. As Csikszentmihalyi et al. point out: "Unless a person wants to pursue the difficult path that leads to the development of talent, neither innate potential nor all the knowledge in the world will suffice."[51] Not only does an aspiring expert need to be strongly motivated to perform well, in the face of adversity and over a long period of

---

[47] Ericsson, K. Anders, "The Influence of Experience and Deliberate Practice on the Development of Superior Expert Performance," in Ericsson, K. Anders (ed.), *The Cambridge Handbook of Expertise and Expert Performance* (Cambridge: Cambridge University Press, 2006), 683–704, 693.

[48] This seems to be unaddressed in the action phase model because 'action' covers such a broad range of activities.

[49] Note that changing plans in such a situation is not a matter of changing goal commitments – which in this example remains stopping the fire – but rather to the 'when, where, and how' details of goal striving.

[50] Krampe, Ralf and Charness, Neil, "Aging and Expertise," in Ericsson, K. Anders (ed.), *The Cambridge Handbook of Expertise and Expert Performance* (Cambridge: Cambridge University Press, 2006), 723–742, 733.

[51] Csikszentmihalyi, Mihaly, Rathunde, Kevin, and Whalen, Samuel, *Talented Teenagers: The Roots of Success and Failure* (New York: Cambridge University Press, 1993), 31–32.

time, but even after achieving expertise a high level of motivation is still required to maintain one's expertise.

Furthermore, grit is of special importance to skill acquisition and the attainment of expertise. Duckworth claims there is a relationship between grit and deliberate practice, as "grittier competitors accumulate more hours of deliberate practice over the course of years."[52] Expertise is definitely a long-term goal, and one has to persevere over long periods of time beset with lots of challenges, failures, frustrations, obstacles, setbacks, etc. Those with high grit will meet the inevitable failures and setbacks in skill acquisition with a search for alternative strategies for pursuing the goal, while those low in grit are more likely to give up on the goal.[53]

Skill Acquisition: Automaticity and Dual-Process Theories of Cognition

In order to make progress in learning a skill, the currently effortful tasks need to become effortless, in order to free up your attention to handle more complicated tasks. As Daniel Kahneman explains, you have "a limited budget of attention that you can allocate to activities, and if you try to go beyond your budget, you will fail. It is the mark of effortful activities that they interfere with each other, which is why it is difficult or impossible to conduct several at once."[54] With practice, tasks can be accomplished more effectively and more efficiently. This allows a person to devote less attention to the tasks at hand without any reduction in performance, and to shift that attention to other matters. This phenomenon is referred to as automaticity, which is usually characterized by features of an action such as it requiring little effort or attention, occurring

---

[52] Duckworth, Angela and Gross, James J., "Self-Control and Grit: Related but Separable Determinants of Success," *Current Directions in Psychological Science*, 23:5 (2014), 319–325, 320.

[53] However, having the requisite motivation is determined by more than one's own level of grit. Social support can either help or hinder the development of expertise in certain domains, as well as an individual's motivation to achieve expertise. One key group in the social support of expertise is parents. Since the development of expertise takes considerable time it helps to start young, and supportive parents can have a big impact on this stage of development. Teachers are another key group that can help to motivate students in acquiring skills. Though one's social class or economic status will likely have an impact in terms of affording coaches and training. Social support can of course work both ways, as there are ways in which society can discourage individuals and groups from the achievement of expertise. There are several issues related to social support for expertise, such as social biases (e.g. gender, race, and social class) in who is publicly recognized as an expert; and in respect to supporting groups and individuals in their striving to attain expertise. For example, there are numerous gender biases affecting what professions women are encouraged, or discouraged, in pursuing.

[54] Kahneman, Daniel, *Thinking, Fast and Slow* (New York: Farrar, Straus and Giroux, 2011), 23.

without much (or any) conscious awareness or intention, and happening spontaneously.[55] Practice allows us to make progress on tackling ever more difficult tasks by tapping into automaticity.[56] Novices learning a skill will have to pay a lot of attention to what they are doing, and attention is a scarce resource. Due to limitations in our short-term or working memory, we can only focus our attention on a limited number of activities at one time. For example, you are not going to be able to pay full attention to changing lanes in heavy traffic at fast speeds if you still have to pay a lot of attention to changing gears. You need that changing of gears to become effortless, so that you can focus your effort on the more demanding task of dealing with heavy traffic.[57] Importantly, as this example suggests, often it is only aspects of a performance, not the whole performance, which becomes automatic. Some aspects of the performance becoming automatic (like changing gears) enables other aspects of the performance to be carried out with greater flexibility and control (as in responding to the actions of other drivers in fast moving traffic).

The contrast between effortful and effortless actions is captured by dual-processes theories of cognition.[58] The first type of cognition is characterized as automatic, intuitive, fast, and effortless; while the second is cognition that is deliberate, analytic, slow, and effortful. Kahneman distinguishes the two processes as System 1 (automatic) and System 2 (deliberate).[59] However, while much of the dual-process literature makes it sound as if you are guided

[55] It should be noted that these are common features associated with automaticity, but not all of these features are necessarily instantiated at the same time. See, for example, Bargh, John, "The Four Horsemen of Automaticity: Awareness, Intention, Efficiency, and Control in Social Cognition," in Wyer, R. S. and Srull, T.K. (eds.), Handbook of Social Cognition Vol. 1 (Hillsdale, NJ: Erlbaum, 1994), 1–40.

[56] Feltovich, Paul J., Prietula, Michael J., and Ericsson, K. Anders, "Studies of Expertise from Psychological Perspectives," in Ericsson, K. Anders (ed.), The Cambridge Handbook of Expertise and Expert Performance (Cambridge: Cambridge University Press, 2006), 41–68, 53.

[57] My thanks to a reviewer who drew my attention to this quote from Alfred North Whitehead: "It is a profoundly erroneous truism, repeated by all copy-books and by eminent people when they are making speeches, that we should cultivate the habit of thinking what we are doing. The precise opposite is the case. Civilization advances by extending the number of important operations which we can perform without thinking about them." Whitehead, Alfred North, An Introduction to Mathematics (New York: Henry Holt and Company, 1911), Chapter 5.

[58] Though, as I will bring out later in this section, it is more accurately described as cognitive processes that range on a continuum from effortful to effortless.

[59] Kahneman, Daniel, Thinking, Fast and Slow (New York: Farrar, Straus and Giroux, 2011). For concerns regarding dual-process theory, see Keren, Gideon and Schul, Yaccov, "Two Is Not Always Better Than One: A Critical Evaluation of Two-System Theories," Perspectives on Psychological Science 4 (2009), 533–550. For a defense of dual-process theories, see Evans, Jonathan and Stanovich, Keith, "Dual-Process Theories of Higher Cognition: Advancing the Debate," Perspectives on Psychological Science 8:3 (2013), 223–241.

by either one process or the other, a more nuanced view sees the two systems as working together, as I will show with skill acquisition.[60]

Deliberate practice clearly involves a transition from deliberate to automatic processing, as Ericsson notes that "[c]onsistent with the mental demands of problem solving and other types of complex learning, deliberate practice requires concentration that can be maintained only for limited periods of time"[61], and furthermore, "the requirement for *concentration* sets deliberate practice apart from both mindless, routine performance and playful engagement, as the latter two types of activities would, if anything, merely strengthen the current mediating cognitive mechanisms, rather than modify them to allow increases in the level of performance."[62] Chess players, for example, when engaging in deliberate practice will spend time studying opening moves and playing through past games played by grandmasters (to see if the move they made turns out to be the same move made by the expert player). This kind of study takes focused concentration, as you are trying to figure out the mistakes you are prone to make, and how to correct them. Ericsson notes that the effect this has is that "individuals refine their representations and can access or generate the same information faster. As a result, chess masters can typically recognize a superior move virtually immediately, whereas a competent club player requires much longer to find the same move by successive planning and evaluation rather than recognition."[63] Deliberate practice also enables a transition from deliberate control over a performance to a performance handled by automatic processes, as those previously effortful tasks become effortless.

Automaticity thus enables, though by no means guarantees, reliably accurate intuitive judgments about how to act in a situation.[64] One

---

[60] See Christensen, Wayne et al., "Cognition in Skilled Action: Meshed Control and the Varieties of Skill Experience," *Mind & Language* 31:1 (2016), 37–66. I'll begin with the less nuanced version of skill acquisition and dual-processes, and then move to the more nuanced version described by Christensen.

[61] Ericsson, K. Anders "The Influence of Experience and Deliberate Practice on the Development of Superior Expert Performance," in Ericsson, K. Anders (ed.), *The Cambridge Handbook of Expertise and Expert Performance* (Cambridge: Cambridge University Press, 2006), 683–704, 699.

[62] Ericsson, K. Anders, "The Influence of Experience and Deliberate Practice on the Development of Superior Expert Performance," in Ericsson, K. Anders (ed.), *The Cambridge Handbook of Expertise and Expert Performance* (Cambridge: Cambridge University Press, 2006), 683–704, 692.

[63] Ericsson, K. Anders, "The Influence of Experience and Deliberate Practice on the Development of Superior Expert Performance," in Ericsson, K. Anders (ed.), *The Cambridge Handbook of Expertise and Expert Performance* (Cambridge: Cambridge University Press, 2006), 683–704, 697.

[64] Here it will be important to note that it does not follow that all intuitive judgments are reliable. Robin Hogarth argues that what all intuitive judgments have in common is a lack of conscious awareness about how those judgments came about, since they were not the result of deliberate effort. Such judgments come about in a spontaneous manner, and people often feel a sense of

important thing to keep in mind about the talk of intuition in expertise is that the ability of the expert to reliably act well on an intuitive level is due to having an immense amount of experience and practice.[65] Skills are context sensitive, and the accuracy of the intuitive judgments that arise in expertise is due to the great familiarity the expert has in operating in these kinds of situations. For example, the chess expert can have a reliable intuition about what move to make in a situation because of her familiarity with being faced with this kind of board position before. The grounding of intuitions in this way is the reason why the intuitive judgments of experts can be highly reliable.

It is important to note here a limiting condition on the development of reliable intuitions arising out of experience and practice. Kahneman points out that we cannot necessarily expect expertise to be achieved in all domains. He draws our attention to this in his overall description of what is required to develop accurate intuitive judgments:

> The acquisition of skills requires a regular environment, and adequate opportunity to practice, and rapid and unequivocal feedback about the correctness of thoughts and actions. When these conditions are fulfilled, skill eventually develops, and the intuitive judgments and choices that quickly come to mind will mostly be accurate.[66]

As noted in other accounts of skill acquisition, practice and feedback are essential.[67] But in order to get useful feedback when one practices, there needs to be some predictability in the environment itself, in the sense that "there are stable relationships between objectively identifiable cues and subsequent events or between cues and the outcomes of possible

---

confidence about them. However, not all intuitions at this level of automatic processes are equally accurate or reliable, despite one's confidence in them. Hogarth, Robin M., *Educating Intuition* (Chicago: University of Chicago Press, 2000).

[65] Importantly, this view of intuitions should not be associated with the social intuitionism of Jonathan Haidt. Although he views moral judgments as the result of automatic processes, for him they are not the product of experience and practice. He also does not think that conscious deliberation can play much of a role in shaping our intuitions, which is contrary to the role that deliberative thinking plays in practice and acquiring skills. I will discuss his view in more detail in the next chapter.

[66] Kahneman, Daniel, *Thinking, Fast and Slow* (New York: Farrar, Straus and Giroux, 2011), 416.

[67] "Whether professionals have a chance to develop intuitive expertise depends essentially on the quality and speed of feedback, as well as on sufficient opportunity to practice." Kahneman, Daniel, *Thinking, Fast and Slow* (New York: Farrar, Straus and Giroux, 2011), 241. Kahneman, as an example, compares learning how to drive a car with learning how to pilot large ships in a harbor. The latter is more difficult to learn in part because of the longer delay between actions and noticeable consequences, which leads to slower feedback on one's attempt to pilot.

actions."[68] Practice and feedback are what enable one to pick up on these cues at an intuitive level. However, if there is not regularity between cues and subsequent events or outcomes, then recognition of those cues will not help you to figure out what to do next. For example, Kahneman argues that there does not seem to be enough regularity to the stock market environment to make it predictable, thus one cannot develop expertise in predicting stock prices.[69] But when there is some regularity to your environment, intuitive judgment can develop as you recognize cues from similar past experiences, and the outcome of actions that were taken in response.

All of this shows how we can develop automatic processes to generate better and more reliable performances and judgments. However, it would be a mistake to think that automatic processes always improve our behavior. Fujita et al. draw our attention to the fact that:

> work on automatic processes has suggested that a lot of information processing appears to occur "behind the scenes." That they can operate efficiently and with minimal conscious guidance leads to the possibility that automatic processing may promote thoughts, feelings, and behaviors that are inconsistent with people's conscious intentions and desires. The efficiency and lack of awareness of such processes may render people unable to intervene and to disrupt such undesired processing.[70]

Racial stereotypes, for example, can have an influence on people who would otherwise sincerely disavow racist attitudes, and such stereotypes stem from automatic processes, and can be difficult to change.[71] As Fujita points out, it is work like this that has led both to the implication that automatic processing is in some sense 'out of our control', and that 'deliberate' processing should thus be understood by contrast as 'controlled'.[72]

However, control should not be equated with the use of deliberative rather than automatic processes.[73] We have already seen how automatic

---

[68] Kahneman, Daniel and Klein, Gary, "Conditions for Intuitive Expertise: A Failure to Disagree," *American Psychologist* 64:6 (2009), 515–526, 524.
[69] Kahneman, Daniel, *Thinking, Fast and Slow* (New York: Farrar, Straus and Giroux, 2011), 233.
[70] Fujita, Kentaro, Trope, Yaacov, Cunningham, William A., and Liberman, Nira, "What Is Control? A Conceptual Analysis," in Sherman, Jeffrey W., Gawronski, Bertram, and Trope, Yaacov, *Dual-Process Theories of the Social Mind* (New York: The Guilford Press, 2014), 50–65.
[71] I will address how we can change some of these problematic responses in Chapter 5.
[72] For several examples from the psychological and cognitive science literature on automaticity that contrast automatic processes with controlled processes, see Wu, Wayne, "Mental Action and the Threat of Automaticity," in Clark, Andy, Kiverstein, Julian, and Vierkant, Tillman (eds.), *Decomposing the Will* (Oxford: Oxford University Press, 2013), 244–261.
[73] Fujita claims that control can also be understood as 'goal-directed', such that we are in control when our actions are furthering our goals. Being out of control is by contrast the sense that our actions are

processes can serve goal achievement with the effects of implementation intentions, in effect exerting control by setting up a preferred response to a situation to trigger automatically. We have also seen how deliberate processes can serve goal achievement with goal setting and the creation of implementation intentions, along with deliberate practice more specifically in skill acquisition. On the other hand, sometimes deliberate processing can actually undermine goal achievement, for example when a skilled performer starts to think too self-consciously about the performance and 'chokes'. There are other examples where introspection on our reasons or preferences can actually lead us to make worse choices.[74] In which case, it does not centrally matter to issues of control whether actions are guided by more deliberate or automatic processes, but rather whether those actions enhance goal setting and striving.[75]

---

not in alignment with our goals. He further claims that much of the literature on dual-processes has conflated these two meanings of control – as not-automatic and as goal-directed, and gives evidence that these two are conceptually independent. Fujita, Kentaro, Trope, Yaacov, Cunningham, William A., and Liberman, Nira, "What Is Control? A Conceptual Analysis," in Sherman, Jeffrey W., Gawronski, Bertram, and Trope, Yaacov, *Dual-Process Theories of the Social Mind* (New York: The Guilford Press, 2014), 50–65. See also Moskowitz, Gordon B., "The Implicit Volition Model: The Unconscious Nature of Goal Pursuit," in Sherman, Jeffrey W., Gawronski, Bertram, and Trope, Yaacov, *Dual-Process Theories of the Social Mind* (New York: The Guilford Press, 2014), 400–422.

[74] Gordon Moskowtiz suggests that "conscious processing can alter the meaning of the goal, because deliberation can recruit interpretive biases that yield changes to how the goal is framed or understood" and that "[c]onsciousness may at times be an obstacle to a goal better pursued implicitly; it can lead one astray by focusing one's attention on irrelevant information or causing one to rationalize an inappropriate response." Moskowitz, Gordon B., "The Implicit Volition Model: The Unconscious Nature of Goal Pursuit," in Sherman, Jeffrey W., Gawronski, Bertram, and Trope, Yaacov, *Dual-Process Theories of the Social Mind* (New York: The Guilford Press, 2014), 400–422, 415 and 416. For other examples, see: Wilson, T. D., Lisle, D. J., Schooler, J. W., Hodges, S. D., Klaaren, K. J., and LaFleur, S. J., "Introspecting About Reasons Can Reduce Post-Choice Satisfaction," *Personality and Social Psychology Bulletin*, 19 (1993), 331–359; and Wilson, T. D. and Schooler, J. W., "Thinking Too Much: Introspection Can Reduce the Quality of Preferences and Decision," *Journal of Personality and Social Psychology*, 60 (1991), 181–192.

[75] This is also one of the reasons why I think the dual-process distinction is better captured in terms of 'effortful' versus 'effortless' cognitive processes, as it lacks connotations of a potentially in-control (i.e. deliberate) and out-of-control (i.e. automatic) contrast. Furthermore, as I will detail below, a performance can involve both effortful (e.g. changing lanes while driving) and effortless (e.g. changing gears) processes at the same time. That this can be the case is obscured by the language of deliberate and automatic processes, as it tends to imply an either-or situation where one type of process or the other is in 'control'. Effortless versus effortful processing instead suggests a continuum of effort rather than a stark contrast or dualism. For example, one can expend effort now (planning implementation intentions) to reduce effort later on a different task (choosing the right food while on a diet). You can also expend effort now (deliberate practice) to be able to do the same task later with reduced effort (changing gears). Control is then about goal-directedness, regardless of how much effort is involved with actions you take in striving towards your goals. Though, for sake of ease, I'll continue to refer to automatic and deliberate processes.

We should be in a better position now to understand the interplay of 'deliberate' (i.e. effortful) and 'automatic' (i.e. effortless) processes in skilled action. Automaticity and intuitive judgment are well known forms of effortless processing that develop from skill acquisition, but what is often left out of the picture in such discussions are the ways in which our deliberative processes are still involved in skilled performance. It comes across as if the use of automatic processes means there is no more need to expend deliberate effort in the performance, which is not the case. So, it is now time to balance out that picture by showing how skill acquisition improves the use of our deliberative processes, and how the two types of processes work in concert. Initially, as previously discussed, performance in a skill will take a lot of cognitive control and attention, so little cognitive resources are left over for strategic monitoring. But as performance becomes more automatic in its implementation, cognitive resources are freed up. These resources might be freed up for engaging in multi-tasking, like carrying on a conversation (deliberate) while driving (automatic).[76] But importantly for skill acquisition, one's attention is now freed up for more control over the performance, such as being able to pay closer attention to traffic patterns or road conditions while driving. Christensen, Sutton, and Mcilwain suggest a hierarchical structure to skilled performance along these lines, by identifying three types of control that might be involved in the performance:[77]

> *Higher strategic control* involves overall control of the primary skill in relation to its goals. In the case of driving this includes navigation to the destination. *Situation control* involves the control of action in relation to the immediate situation. In the case of driving this involves proximal control of the car in relation to features of the situation, including maneuvers like accelerating to traffic speed, maintaining lane position, maintaining a safe distance to other cars, changing lanes, and so on. *Implementation control* involves performing actions that achieve situation control, which in the case of driving includes steering, accelerating, braking, changing gears, and so on.[78]

---

[76] Furthermore, you are unlikely to be able to recount all the driving conditions you experienced afterwards, since you were not paying explicit attention to them. Dual-process cognition also explains how we can be paying conscious attention to one matter while simultaneously engaged in another activity.

[77] However, their discussion is limited to control in the action phase, and with respect specifically to actions which involve the exercise of skill.

[78] Christensen, Wayne, Sutton, John, and Mcilwain, Doris J. F., "Cognition in Skilled Action: Meshed Control and the Varieties of Skill Experience," *Mind & Language* 31:1 (2016), 37–66, 49.

In these terms, the benefit of automaticity can be seen when one no longer needs to pay close attention to implementation control of the car, thus freeing up one's attention to better focus on situational control. Situational control can benefit too from automaticity, freeing up one's attention for higher strategic control. Though part of the hierarchical structure also implies that as you move up the hierarchy, the control involved becomes for the most part more deliberate and admits less potential for automaticity.[79] Though even with higher strategic control, like navigation, this can become automatic – at least with very familiar situations, like navigating home. Sometimes this automaticity even goes awry – like driving on 'autopilot' and going home when you actually meant to go somewhere else.[80] Exerting control in one or more of its many forms in the action phase will also have consequences for the final phase of evaluation (phase 4). It will be a time to reflect on whether the goal was achieved, and potentially an analysis of the effectiveness of the chosen plans and actions taken in striving for it. Of further consequence is whether one had to exercise effortful self-control while acting, due to a potential goal conflict.[81] Studies

[79] First, it is worth noting that the relationship they describe between the elements of the 'action' hierarchy, such that you move top-down from more deliberate to more automatic processes, is not a feature of the relationship between goals on a goal hierarchy. So, this shows another difference between the two forms of hierarchical structured control. Second, while they are a bit skeptical about the degree to which situation control can be automated, from my own experience the driving examples they use are clearly tasks that can become automatic. See also Fridland who argues that this kind of control, which she refers to as "selective, top-down, automatic attention," can become automatic. She claims that "[t]his kind of attention is responsible for selecting the relevant features in an environmental array that a skilled agent should gather information about and respond to, given her goals, plans, and strategies. Importantly, this kind of attention improves with training, is automatic, and is sensitive to the semantic content of the intentional states of the agent." Fridland, Ellen, "They've Lost Control: Reflections on Skill," *Synthese*, 191 (2014), 2729–2750, 2746.

[80] This account of the hierarchical structure of control in a skilled performance reflects the previous discussion of goal hierarchies, insofar as the higher systems provide direction for the lower systems on the hierarchy. Higher strategic control is related to exercising the skill on behalf of some subgoal of the agent, such as wanting to drive to a specific destination. Higher strategic control will then provide direction for situation control and one's attention, such as planning how to reach one's destination given one's current situation. Likewise, situation control will then determine what context-specific maneuvers to perform for implementation control. This structure reflects the fact that plans for how to achieve the subgoal that one is striving for must be sensitive to context.

[81] Not all exercises of self-control in avoiding conflict need be effortful. Implementation intentions, for example, are a way of avoiding the potential goal conflict by cueing up a specific behavior to take when you are put in the potential conflict situation (e.g. you reach automatically for the fruit instead of the dessert, thus experiencing no conflict in the moment). This is one of the benefits of pairing mental contrasting (where you elaborate a significant obstacle to achieving your goal) with implementation intentions (where you figure out in advance what to do, so you have an automatic response) – for it is a way of seeing the conflict in advance and planning how to resolve it before the time comes. See Fishbach, Ayelet and Converse, Benjamin A., "Identifying and Battling Temptation," in Vohs, Kathleen D. and Baumeister, Roy F. (eds.), *Handbook of Self-Regulation: Research, Theory, and Applications*, Second Edition (New York: The Guilford Press), 244–260.

have documented an effect where after an effortful exercise of self-control, it seems to become more difficult to engage in another act of effortful self-control soon after (especially with a similar task). Early experiments indicated that willpower (i.e. effortful self-control) was like a muscle – it gets weakened after repeated use (a phenomenon referred to as ego depletion).[82] However, there have recently been numerous failures to replicate the findings of the experiments that indicated it was like a muscle or a finite resource that gets depleted and takes time to renew. That there is often a refractory period after effortful self-control, though, is a phenomenon that has still been well documented, despite the failure of attempts to explain this phenomenon in terms of a muscle or a limited resource.[83]

It has been found that affirming one's core values, and reframing effort as something fun or an expression of one's 'willpower', are ways to prevent self-control fatigue.[84] Some of these methods for overcoming self-control fatigue involve changing how situations and events are construed. When you reaffirm your core values after acting (in phase 4 of evaluation), you change how you are construing the event, as you are viewing it as an expression of your most important values. Likewise, with construing your effortful self-control as an expression of your 'willpower' – a quality that people like to associate themselves with. This 'high' level of construal draws your attention to your action having contributed to your most important desires and goals, as opposed to a 'low' level of construal that draws your attention to how much effort it took to accomplish that goal.[85]

---

[82] Baumeister, Roy F., Vohs, Kathleen D., and Tice, Dianne M., "The Strength Model of Self-Control," *Current Directions in Psychological Science*, 16:6 (2007), 351–355.

[83] One of the more promising explanations for this refractory side-effect of effortful self-control explains it as a change in one's motivation, resulting from viewing the effort involved as a drawback of pursuing that goal. It is essentially a shift in goal priorities, in the evaluation phase (action phase 4), towards more immediately gratifying goals and away from the more long-term (though also more valued) goals. See Inzlicht, Michael, Berkman, Elliot, and Elkins-Brown, Nathaniel, "The Neuroscience of 'Ego Depletion': How the Brain Can Help Us Understand Why Self-control Seems Limited," in Harmon-Jones, Eddie and Inzlicht, Michael (eds.), *Social Neuroscience: Biological Approaches to Social Psychology* (New York: Routledge, 2016), 101–123.

[84] Inzlicht, Michael, Berkman, Elliot, and Elkins-Brown, Nathaniel, "The Neuroscience of 'Ego Depletion': How the Brain Can Help Us Understand Why Self-control Seems Limited," in Harmon-Jones, Eddie and Inzlicht, Michael (eds.), *Social Neuroscience: Biological Approaches to Social Psychology* (New York: Routledge, 2016), 101–123.

[85] This approach to understanding self-control fatigue can then also be understood in terms of construal level theory, which distinguishes between 'high' and 'low' ways of construing events. A 'high' level construal focuses on the more abstract and distant goals and values that structure one's actions (i.e. why you're doing it), whereas a 'low' level construal focuses instead on the more concrete and immediate means you are taking for reaching those goals (i.e. how you're going to do it). See Trope, Yaacov and Liberman, Nira, "Construal-Level Theory of Psychological Distance," *Psychological Review*, 117:2 (2010), 440–463. Also, Büttner, Oliver B., Wieber, Frank,

As another example, having both fruit and cake as options in the buffet line will likely cause a conflict in the dieter between immediate gratification with the cake or acting in alignment with one's more long-term goal of losing weight by choosing the fruit. Of course, taken by itself, one piece of cake is not going to sabotage the long-term goal of losing weight, which suggests that perhaps getting the cake this time is not in conflict with the long-term goal. But if that is how you think each time you are presented with this choice, then you will likely undermine the more valued goal over time. However, as Fishbach and Converse point out, if instead "a person considers multiple opportunities to act and expects to make consistent choices at each opportunity," thus stepping back and seeing this instance of behavior in terms of how it relates to an overarching goal in the long term, then it will be easier to identify the conflict and to choose appropriately.[86] Changing the levels at which an event is construed has been shown to affect the motivational strength of goals, like in the examples above of combatting self-control fatigue.[87]

Skillfulness: Schemas and Mental Models

The way in which we construe events also shapes our knowledge, and experts in a skill differ from novices both in the content and the organization of their knowledge. The term 'schema' is used by psychologists to refer to how we organize knowledge, including how such knowledge is stored and later retrieved.[88] Since we are constantly presented with an overwhelming amount of information regarding ourselves and our current environment, and we cannot make sense of all of it at once, we need a way to organize the information we are presented with, and we do this by forming schemas. Schemas organize our information into different categories and help us to interpret the world around us. A simple example is

Schulz, Anna Maria, Bayer, Ute C., Florack, Arnd, and Gollwitzer, Peter M., "Visual Attention and Goal Pursuit: Deliberative and Implemental Mindsets Affect Breadth of Attention," *Personality and Social Psychology Bulletin*, 40:10 (2014), 1248–1259.

[86] Fishbach, Ayelet and Converse, Benjamin A., "Identifying and Battling Temptation," in Vohs, Kathleen D. and Baumeister, Roy F. (eds.), *Handbook of Self-Regulation: Research, Theory, and Applications*, Second Edition (New York: The Guilford Press), 244–260.

[87] Fishbach, Ayelet and Converse, Benjamin A., "Identifying and Battling Temptation," in Vohs, Kathleen D. and Baumeister, Roy F. (eds.), *Handbook of Self-Regulation: Research, Theory, and Applications*, Second Edition (New York: The Guilford Press), 244–260.

[88] Cantor, Nancy, "From Thought to Behavior: 'Having' and 'Doing' in the Study of Personality and Cognition," *American Psychologist*, 45:6 (1990), 735–750.

having a schema for a cat – something that is furry, has four legs, a tail, whiskers, makes purring sounds, etc. This schema can include both these generic details, as well as more specific information like the features and personalities of the cats you have kept as pets. There will be a lot of overlap between people with the generic details in a simple schema like 'cat', though of course there will be a lot more variation when it comes to calling to mind particular cats you have encountered. This schema makes it easy to identify other cats in your future encounters, as the animal in front of you will be compared to your existing schema and will be recognized as a cat if it fits the schema. This also has the effect of making it easy to encode this new information into your memory. However, new experiences can also lead you to revise your present schema, for example when you encounter a cat with only three legs. Finally, schemas do not operate in a purely passive way, as the way we categorize information affects what details we notice in our environment.

Events that we experience are also organized by schemas, and here you can expect that people who experience the same event will have some variation in their schemas for it. People see events from different perspectives, bring their own concerns into interpreting the event, have different associated affective responses to the event, etc. As another example, you have a self-schema – the way you regard yourself, which is likely to be quite different from the schema other people have of you. The self-schema appears to be one of the most complex schema a person has, likely due to us having more experiences of ourselves than anything else.

People vary in their schemas because of their differing experiences, and how those experiences are interpreted in the light of their pre-existing schema. This is especially relevant for understanding skill acquisition. A novice in chess, because of a lack of experience, will start out with fairly crude schemas – it involves a board, some pieces with different shapes and values, it is a competitive game . . . but perhaps not much more than that. An expert in chess, by contrast, has very complex schemas for representing chess board positions, given all the experience she has. Further experience allows one to update existing schemas, and to nuance that organizational structure with new information. This then allows someone to notice things in future experiences that she did not notice before, because of the way schemas influence the details that we notice. Take, for example, learning to drive a stick-shift. Initially it helps to follow some simple rules that determine when it is time to shift gears once you reach a certain speed. With some experience driving stick-shifts, you will get accustomed to the different sounds the engine makes, at which point you should try instead to let the engine noises clue you in as to when to shift gears. But it would not be helpful to give those instructions to complete novices, as their schema do not include finer-grained details like when an engine sounds like it is racing.

A final important aspect of schemas is that the more you use a schema to organize your experience, the easier it is to call it to mind. So, schemas vary in their accessibility, and a schema that is frequently used is said to be 'chronically accessible'. This is then another way in which people can vary with respect to schemas, in terms of their accessibility. This highlights how schemas can affect the way we perceive situations, as the more accessible a schema is, the more you are likely to be viewing the world through that schema.[89] This is one of the ways schemas influence self-regulation, by affecting levels of motivation. To go back to the earlier example of dieting, a schema involving healthy eating, if it is repeatedly invoked, will easily come to your mind. Here we can see the further role of schemas in skill acquisition. Schemas develop as one learns a skill, as you are gaining knowledge in the skill domain, and this will in turn change how you view situations – such as noticing details or options you missed before. Further, with repeated practice, as that schema becomes activated more often, it can become chronically accessible, which in turn helps with sustaining a high motivation.

These highly developed schemas constructed from experience and practice make it easier to react appropriately in similar situations in the future. When you recognize that you have been in this situation before, and you have acted successfully in past situations like this one, then you do not need to stop and deliberate about what to do next. Essentially, you are pattern matching between your current situation and the schemas you have acquired through training and experience. This lack of needing to stop and deliberate is supported by the recognition-primed decision model, which was developed with extensive research on the decision making of fireground commanders.[90] The model was developed to account for how experts made

[89] Social cognitive theorists like Mischel and Shoda propose that personality variation is understood in terms of how we construe situations, along with our "if-then" behavior patterns. For example, somebody trying to control their temper might follow the plan of "if somebody is insulting me, then I will just walk away." But whether somebody is insulting you depends in part on how you construe someone else's behavior. Furthermore, how we construe situations will be affected by which schemas are more accessible. Mischel, W. and Shoda, Y., "A Cognitive-Affective System Theory of Personality: Reconceptualizing Situations, Dispositions, Dynamics, and Invariance in Personality Structure," *Psychological Review*, 102 (1995), 246–268.

[90] Fireground commanders are those commanding firefighters on the scene of a fire. They have to arrive at decisions about how to coordinate the activities of the firefighters to contain the fire and

decisions in situations where there is a lot at stake and decisions have to be made in a short period of time (like with fighting fires). Because of extensive past experience, what the decision maker recognizes "includes the type of situation this is, what to expect from the situation (expectancies), suitable goals, typical courses of action (COAs), and relevant cues."[91] So practice and experience shapes the schemas of the learner, both in terms of their knowledge base but also how they construe situations:

> Because they have more and better organized knowledge in a domain, experts perceive things differently than do novices. They perceive different affordances. Perception of affordances is highly influenced by the amount of experience that one has with similar situations.[92]

Experience not only changes how experts view a situation, it also enables them to efficiently and effectively respond to the situation. A skilled chess player can know which moves to make because of her experiences in playing the game: being in a variety of situations, seeing the possible moves, and knowing which moves worked and which did not. This allows her to have an immediate intuitive response about what to do next in the situation. As Cantor notes, "[i]ndividuals are particularly facile in their domains of expertise at retrieving "facts" and at organizing new information in terms of their schemas; they find it almost impossible not to think in these terms when in relevant situations, and their familiar schemas provide a ready, sometimes automatically available plan of action in such life contexts."[93]

As important as pattern recognition is to expert performance, however, it does not suffice to explain the decision-making capabilities of those with

---

keep everyone safe, based on the behavior of the fire and the skills of their firefighters (amongst other factors). "Data analysis found that approximately 80% of the commanders' decisions were recognition-based. In fact, some interviewees said that they never made "decisions" at all." Ross, Karol, Shafer, Jennifer, and Klein, Gary, "Professional Judgments and 'Naturalistic Decision Making'," in Ericsson, K. Anders (ed.), *The Cambridge Handbook of Expertise and Expert Performance* (Cambridge: Cambridge University Press, 2006), 403–419, 407.

[91] Ross, Karol, Shafer, Jennifer , and Klein, Gary, "Professional Judgments and "Naturalistic Decision Making," in Ericsson, K. Anders (ed.), *The Cambridge Handbook of Expertise and Expert Performance* (Cambridge: Cambridge University Press, 2006), 403–419, 406.

[92] Affordances can be understood here in terms of what opportunities a situation presents, such as a chess expert having a better grasp of what moves could be made than a novice when viewing the layout of a chess board. Narvaez, Darcia and Lapsley, Daniel K. "The Psychological Foundations of Everyday Morality and Moral Expertise," in Lapsley, Daniel K. and Power, F. Clark (eds.), *Character Psychology and Character Education* (Notre Dame: IN: University of Notre Dame Press, 2005), 140–165, 150–151.***

[93] Cantor, Nancy, "From Thought to Behavior: 'Having' and 'Doing' in the Study of Personality and Cognition," *American Psychologist*, 45:6 (1990), 735–750, 738.

a high degree of skillfulness. As Anders Jansson points out, in summarizing the work of Conant and Ashby, "the very object of decision making can be regarded as that of control. In order to control a situation, however, a person must develop a model of that situation."[94] What Conant and Ashby were interested in was the designing of a regulator for some system, say designing a regulator of airport traffic when planes are arriving and departing constantly. How can you best regulate such a system of traffic? Their answer is that to regulate it well, it is necessary that one has an accurate model of the system (which had hitherto been viewed as optional but not crucial). Conant and Ashby provide a proof for their theorem, which:

> shows, under very broad conditions, that any regulator that is maximally both successful and simple must be isomorphic with the system being regulated... Making a model is thus necessary. The theorem has the interesting corollary that the living brain, so far as it is to be successful and efficient as a regulator for survival, must proceed, in learning, by the formation of a model (or models) of its environment.[95]

This idea is of course quite central to cybernetics and control theory in what it takes to be effective in self-regulation. You can regulate well to the extent that you have an accurate model of the system that you are interacting with.[96] In chess, for example, as players increase their skill, "they become increasingly able to encode and manipulate internal representations of chess positions to plan the consequences of chess moves, discover potential threats, and even develop new lines of attack."[97] These kinds of detailed schema of the physical and social environment are referred to as mental models, and they play a key role in understanding

---

[94] Jansson, Anders, "Goal Achievement and Mental Models in Everyday Decision Making," in Juslin, Peter and Montgomery, Henry (eds.), *Judgment and Decision Making: Neo-Brunswikian and Process-Tracing Approaches* (London: Lawrence Erlbaum Associates, 1999), 23–43, 25. Also, Conant, Roger C. and Ashby, W. Ross, "Every Good Regulator of a System Must Be a Model of that System," *International Journal of Systems Science*, 1:2 (1970), 89–97.

[95] Conant, Roger C. and Ashby, W. Ross, "Every Good Regulator of a System Must Be a Model of that System," *International Journal of Systems Science*, 1:2 (1970), 89–97, 89.

[96] I will merely note here what I will come back to in later chapters, which is that often what we want to control is internal to our own intrapersonal processes and behavior, such as our emotions or reactions to situations, either directly as a goal or indirectly as a means to exert better control over the external social or natural environment. In which case, what we need an accurate model of is our own self, and that may give self-inquisitiveness (to find out about what makes us 'tick') a central role to play in self-regulation.

[97] Ericsson, K. Anders, "Protocol Analysis and Expert Thought: Concurrent Verbalizations of Thinking during Experts' Performance on Representative Tasks," in Ericsson, K. Anders (ed.), *The Cambridge Handbook of Expertise and Expert Performance* (Cambridge: Cambridge University Press, 2006), 223–241, 233.

the relevant factors of situations. Mental models are defined as "mechanisms whereby humans are able to generate descriptions of system purpose and form, explanations of system functioning and observed system states, and predictions of future states."[98] A 'system' in this sense represents the dynamic environment a person is operating in, such as a player facing an opponent in a chess match or a firefighter facing a wildfire. The person is interacting with the 'system', and the system can change in response to what the person does. These mental models are how performers exert better situational control, as described in the previous section.

These mental models are a type of schema, but they also involve a bit of abstraction away from one's particular experiences.[99] As Mica Endsley points out about mental models, "although they grow and evolve with experience, largely represent static knowledge about the system – its significant features, how it functions, how different components affect others, and how its components will behave when confronted with various factors and influences."[100] Mental models provide knowledge about what are likely to be relevant features in a system, help to more efficiently process new information about that system, and allow forecasting how that system is likely to change in the near future. For example, "studies of expert fire fighters have shown that experts interpret any scene of a fire dynamically, in terms of what likely preceded it and how it will likely evolve. This kind of understanding supports efforts to intervene in the fire."[101] These mental models provide the information we need to exert control over situations.

Beyond the role of mere experience, Seligman, Railton, Baumeister, and Sripada's work on prospection helps to explain how these mental models get built.[102] As discussed earlier with regard to the use of forethought in

---

[98] Rouse, William B. and Morris, Nancy M. (1985). "On Looking into the Black Box: Prospects and Limits in the Search for Mental Models" (No. DTIC #AD-A159080). Atlanta, GA: Center for Man-Machine Systems Research, Georgia Institute of Technology.

[99] "The useful utilization of events as familiar requires a degree of appropriate abstraction, both in the event features utilized and in the memory organization imposed on the memory models themselves." Feltovich, Paul J. Prietula, Michael J., and Ericsson, K. Anders , "Studies of Expertise from Psychological Perspectives," in Ericsson, K. Anders (ed.), *The Cambridge Handbook of Expertise and Expert Performance* (Cambridge: Cambridge University Press, 2006), 41–68, 54.

[100] Endsley, Mica, "Expertise and Situation Awareness," in Ericsson, K. Anders (ed.), *The Cambridge Handbook of Expertise and Expert Performance* (Cambridge: Cambridge University Press, 2006), 633–651, 638.

[101] Feltovich, Paul J., Prietula, Michael J., and Ericsson, K. Anders, "Studies of Expertise from Psychological Perspectives," in Ericsson, K. Anders (ed.), *The Cambridge Handbook of Expertise and Expert Performance* (Cambridge: Cambridge University Press, 2006), 41–68, 52.

[102] Seligman, Martin, E. P., Railton, Peter Baumeister, Roy F., and Sripada, Chandra, "Navigating into the Future or Driven by the Past," *Perspectives on Psychological Science* 8:2 (2013), 119–141.

goal setting and planning, prospection involves generating representations of future possibilities, as with the example of firefighters above. It is a matter of having expectations of the form "*if* in circumstance C and state S, *then* behavior B has outcome O with probability p."[103] These expectations can then guide future behavior, such as intervening in a fire. Furthermore, the more accurate the expectations, the better one can be guided by prospection. So mental models provide knowledge about a system to help generate accurate prospection.

How does experience help one to arrive at such a model? Their answer is that there is a feedback loop when one is guided by our representations of future possibilities. You start off with an expectation of what will happen when you act in a particular way, and if that expectation shows itself to be mistaken, then you try to correct your expectation. The next time you act, it is on the basis of this updated expectation, which is open to further revision based on your observation of how things turn out after acting. In sum, having an expectation "transforms experience into experimentation —continuously generating a 'test probe' so that the next experience always involves an implicit question and supplies an answer, which can then function as an error-reducing 'learning signal'."[104] You are essentially learning from experience. Gilbert Ryle gives a nice illustration of this with how a skilled mountaineer walks over difficult terrain.[105] She is testing the terrain (i.e. her model of the environment) with each step she takes. When things do not go as expected, she is prepared to update her mental model and change her approach, and this will carry forward in her future behavior. As Ryle points out, "It is of the essence of intelligent practices that one performance is modified by its predecessors. The agent is still learning."[106]

For another application of this to skill, Seligman et al. refer to the work of Yarrow, Brown, and Krakauer on elite athletes, which showed that they "act through a continuously updated, largely unconscious or "implicit" action-guiding forward model of their situation and its possibilities."[107]

[103] Seligman, Martin E. P., Railton, Peter, Baumeister, Roy F., and Sripada, Chandra, "Navigating into the Future or Driven by the Past," *Perspectives on Psychological Science* 8:2 (2013), 119–141, 124.
[104] Seligman, Martin E. P., Railton, Peter, Baumeister, Roy F., and Sripada, Chandra, "Navigating into the Future or Driven by the Past," *Perspectives on Psychological Science*, 8:2 (2013), 119–141, 124.
[105] Ryle, Gilbert, *The Concept of Mind* (New York: Routledge, 2009), 30.
[106] Ryle, Gilbert, *The Concept of Mind* (New York: Routledge, 2009), 30.
[107] Seligman, Martin E. P., Railton, Peter, Baumeister, Roy F., and Sripada, Chandra, "Navigating into the Future or Driven by the Past," *Perspectives on Psychological Science*, 8:2 (2013), 119–141, 124. Yarrow, Kielan, Brown, Peter, and Krakauer, John W., "Inside the Brain of an Elite Athlete:

Importantly, this generating and updating of expectations to provide a model of one's environment often happens spontaneously and unconsciously, even though it can be done through conscious deliberation as well.[108] Since this intelligent behavior can occur unconsciously, there should not be a concern that the automatic and unconscious processes involved in skilled behavior will result in that behavior being a matter of mindless habit.[109]

One final use of mental models worth highlighting, in comparison to its use in automatic processing above, is the more deliberate ability to run mental simulations of situations and possible courses of action to take in response. For mental models to help with action guidance, new situations do not need to map on exactly to previous situations, but there needs to be a number of relevantly similar features in the current situation when compared to the model. The expert, especially when faced with a somewhat unfamiliar situation, can run a kind of mental simulation on the initial course of action (COA) that occurs to her. According to the recognition-primed model of decision making:

> Mental simulation is the process of consciously envisioning a sequence of events, such as imagining how a COA [course of action] will play out. This allows a decision maker who knows enough to make accurate predictions to see what the consequences of a particular COA might be … If the first COA evaluated is found wanting, the expert generates a second and so on, evaluating each in turn but never comparing options against each other.[110]

Initially, one should not necessarily expect expert-level performance from an expert facing a unique situation, even if experts will reliably perform better than non-experts in such situations. Expertise is limited to a certain background of experience.[111] Because expertise develops out of concrete experience, experts will be at their best when facing relatively familiar

---

The Neural Processes that Support High Achievement in Sports," *Nature Reviews Neuroscience*, 10:8 (2009), 585–596.

[108] Seligman, Martin E. P., Railton, Peter, Baumeister, Roy F., and Sripada, Chandra, "Navigating into the Future or Driven by the Past," *Perspectives on Psychological Science*, 8:2 (2013), 119–141, 125.

[109] Perhaps of note is an insight by Ryle that "[t]o be intelligent is not merely to satisfy criteria, but to apply them; to regulate one's actions and not merely to be well-regulated." Ryle, Gilbert, *The Concept of Mind* (New York: Routledge, 2009), 17.

[110] Ross, Karol, Shafer, Jennifer, and Klein, Gary ,"Professional Judgments and "Naturalistic Decision Making," in Ericsson, K. Anders (ed.), *The Cambridge Handbook of Expertise and Expert Performance* (Cambridge: Cambridge University Press, 2006), 403–419, 406–407.

[111] Chi, Michelene T. H., "Two Approaches to the Study of Experts' Characteristics," in Ericsson, K. Anders (ed.), *The Cambridge Handbook of Expertise and Expert Performance* (Cambridge: Cambridge University Press, 2006), 21–30, 24.

situations.[112] Thus, experts also need to be aware of when they are facing situations that include unique features, so as to adjust their performance. While they may not perform as well in truly unique situations, they will still fare better than novices. Overall, the research indicates that "Most people do not operate at the level of novice all the time or expert all the time, but rather move around in between, using combinations of cognitive mechanisms depending on the situation at hand and the availability of key constructs (e.g. mental models and schema)."[113]

Skillfulness: Articulation and Codification of Knowledge

Mental simulation is another place where we see the interplay between automatic (System 1) and deliberative (System 2) processes in expert performance.[114] The courses of action that experts are simulating are drawn from their experience and occur to them at an intuitive level. So while experts might be able to articulate some of the process of mental simulation itself, they still cannot necessarily explain why they saw situations in a particular light, or why a particular course of action occurred to them.[115] The psychological research demonstrates that "experts often cannot articulate their knowledge because much of their knowledge is tacit and their overt intuitions can be flawed."[116] One reason for the difficulty

---

[112] However, it should be noted that 'familiar' is not necessarily the same as 'easy', and familiar situations may be difficult enough to always require a high degree of deliberate effort in situational control. See Christensen, Wayne, Sutton, John, and Mcilwain, Doris J. F., "Cognition in Skilled Action: Meshed Control and the Varieties of Skill Experience," *Mind & Language*, 31:1 (2016), 37–66, 52.

[113] Endsley, Mica, "Expertise and Situation Awareness," in K. Anders Ericsson (ed.), *The Cambridge Handbook of Expertise and Expert Performance* (Cambridge: Cambridge University Press, 2006), 633–651, 640. This is a good point to keep in mind for application to virtue, as it should lessen the amount of idealization we have with virtue possession, as there is a tendency to over-idealize virtue as something that once possessed will enable us to act well in whatever situations we face.

[114] Kahneman claims that the "process involves both System 1 and System 2. In the first phase, a tentative plan comes to mind by an automatic function of associative memory – System 1. The next phase is a deliberate process in which the plan is mentally simulated to check if it will work – an operation of System 2." Kahneman, Daniel, *Thinking, Fast and Slow* (New York: Farrar, Straus and Giroux, 2011), 237.

[115] Ericsson points out that "they cannot report why only one of several logically possible thoughts entered their attention, they must make inferences or confabulate answers to such questions." Ericsson, K. Anders, "Protocol Analysis and Expert Thought: Concurrent Verbalizations of Thinking during Experts' Performance on Representative Tasks," in Ericsson, K. Anders (ed.), *The Cambridge Handbook of Expertise and Expert Performance* (Cambridge: Cambridge University Press, 2006), 223–241, 230.

[116] Chi, Michelene T. H., "Two Approaches to the Study of Experts' Characteristics," in Ericsson, K. Anders (ed.), *The Cambridge Handbook of Expertise and Expert Performance* (Cambridge: Cambridge University Press, 2006), 21–30, 24. Also, it is important to note that "tacit

in articulation is that intuitions arising out of expertise "are due to highly valid cues that the expert's System 1 has learned to use, even if System 2 has not learned to name them."[117] That is, being asked to give an explanation of one's actions involves deliberate processes. However, since the recognition of the situational cues and the resulting intuitive judgments are partially based on automatic processes, an expert cannot necessarily explain that part of her cognitive process. Furthermore, as discussed earlier, implementation control and even situation control during skilled performance can become automatic, and thus those parts of the skilled performance are not necessarily available to conscious introspection or for explanation on the part of the performer.[118] It is also important to keep in mind that being able to accurately explain the basis of one's actions is a different task from the performance itself, and so doing well in a performance does not necessarily translate into giving a good explanation.[119]

Even when experts are able to articulate an explanation, the explanations are often inconsistent with the observed behavior of the experts. These problems occur both when experts are asked about a specific task they just performed and when asked in general about their methods.[120] Of particular difficulty is getting an answer to the question of why the expert

knowledge is not viewed as an automatic response produced from repeated exposures to the same patterns of stimuli. Rather, it is viewed as an adaptive intellectual resource stemming from the active interaction between individuals and their dynamic environment." Cianciolo, Anna T., Matthew, Cynthia, Sternberg, Robert J., and Wagner, Richard K., "Tacit Knowledge, Practical Intelligence, and Expertise," in Ericsson, K. Anders (ed.), *The Cambridge Handbook of Expertise and Expert Performance* (Cambridge: Cambridge University Press, 2006), 613–632, 617.

[117] Kahneman, Daniel, *Thinking, Fast and Slow* (New York: Farrar, Straus and Giroux, 2011), 240.
[118] Researchers involved with expert decision making maintain that "expert knowledge is largely tacit knowledge and can be difficult for the expert to share when asked. We cannot tell someone how to perform largely unconscious processes." Ross, Karol, Shafer, Jennifer, and Klein, Gary, "Professional Judgments and "Naturalistic Decision Making," in K. Anders Ericsson (ed.), *The Cambridge Handbook of Expertise and Expert Performance* (Cambridge: Cambridge University Press, 2006), 403–419, 412.
[119] Ryle makes this point when discussing skill, saying "the capacity to perform and to appreciate an operation does not necessarily involve the ability to formulate criticisms or lessons. A well-trained sailor boy can both tie complex knots and discern whether someone else is tying them correctly or incorrectly, deftly or clumsily. But he is probably incapable of the difficult task of describing in words how the knots should be tied." Ryle, Gilbert, *The Concept of Mind* (New York: Routledge, 2009), 43.
[120] Ericsson notes that "[w]hen experts are asked to describe their general methods in professional activities, they sometimes have difficulties, and there is frequently poor correspondence between the behavior of computer programs (expert systems) implementing their described methods and their observed detailed behavior when presented with the same tasks and specific situations." Ericsson, K. Anders, "Protocol Analysis and Expert Thought: Concurrent Verbalizations of Thinking during Experts' Performance on Representative Tasks," in Ericsson, K. Anders (ed.), *The Cambridge Handbook of Expertise and Expert Performance* (Cambridge: Cambridge University Press, 2006), 223–241, 231.

responded one way rather than another, as one study revealed that "participants' responses to 'why-questions' after responding in a task were in many circumstances as inaccurate as those given by other participants who merely observed these individuals' performance and tried to explain it without any memory or first-hand experience of the processes involved."[121] In short, experts are primarily identified by their perform-ance, for experts are not necessarily reliable at providing accurate accounts of the factors guiding their performance, and this gives us a reason to be cautious about requiring articulation as a condition for expertise.

However, it is important to note that the research does not support the stronger conclusion that experts can never accurately articulate their reasons for action.[122] One of the advantages of the hierarchical account of skilled performance is that it shows which aspects are more likely conscious and available to the agent for use, as Fridland points out, in "practical reasoning, deliberation, reflection, and inference."[123] While some forms of control exercised in performance may be automatic, higher strategic control is unlikely to be automatized, and thus a performer should be able to articulate how the overall performance is linked to her specific goals. Because there is a lot of situational variability, situational control will often require deliberate effort of the kind which the performer can report. Furthermore, deliberate practice should admit of even more consciously available information to the performer than in an actual performance. This provides a more balanced picture of what our expectations should be when it comes to articulating what one knows how to do.

[121] Ericsson, K. Anders, "Protocol Analysis and Expert Thought: Concurrent Verbalizations of Thinking during Experts' Performance on Representative Tasks," in Ericsson, K. Anders (ed.), *The Cambridge Handbook of Expertise and Expert Performance* (Cambridge: Cambridge University Press, 2006), 223–241, 230.

[122] Despite these problems, there is a kind of reporting that experts can do about their thought process which does appear to be reliable. Instead of asking experts to explain their behavior after performing some task, experts are asked to 'think aloud' while engaged in performance of the task. While these verbalizations are far more accurate than after the fact explanations, they are not particularly detailed. The reason is that in 'think aloud' experiments "participants were not asked to describe or explain how they solve these problems and do not generate such descriptions or explanations. Instead, they are asked to stay focused on generating a solution to the problem and thus only give verbal expression to those thoughts that spontaneously emerge in attention during the generation of the solution." Ericsson, K. Anders, "Protocol Analysis and Expert Thought: Concurrent Verbalizations of Thinking during Experts' Performance on Representative Tasks," in Ericsson, K. Anders (ed.), *The Cambridge Handbook of Expertise and Expert Performance* (Cambridge: Cambridge University Press, 2006), 223–241, 228.

[123] Fridland, Ellen, "They've Lost Control: Reflections on Skill," *Synthese*, 191 (2014), 2729–2750, 2745.

While there was an early hope in expertise research that the knowledge of experts could be extracted and rules could be developed that would greatly reduce the time and practice required to attain expertise, some of the problems with getting experts to fully articulate their knowledge reduced that hope.[124] There are further problems with trying to map out this knowledge given the complexity of the mechanisms that mediate expert performance. One researcher reports:

> For example, Allen Newell (personal communication) described a project in which one of his graduate students in the 1970s tried to elicit all the relevant knowledge of a stamp collector. After some forty hours of interviews, Newell and his student gave up, as there was no sight of the end of the knowledge that the expert had acquired. As it may be difficult, perhaps impossible, to describe all the knowledge and skills of experts.[125]

It is important to keep realistic expectations of our ability to describe the knowledge of experts. Of course, the research on expertise can extract some of the knowledge of experts, which helps to improve skill acquisition at all levels of performance, but there is no substitute for the roles of deliberate practice and experience in a variety of situations to achieve expertise.[126]

In sum, skill acquisition turns out to be fundamentally a matter of deliberate practice, where one strives to improve one's skill by trying to correct for errors and to overcome one's current limitations. Part of what deliberate practice allows you to do is to take previously effortful tasks and make them effortless. This aspect of automaticity can enable accurate intuitive judgment but can also limit our ability to introspect and

---

[124] Furthermore, the discovery of the complex of adaptations that mediate expert performance dispelled "the hope that it would be possible to extract the accumulated knowledge and rules of experts and then use this knowledge to more efficiently train future experts and, thus, reduce the decade or more of experience and training required for elite performance." Feltovich, Paul J., Prietula, Michael J., and Ericsson, K. Anders, "Studies of Expertise from Psychological Perspectives," in Ericsson, K. Anders (ed.), *The Cambridge Handbook of Expertise and Expert Performance* (Cambridge: Cambridge University Press, 2006), 41–68, 61. In addition, Polanyi is often credited as "the first critic who saw that nonconscious and intuitive mediation limits the possibility of eliciting and mapping the knowledge and rules that mediates experts' intuitive actions." Ericsson, K. Anders "An Introduction to *Cambridge Handbook of Expertise and Expert Performance*: Its Development, Organization, and Content," in Ericsson, K. Anders (ed.), *The Cambridge Handbook of Expertise and Expert Performance* (Cambridge: Cambridge University Press, 2006), 3–20, 12.

[125] Ericsson, K. Anders, "Protocol Analysis and Expert Thought: Concurrent Verbalizations of Thinking during Experts' Performance on Representative Tasks," in Ericsson, K. Anders (ed.), *The Cambridge Handbook of Expertise and Expert Performance* (Cambridge: Cambridge University Press, 2006), 223–241, 235–236.

[126] Feltovich, Paul J., Prietula, Michael J., and Ericsson, K. Anders, "Studies of Expertise from Psychological Perspectives," in Ericsson, K. Anders (ed.), *The Cambridge Handbook of Expertise and Expert Performance* (Cambridge: Cambridge University Press, 2006), 41–68, 61.

articulate our reasons for action. At the same time, when tasks become effortless, that allows us to focus our attention on other aspects of our practice or performance for better control. So, both deliberate practice and skillful performances involve an interplay between automatic and deliberate processes in skill acquisition. Furthermore, experience also helps us to refine our mental representations (in terms of schemas and mental models) of the skill domain. Frequent experience can make schemas 'chronically accessible', influencing how we perceive situations through the perspective of that schema. We also update our mental models with experience, as we are refining them as we practice or perform our skill. All of these aspects are important to account for in any philosophical theory involving skill.

Dreyfus on Expertise

The Dreyfus model of skill acquisition is probably the most well-known philosophical account of expertise, and it has been extended into accounts of ethical expertise.[127] It represents a phenomenological approach to understanding expertise. While the psychological research partially supports their view, it also provides a corrective for all those things the Dreyfus model leaves out, as the Dreyfus account overemphasizes the role of automatic processes and mostly neglects the deliberative processes. The following section presents a very brief outline of the Dreyfus model, and then points out those features of skilled performance that the model neglects.[128]

The Dreyfus model divides skill acquisition into five stages: novice, advanced beginner, competent performer, proficient performer, and expert. At the initial stages of skill acquisition, novices follow simple and context-free rules, such as, in cases of driving, "shift into second gear at ten m.p.h.," or use the two-second rule in judging how much space to leave between you and the car in front of you. Since the rules at this stage are

---

[127] See Dreyfus, Hubert, "Overcoming the Myth of the Mental: How Philosophers Can Profit from the Phenomenology of Everyday Expertise," *Proceedings and Addresses of the American Philosophical Association*, 79:2 (2005), 47–65. Dreyfus, Hubert, "Could Anything Be More Intelligible Than Everyday Intelligibility? Reinterpreting Division I of Being and Time in the Light of Division II," in Faulconer, James E. and Wrathall, Mark A. (eds.), *Appropriating Heidegger* (Cambridge, UK: Cambridge University Press, 2000). Dreyfus, Hubert, *What Computers Still Can't Do: A Critique of Artificial Reason* (Cambridge: MIT Press, 1992). Dreyfus, Hubert and Dreyfus, Stuart, "The Ethical Implications of the Five-Stage Skill-Acquisition Model," *Bulletin of Science, Technology & Society*, 24:3 (2004), 251–264.

[128] Some further critiques of the Dreyfus model, particularly the way it ignores the distinction between *techne* and *phronesis*, will be discussed in Chapter 4.

context-free, however, they are apt to fail in a variety of different circumstances, such as when driving in the rain or in heavy traffic. As the novice gains experience, she discovers new features of situations, or someone else points them out, as relevant. Instead of relying only upon rules, the advanced beginner starts using maxims, which are not context-free like rules, but rather take into account the new features of situations of which the advanced beginner is aware. A maxim for driving might be "when the engine sounds like its racing shift up in gear." This maxim refers to the situational aspect of engine sounds, which it takes experience to recognize, and so this type of instruction is inappropriate for novices.

Even these maxims have their limitations, however, for the number of situational factors can become overwhelming. Moving beyond maxims requires making choices about what the most relevant factor is in a situation, and this is done by adopting a specific plan or perspective. According to the Dreyfus model, the competent performer feels responsible for both the choice of perspective and the outcome of that choice, and thus becomes emotionally involved in the experience of the outcome. "An outcome that is clearly successful is deeply satisfying and leaves a vivid memory of the plan chosen and of the situation as seen from the perspective of the plan. Disasters, likewise, are not easily forgotten."[129] These outcomes provide the feedback that a person needs in order to improve her skill. The feedback, if positive, reinforces making that choice again in a similar situation. The feedback, if negative, prompts the person to make a different choice in that situation. While the competent performer has to make up rules to help her decide what plan or perspective to adopt in order to focus in on the relevant features of a situation, the proficient performer no longer uses rules or even makes a choice about a plan. The proficient performer simply experiences the situation in the light of a certain perspective, without making a conscious decision about the most appropriate perspective to take in the situation.

The final stage is that of expertise. Dreyfus discovered that one of the hallmark features of expertise is an intuitive form of decision-making. By 'intuition', he is "referring to the understanding that effortlessly occurs upon seeing similarities with previous experiences."[130] The ability of the expert to act well intuitively is due to the expert's experience and

---

[129] Dreyfus, Hubert and Dreyfus, Stuart, *Mind Over Machine: The Power of Human Intuition and Expertise in the Era of the Computer* (Oxford: Basil Blackwell, 1986), 26.
[130] Dreyfus, Hubert and Dreyfus, Stuart, *Mind Over Machine: The Power of Human Intuition and Expertise in the Era of the Computer* (Oxford: Basil Blackwell, 1986), 28.

familiarity with the situation in which she acts. The immediacy of the expert's judgment occurs because of repeated exposure to similar previous experiences, and the outcome of actions taken in those situations.[131] The expert knows what actions are required and how to perform them in that situation without detached calculation or having to weigh alternatives. An expert driver will shift gears when appropriate without even being aware of it. Dreyfus also found that experts frequently were not able to give an account of how they knew what to do. One might be an expert skier but find it quite difficult to teach others how to ski. On the Dreyfus account, since experts generally act well without applying rules and principles, it is no surprise that experts often find it difficult to explain their actions by reference to principles. Dreyfus explicitly argues against any articulation requirement for expertise:

> Rationalists say that one must be able to articulate the principles underlying any rational decision. We say, not unless you build it into your definition of rational. If you mean anybody must be able to articulate the principles underlying a decision that they make that turns out to be a good decision based on past experience, and even perhaps the best decision as shown by playing out a game or doing an autopsy, then it is just false – a mistake that starts with Socrates and Plato – to hold that such a decision makes somebody able to articulate his principles.[132]

Of course, some experts are articulate or good at teaching others, but these abilities are not in any way necessary for expertise.

The Dreyfus account certainly captures the aspects of skilled performance that become automatic, but it also overgeneralizes expert performance on the basis of only those aspects. Dreyfus seems sometimes at pains to avoid talk of deliberation and choice with regard to expertise. It is mainly at the early stages of skill acquisition that Dreyfus acknowledges the role of deliberation and the need to make conscious choices between alternatives. But the deliberative processes are seen as a crutch that the performer eventually needs to let go of in order to improve her level of skill, and where expertise is only understood in terms of automatic processes. However, Dreyfus underestimates the role of deliberative processes in skill acquisition and performance in two main respects: (1) the degree to which practice must be 'deliberate practice' involving self-regulating behavior in

---

[131] Dreyfus, Hubert and Dreyfus, Stuart, "Towards a Phenomenology of Ethical Expertise," *Human Studies*, 14 (1991), 229–250, 235.

[132] Dreyfus, Hubert in Dreyfus, Hubert and Dreyfus, Stuart, "Sustaining Non-Rationalized Practices: Body-Mind, Power, and Situational Ethics. Interview Conducted by Bent Flyvbjerg, *Praxis International*, 11 (1991), 93–113,111–112.

both the early *and* advanced stages of skill acquisition; and (2) the role of deliberative processes in both strategic and situational control over a skilled performance.

First, the initial stages of skill development on the Dreyfus model are characterized in terms of rule-following. A novice relies on context-free rules, at least until she gains enough experience that she can use more sophisticated rules that refer to situational cues that she has learned to recognize. While this is certainly a familiar aspect of learning a skill, what is not mentioned is the role of deliberate practice and the need for self-regulating behavior. That is, the focus on the Dreyfus model is what performance is like at each stage of skill development, rather than the factors that enable one to improve (beyond needing more experience). Second, the main deliberative factor in expertise on the Dreyfus model is the rule-following of the novice and advanced beginner, which is something that needs to be left behind to progress to higher levels of skill. Thus, on the Dreyfus model, there seems to be no important deliberative aspects that carry over into higher levels of performance. However, improvement in one's level of skill always requires deliberate aspects such as deliberate practice and self-regulating behavior. As Darcia Narvaez points out, "[c]oaching self-regulation requires enlisting the deliberative mind to help the intuitive mind. Armed with theoretical knowledge, the deliberative mind, for example, plays a critical role in learning by selecting the environments from which the intuitive mind learns effective behaviors, thereby accelerating implicit learning."[133] So while rule-following does drop out of the picture at higher levels of skill, not all deliberative aspects from the initial stages drop out (such as mental modeling). These are important features of expertise that are absent in the Dreyfus model, and certainly skew the view towards an overemphasis on automatic processes.

Second, while expert performance displays automaticity with respect to implementation control, some situational control and most strategic control requires the use of deliberative processes. For example, you may be driving on 'auto-pilot' on the way home when you get an emergency call from a friend or from work, and then you have to decide whether to change your destination. You have to deliberate about the competing goals in this situation, and how you will direct the exercise of your skill (i.e. strategic control). Or take for example driving in bad weather and coming

---

[133] Narvaez, Darcia, "Integrative Ethical Education," in Killen, Melanie and Smetana, Judith (eds.), *Handbook of Moral Development* (Mahwah, NJ: Erlbaum, 2006), 703–733, 723.

up behind someone driving slowly. Will you attempt a somewhat risky maneuver to pass the slow driver (perhaps because you are in a rush somewhere), or would you rather play it safe and just drive slower?

Similarly, you will likely need to pay some attention to the present situation when driving in bad weather (i.e. situation control). While Dreyfus does acknowledge that in unfamiliar situations even an expert will have to switch to a deliberative approach, these instances count as rare exceptions for him. Otherwise he treats deliberation as something that interferes with the smooth running of one's automatic processes. However, truly familiar situations where there is no variation to pay attention to are likely the rare exceptions instead. Team sports are a good example of this, as players are rarely faced with the exact same team along with individual matchups, using the exact same offensive and defensive tactics, etc. Furthermore, automatic processes are not necessarily disrupted by the use of deliberation. As Christensen et al. note, for example, "a driver can simultaneously have heightened awareness of nearby cars during a passing maneuver and low awareness of changing gears."[134] Or, to put the point differently, you are able to have a heightened awareness of the location of other cars (deliberate situation control) precisely because you do not need to pay any attention to changing gears (automatic implementation control). If it required a lot of your attention to change gears correctly, say because you are not used to driving a stick shift, then you would not be able to also pay greater attention to what the other cars around you are doing. So, it is important to keep in mind that one of the main benefits of automaticity is that it frees up your attention for other aspects of your performance, and not that it serves mainly to make deliberative processes unnecessary as the Dreyfus account implies.[135]

---

[134] Christensen, Wayne, Sutton, John, and Mcilwain, Doris J. F., "Cognition in Skilled Action: Meshed Control and the Varieties of Skill Experience," *Mind & Language*, 31:1 (2016), 37–66, 50.

[135] Interestingly, Ellen Fridland extends this kind of critique of Dreyfus to Jason Stanley's attempts to reduce know-how to propositional knowledge, arguing that "[s]urprisingly then, for very different reasons and with very different agendas, both Stanley and the Dreyfus end up with an inadequate account of skill for the very same reason: both are overzealous in reducing control to an unintelligent, mechanistic, stimulus-response process." Fridland, Ellen, "They've Lost Control: Reflections on Skill," *Synthese*, 191 (2014), 2729–2750, 2742. I do not tackle Stanley's account here, both because it has not been extended to ethical expertise as has the views of Dreyfus and Annas, and because I agree with Fridland that there has already been a sufficient critique on Stanley's attempt to account for know-how and skill purely in terms of propositional knowledge.

Annas on Expertise

Julia Annas is one of the few modern writers on virtue to defend a skill model of virtue. While elements of her account of virtue will be discussed in later chapters, what is of concern here is the view of skills and expertise that she is working from. She relies on an intellectual account of expertise, which portrays expertise as if it were primarily a matter of deliberative processes. Her view can thus help correct for how the Dreyfus account underemphasizes the role of deliberative processes in expertise. Though, like Dreyfus, she also overgeneralizes, but instead with respect to the role of deliberation. Annas' discussion draws mainly on Socratic and Stoic ideas about the nature of skills and expertise. According to Annas, there are three necessary elements of a genuine skill: the skill must be teachable, there must be unifying principles underlying the skill that the expert can grasp, and experts should be able to give an account of skilled actions. As Annas notes, these three elements are also connected, "since a teacher can scarcely teach if she is completely inarticulate about her subject, and what is taught must be a unified body of practical knowledge rather than a bunch of unconnected practical tips, if it is an expertise that we have."[136]

The first element is that the skill is teachable, by which Annas also means that an expert can teach it. Since the expert has learned something, she should be able to teach what she has learned to someone else. The expert has learned the theory behind the skill. This contrasts with what Socrates refers to as a 'knack', which is something that can be picked up merely by trying to do it yourself, or by watching someone else do it. Knacks lack the intellectual component that is found in skills.[137] Rhetoric and cooking are putative examples of mere knacks. Genuine skills have a strong intellectual component, and this is what the expert is able to teach.

Annas is surely correct that skills are teachable, as coaches and trainers can provide essential feedback and deliberate practice routines for improvement. As Annas rightly notes: "aspiration leads the learner to strive to *improve*, to do what he is doing better rather than taking it over by rote from the teacher."[138] Virtue, while considered to involve habitual actions, is not mere mindless or route repetition. However, Annas is also making a stronger claim, that the expert, in virtue of her expertise, should be able to

---

[136] Annas, Julia, "The Structure of Virtue," in DePaul, Michael and Zagzebski, Linda (eds.), *Intellectual Virtue* (Oxford: Clarendon Press, 2003), 15–33, 18.
[137] Annas, Julia, *Intelligent Virtue* (Oxford: Oxford University Press, 2011), 20.
[138] Annas, Julia, *Intelligent Virtue* (Oxford: Oxford University Press, 2011), 18.

teach others. She goes as far as to say that "we do in fact deny that someone is an expert if she is inarticulate about her subject, unable to teach it or unable to express more than isolated tips about its practice."[139] The psychological research, though, does not appear to support this stronger claim:

> Although it is tempting to believe that upon knowing how the expert does something, one might be able to 'teach' this to novices directly, this has not been the case (e.g., Klein & Hoffman, 1993). Expertise is a long-term developmental process, resulting from rich instrumental experiences in the world and extensive practice. These cannot simply be handed to someone.[140]

Part of the difficulty in teaching is that expertise is not primarily an intellectual grasp of theory, but the development of a number of cognitive adaptations (many of which are automatic processes) that result from experience and practice. There is no way to gain this kind of knowledge except by going through the same kind of process. Furthermore, one weakness of experts appears to be that they have trouble predicting novice performance, perhaps because they cannot easily take on the perspective of a novice attempting a task. Certainly, a good teacher needs to be able to appreciate the perspective of a novice, in order to provide helpful guidance at that stage of skill development. Being an expert seems to carry an inherent disadvantage in that regard. However, one should not overstate the case, as experts can be good teachers. It is just not the case, as Annas claims, that expertise necessarily translates into being able to teach well. For example, many in academia should be familiar with professors that are good at research, but not so good at teaching. Being a good teacher requires an additional skill set beyond being able to perform well yourself.

The second element expands upon the intellectual component found in teaching. To possess a skill requires what Annas refers to as having "a unified grasp of its field."[141] This implies that there are principles that unify the field of a skill, and that the expert has a grasp of these principles. There is no such thing as having expert knowledge of only part of the field. One could not claim to be an expert at something as narrow as only being able to fix

[139] Annas, Julia, "The Structure of Virtue," in DePaul, Michael and Zagzebski, Linda (eds.), *Intellectual Virtue* (Oxford: Clarendon Press, 2003), 15–33, 33.
[140] Feltovich, Paul J., Prietula, Michael J., and Ericsson, K. Anders, "Studies of Expertise from Psychological Perspectives," in Ericsson, K. Anders (ed.), *The Cambridge Handbook of Expertise and Expert Performance* (Cambridge: Cambridge University Press, 2006), 41–68, 46. Klein, Gary A. and Hoffman, Robert R., "Seeing the Invisible: Perceptual-Cognitive Aspects of Expertise," in Rabinowitz, Mitchell (ed.), *Cognitive Science Foundations of Instruction* (Hillsdale, NJ: Erlbaum, 1993).
[141] Annas, Julia, "Virtue as a Skill," *International Journal of Philosophical Studies*, 3:2 (1995), 227–243, 231.

Toyotas, or to claim, as Ion does, only to know Homer and not much of any other poet. Annas gives further examples of this demanding condition:

> The expert in the language will have mastery of all that is needed to understand the language, and, moreover, will see how it is all unified. Similarly, someone learning a practical skill like building will pick up bits of know-how and technique here and there; the expert, however, will have mastery of everything relevant to that kind of building, and will have unified that mastery so as to be able to understand his own and others' successes and mistakes, and to be able to apply his skill in new situations without further learning being required.[142]

Expertise requires understanding the principles that govern the entire field, and not just some parts of it. This unified grasp is what allows experts to deal with unfamiliar situations in the way that someone who has simply memorized a set of rules cannot, since it enables them to act well with regard to all areas of the field.

However, the expertise literature throws some doubt on experts having a 'unified grasp of the field'. It is not just the case that expertise is domain-limited, but it is also limited even within a domain. Although Annas relies on medicine as the main example of a 'genuine' skill that fits her account of skills, "studies showed that the same physician can demonstrate widely different profiles of competence, depending on his or her particular experiential history with different types of cases."[143] Expertise arises out of experience, and one's experience places a limiting factor on which situations one can display expert-level performance. Annas, by contrast, thinks that expertise is a matter of an intellectual grasp of principles in a domain, such that once you grasp the principles, you are no longer limited in acting at the level of an expert, as no further learning is required. She is surely correct in thinking that experts should be able to generalize to some extent from their experiences, such that they would have some idea of how to act well in unfamiliar situations. But it is important not to overestimate how well experts will react in novel situations, since their expertise is still linked to a certain history of experience.[144]

---

[142] Annas, Julia, "The Structure of Virtue," in DePaul, Michael and Zagzebski, Linda (eds.), *Intellectual Virtue* (Oxford: Clarendon Press, 2003), 15–33, 18.

[143] Feltovich, Paul J., Prietula, Michael J., and Ericsson, K. Anders, "Studies of Expertise from Psychological Perspectives," in Ericsson, K. Anders (ed.), *The Cambridge Handbook of Expertise and Expert Performance* (Cambridge: Cambridge University Press, 2006), 41–68, 47.

[144] For example, "[t]he experienced pilot who has never encountered or been trained for a particular anomaly will be challenged to process information in working memory to determine what is happening, and may be inefficient in searching for relevant information to solve the problem, in much the same way as when she was a novice pilot (although it is likely that she will not be as bad off as

The third element of a genuine skill further develops the previous intellectual components, by requiring that experts have the ability to 'give an account' of their actions. Giving an account, according to Annas, means "that the person with a skill be able explicitly to explain and justify her particular decisions and judgements, and to do so in terms of some general grasp of the principles which define that skill."[145] The expert needs to be able to articulate the reasons for her actions, and this explanation should draw upon the expert's grasp of the principles underlying the skill. Although this condition could be thought of as requiring merely that the principles are articulable, rather than requiring that the expert can actually articulate the reasons herself, Annas explicitly describes this requirement in terms of the expert being able to articulate the reasons for her actions.

As discussed earlier, however, research shows that experts cannot be relied on to accurately articulate their reasons for action.[146] Skilled performance requires that some aspects of the performance are automatic, so that attention can be focused on the other aspects, and the use of automatic processes means not all of what the expert does is open to introspection and articulation. Not only is the articulation requirement controversial, but overall the three essential elements form a high intellectual standard for skills that strikes people as counterintuitive, and Annas tries to defend herself from this kind of objection:

> For at this point someone will claim that he has learnt to be a plumber just by watching old Joe over there, without explicitly learning anything, and without working out any general principles unifying the field of practice. This kind of counterexample, however, misses the point. For what concerns Socrates is not the intuitive conception of skills, but the intellectual structure of cases which are admittedly cases of genuine skills.[147]

Annas acknowledges that there seem to be cases of people who acquire a skill without perhaps explicitly learning anything, and even more likely

---

a complete novice). Most people do not operate at the level of novice all the time or expert all the time, but rather move around in between, using combinations of cognitive mechanisms depending on the situation at hand and the availability of key constructs (e.g., mental models and schema)." Endsley, Mica, "Expertise and Situation Awareness," in Ericsson, K. Anders (ed.), *The Cambridge Handbook of Expertise and Expert Performance* (Cambridge: Cambridge University Press, 2006), 633–651, 640.

[145] Annas, Julia, "Virtue as a Skill," *International Journal of Philosophical Studies* 3:2 (1995), 227–243, 233.

[146] As Paul Bloomfield notes, "[s]ometimes, if doctors are asked why they go on as they do, at some point they end up giving the same answer that practitioners of cookery give, the same one that Socrates finds distinctive of knacks: 'Because it works'. (This point seems strangely missing in *Gorgias*.)" Bloomfield, Paul, *Moral Reality* (Oxford: Oxford University Press, 2001), 61.

[147] Annas, Julia, "Virtue as a Skill," *International Journal of Philosophical Studies*, 3:2 (1995), 227–243, 232.

without having some unified grasp of principles underlying the skill. These sorts of cases appear to be counter-examples to Annas's account, since the high intellectual standards are not necessary for acquiring those skills.

Annas's reply is that genuine skills do exhibit the intellectual structure described, and those are the skills to which Socrates refers. This response seems to imply that what is wrong with this type of example is that the putative skill is not a genuine skill, and hence does not represent a counter-example to her claims about the structure of skills. While this type of response may be appropriate with regard to some putative skills, it becomes problematic if every alleged counter-example is simply dismissed by defin-ition as not a genuine skill if it lacks the proper intellectual requirements.

Annas, however, does not respond in this way to all counter-examples. Annas allows there to be differences in the structure of genuine skills, which is a point especially relevant to the third intellectual element of skills, for:

> Even more than the other conditions, it is clear that this idea – that a skill involve a rational ability to explain and defend one's exercise of it – is likely to be quite false of a number of examples of actual skills. For this condition excludes an inarticulate ability from being a skill; and this certainly seems to flout our everyday intuitions about what is and what is not a skill. But once again we must ask, "Does this matter?" It is clear that Socrates is not interested in skills for their own sake. He is concerned with the idea that virtue is, or is like, a skill, and so he is concerned with the intellectual structure that some skills, at any rate, display.[148]

Annas admits that the requirement of giving an account is not true for a number of actual skills. For Annas, this result is not problematic, so long as there are some skills that do display these strong intellectual components, because it is those kinds of skills that she thinks share a structure similar to virtue. So, her claims should not be read as applying to everything we might label a skill.

That there are skills that display the three intellectual components, however, is far from clear. One of the skills she does mention is medicine, but evidence from the medical field calls into question experts displaying all of these strong intellectual components.[149] For example:

> Bias is probably one of the most serious handicaps of experts, especially in the medical profession ... my colleagues and I found the experienced

---

[148] Annas, Julia, "Virtue as a Skill," *International Journal of Philosophical Studies*, 3:2 (1995), 227–243, 233.

[149] Medicine is also not a good example for her account given the requirement to have a unified grasp of all the principles of the field, which in the case of medicine would be too much for anyone.

physicians to manifest serious biases. We presented several types of cases to specialists, such as hematologists, cardiologists, and infectious disease specialists. Some were hematology cases and others were cardiology cases. We found that regardless of the type of specialized case, specialists tended to generate hypotheses that corresponded to their field of expertise: Cardiologists tended to generate more cardiology-type hypotheses, whether the case was one of a blood disease or an infectious disease[150]

The psychological research thus appears to temper some of Annas's claims about expertise, when she overstates the intellectual aspects. Overall, while Dreyfus and Annas draw our attention to some important aspects of expertise, focusing on automatic or deliberate processes (respectively), they both overstate the importance of that process while also neglecting the importance of the other process. Furthermore, neither grounds their account of skill in self-regulation, which is problematic both for getting a better understanding of skill acquisition and for conceptualizing virtue as a skill (as we will see throughout the remaining chapters).

Conclusion

There are important automatic and deliberative aspects to both skill acquisition and expert performance, and hopefully the above discussion has presented a general, but balanced, approach to this that also enables us to understand how these two aspects interrelate. The psychological research helps to correct those philosophical accounts of expertise that overemphasize one aspect over the other.[151] Because the acquisition of skill is a paradigm case of how people can gain knowledge to improve their behavior, the framework presented in this chapter will serve as a foundation for understanding moral self-regulation and the acquisition of virtue in the next chapter.[152]

---

[150] Chi, Michelene T. H., "Two Approaches to the Study of Experts' Characteristics," in Ericsson, K. Anders (ed.), *The Cambridge Handbook of Expertise and Expert Performance* (Cambridge: Cambridge University Press, 2006), 21–30, 26–27. Hashem, Ahmad, Chi, Michelene T. H., and Friedman, Charles P., "Medical Errors as a Result of Specialization," *Journal of Biomedical Informatics*, 36 (2003), 61–69.

[151] "In expert education, the intuitive mind and the analytical mind are developed together." Narvaez, Darcia, "The Neo-Kohlbergian Tradition and Beyond: Schemas, Expertise and Character," in Carlo, Gustav and Pope-Edwards, Carolyn (eds.), *Nebraska Symposium on Motivation*, Vol. 51: Moral Motivation through the Lifespan (Lincoln, NE: University of Nebraska Press, 2005), 119–163, 253.

[152] However, I should also note that there are additional details of self-regulation and skill acquisition that I will cover in later chapters, to handle some more specific issues.

CHAPTER 2

Moral Virtues as Skills

This chapter follows on the structure of the previous chapter. Following Flanagan's "Principle of Minimal Psychological Realism," I conceptualize moral agency as a specialized form of human agency in general. Insofar as agency is exercised through self-regulation, the same will be true of moral agency. We can attempt to regulate our intrapersonal (or covert) processes, our overt behavior, and our environment to better meet our moral standards. Successful moral self-regulation will include not only the specific moral standards we adopt, but also the strategies we use for conforming to those standards. From there I discuss the acquisition of moral skills (i.e. the moral virtues) as a sophisticated form of self-regulation, to deal with the complexity of morality.[1] Like skilled performers who gradually increase their knowledge within their skill domain, represented by increasingly nuanced and more accessible schemas, we can expect that people will vary with respect to the content and accessibility of their moral schema. The research on expertise will thus inform the moral ideal of the virtuous person. This conception of 'virtue as skill' turns out to have many affinities with neo-Aristotelian accounts of virtue, which are dominant in virtue theory. Neo-Aristotelian accounts of the virtuous person bear a striking resemblance to descriptions of experts. This is perhaps of no surprise given the frequent skill analogies that Aristotle used in explaining virtue. Many of the similarities between this skill model of virtue and neo-Aristotelian accounts of virtue will be brought out in the discussion, as well as the dissimilarities.[2] Furthermore, a virtue as skill model will not necessarily embrace all the virtues common to neo-Aristotelian accounts. I will discuss individuating the virtues on a skill model, how some traits commonly

---

[1] I move to the question of intellectual virtues in Chapter 3.

[2] Though I should note that nothing really hinges on the degree to which the skill model of virtue matches up to neo-Aristotelian accounts, and I will offer in this chapter some rebuttals to the arguments of Aristotle and others that virtues cannot be understood to be skills (even when they grant that there are a lot of similarities).

thought of as 'virtues of will power' will turn out to be excellences of self-regulation more generally. Finally, I will argue that vice, on the contrary, should not be conceptualized as a skill, and that this does not threaten to undermine viewing virtue as skill.

Moral Self-Regulation

Moral behavior is basically self-regulation with reference to specifically moral standards. The importance of moral standards has of course been a focus of ethical theory. However, it is important to note that moral self-regulation only requires having some moral standard or other to conform to, rather than necessarily having a correct moral standard. So, by 'moral standards' I do not intend to set up a contrast here with 'immoral standards'. Rather, I mean to refer to those standards by which we make evaluative judgments with respect to moral actions (as opposed to standards we use to evaluate athletic competitions, musical performances, political debates, etc.). So in that sense, everybody has moral standards, even if they are as corrupt as to permit committing genocide against certain ethnic groups (other than one's own, of course, for that would be viewed as wrong). Thus, one main goal of ethics is to figure out which moral standards ought to be guiding us.[3]

Ethics has also frequently been concerned with moral motivation, though the focus is often on what sorts of thoughts or feelings should prompt moral action (such as impartial considerations of duty or justice, versus partial concerns for love and friendship). That one ought to be highly motivated to achieve moral standards is usually, and unsurprisingly, taken as a given in ethical theory. Perhaps of greater practical concern are the mechanisms by which people internalize moral values such that they rank high on the hierarchy of one's goals. This point is familiar in the rejection of the pursuit of moral goals for purely instrumental reasons, since that would put moral goals lower on the hierarchy, and thus more likely to be compromised for the sake of more valued goals. The action phase model further helps to illuminate the difference between stages of motivation (goal setting) and volition (goal striving), which are often run together. While people set moral goals for themselves (e.g. 'be honest'), I suspect that people are likely to leave it at having set a goal intention,

---

[3] I will pick back up on this issue in Chapter 4 when I discuss the importance of practical wisdom in reflecting on our moral standards.

without further setting implementation intentions to achieve that goal, or otherwise treating the goal as complex enough to require skill acquisition.

Achieving these moral goals will also require self-control, as it is widely recognized that it can be difficult to adhere to moral standards, since morality has to compete with other valued goals. That effortful self-control can have the effect of shifting motivation away from prioritizing moral goals (during the fourth phase of evaluation, as discussed in the previous chapter), however, is a point that is less widely acknowledged in ethics generally. Perhaps virtue theory does better at recognizing this point, given the emphasis it places on developing good habits, where acting in conformity to one's moral standards becomes automatic, and thus the effortless self-control does not have that effect of shifting priorities. Also of relevance is the distinction between self-control and grit, the latter of which receives far less attention. Insofar as we want people to place a high value on achieving moral goals, grit will be important to maintaining a long-term commitment to such goals.

This account of moral self-regulation has some overlap with Tanner and Christen's account of moral intelligence, which makes some use of the framework of social cognitive theory and self-regulation that I covered in the previous chapter.[4] However, as I will argue, they unnecessarily theorize new types of competences for specifically moral self-regulation. They conceive of moral intelligence in terms of five moral competences: moral compass, moral commitment, moral sensitivity, moral problem solving, and moral resoluteness. The moral compass is essentially having moral standards or goals that guide us.[5] Moral commitment reflects how highly valued that moral goal is relative to other goal commitments.

These two ideas of a compass and commitment, though, are already captured in the hierarchical organization of goals, and the phase of goal setting (i.e. commitment). Moral behavior must be guided of course by goals with moral content, and the degree to which one is guided by such goals reflects how highly valued they are. They claim that moral commitment is the central competence, because a more committed individual is

---

4 Tanner, Carmen and Christen, Markus, "Moral Intelligence – A Framework for Understanding Moral Competences," in Christen, Markus, van Schaik, Carel, Fischer, Johannes, and Huppenbauer, Markus (eds.), *Empirically Informed Ethics: Morality between Facts and Norms* (Switzerland: Springer, 2014), 119–136.
5 Tanner and Christen make a similar claim, with respect to their idea of a 'moral compass', to mine that it requires some set of moral standards to operate, rather than a specific set of moral standards. They also explain their concept of the moral compass in terms of moral schemas.

more likely to engage in moral self-regulation. This is true, though it is also true for any goal commitment. After all, a person is motivated by many competing goals, and so the extent to which one is willing to engage in self-regulation on behalf of any particular goal depends in part on how valued that goal is relative to the competing goals, and this is equally true with both moral and non-moral goals. For people who value chess to the extent that 'chess is life',[6] for example, we could expect that they would hold themselves to high standards of performance, be sensitive to the nuances of chess positions, have highly effective automatic and deliberate problem-solving routines, etc. In this sense, there is no need to introduce special 'moral' conceptions of these aspects of self-regulation, as they do not operate differently in the moral case from the non-moral case (and labeling them as specifically 'moral' capacities suggests that they do).[7]

Likewise, I would also resist putting the term 'moral' at the beginning of the other competences. With all these components of self-regulation, there is not a special version of it for conforming to moral standards. For example, self-control will operate the same regardless of the goal being pursued, and so there is no special faculty of 'moral' resoluteness.[8] 'Moral sensitivity' and 'moral problem solving' would be parts of any moral skill acquisition. However, I do not see there being either a general moral sensitivity competence, or a general moral problem-solving competence. All skill acquisition involves developing a greater sensitivity to the relevant factors in that domain, along with greater problem-solving abilities. Furthermore, acquiring skills will require having standards that guide the skill development, a need for commitment to those standards, and the resoluteness to carry through. So competent self-regulation with regard to moral standards enables the acquisition of specific moral skills, like honesty or kindness, which are sensitive to different features of moral relevance and will also require different problem-solving approaches.

Finally, moral motivation on their account is something that is an overarching feature of moral action. They define it as "the desire to bring current state of affairs into line with some valued moral standpoints," such

---

[6] Attributed to Bobby Fischer.

[7] My critique is based on thinking that we should avoid positing new concepts for the moral domain unless it is for an aspect unique to morality. Where you start to get complications with self-regulation of specifically moral standards is with the phenomenon of moral disengagement, which I will discuss further in Chapter 5.

[8] Of course, that is not to imply that people have equal self-control with regard to all aspects of their life. Duckworth has shown that self-control is domain specific, as I will discuss later in this chapter, and I assume someone's self-control could vary with respect to different moral standards.

that one's level of motivation will affect one's moral competences.[9] Motivation on their account is basically a reflection of one's degree of commitment, where greater commitment should show itself in greater levels of sensitivity and resoluteness. While I agree that levels of commitment have this trickle-down effect on other aspects of self-regulation, I think this added step is unnecessary, as having a goal commitment of any kind comes with an intention to bring the current state of affairs into conformity with that goal. This works via a self-sanctioning process, described in the previous chapter, whereby you gain self-satisfaction by achieving goals, but feelings of self-censure when you do not. The other drawback to adding an overarching feature of motivation is that it blurs the distinction between motivation and commitment on the one hand (guided by considerations of desirability and feasibility of goals), and volition on the other hand (guided by concerns of how to achieve one's goal commitments).

Related to the above account is Christen and Alfano's approach to capturing moral agency, which also has some parallels to my account. They conceive of moral agency as having three aspects: (1) a normative frame of reference for evaluating actions and events; (2) the exercise of certain competences that are necessary for moral action; and (3) the exercise of those competences occurring in situated contexts.[10] They claim these aspects roughly match up with three different approaches to studying morality: moral philosophy; personality psychology; and social psychology (respectively). Moral philosophy is certainly engaged in, amongst other things, determining which standards one should adopt to guide moral agency and self-regulation, but it also helps to determine the motivational structure that agents should have.[11] Psychological research on competences helps to illuminate the use of self-regulation and skill acquisition. The third aspect of situational context points to the triadic relationship between person, behavior, and environment.

---

[9] Tanner, Carmen and Christen, Markus, "Moral Intelligence – A Framework for Understanding Moral Competences," in Christen, Markus, van Schaik, Carel, Fischer, Johannes, and Huppenbauer, Markus (eds.), *Empirically Informed Ethics: Morality between Facts and Norms* (Switzerland: Springer, 2014), 119–136, 123.

[10] Christen, Markus and Alfano, Mark, "Outlining the Field – A Research Program for Empirically Informed Ethics," in Christen, Markus, van Schaik, Carel, Fischer, Johannes, and Huppenbauer, Markus (eds.), *Empirically Informed Ethics: Morality between Facts and Norms* (Switzerland: Springer, 2014), 3–28.

[11] This will certainly have implications for determining the kinds of competences we need to acquire for moral agency. But, as noted by the principle of minimal psychological realism, this philosophical endeavor will have to be constrained both by the kinds of psychological competences we can acquire, and by our knowledge of how situational factors influence behavior.

Furthermore, my focus on virtue as a skill can be seen as addressing one of the major research questions they pose for doing empirically informed ethics – dealing with moral complexity. As they note, ethical reasoning usually has the effect of increasing the complexity of moral problems, whereas "a moral appraisal of a situation often has a simplification effect . . . it makes a seemingly complex problem easier to decide."[12] This is precisely what makes skill acquisition necessary in general – dealing with highly complex domains, such that there is a need to find ways to simplify the complexity in order to act well.[13] As discussed in the previous chapter, skill acquisition, through deliberate practice, allows for difficult tasks to be done effortlessly, thus freeing one's attention to focus on more difficult problems. This allows us to handle the complexity incrementally, by making deliberate and effortful processes become intuitive and effortless, which accords with Christen and Alfano's contention that intuition plays an important role in navigating the complexity–simplicity relationship in morality.

Acquiring Virtue as a Skill

The acquisition of virtue will require what is generally involved in acquiring skills. The most important factor is experience. There appears to be no substitute for the approximately 10,000 hours that goes into acquiring expertise.[14] This fits in nicely with the emphasis virtue ethicists place on the time it takes to develop virtues. Aristotle, for example, denied that children have enough lived experience to be said to have virtues or vices.[15]

---

[12] Christen, Markus and Alfano, Mark, "Outlining the Field – A Research Program for Empirically Informed Ethics," in Christen, Markus, van Schaik, Carel, Fischer, Johannes, and Huppenbauer, Markus (eds.), *Empirically Informed Ethics: Morality between Facts and Norms* (Switzerland: Springer, 2014), 3–28, 27. They distinguish between the moral and ethical, as I do, by specifying that morals refer to whatever standards are guiding individuals, while ethics reflects a critical approach to moral standards.

[13] Note that skill acquisition is not the only means to simplify complex situations, as heuristics are another, though less reliable, way. Also, with regard to morality, some people like to adopt a simple 'black and white' approach to viewing moral problems. The problem with this way of simplifying, though, is that one is oversimplifying by merely ignoring the complexity – essentially pretending that complex issues are really simplistic. This is of course not a way to reliably act well, since you are not actually grappling with the complexity, but that does not stop many people from taking just such an approach.

[14] Though as I will point out later, both the acquisition of skill and virtue are a matter of degree, and the 10,000 hours is only meant to approximate what it takes to be operating at the highest levels.

[15] This stands in contrast to those who are surprised that children do not have virtues or vices. For example, John Doris cites the Hartshorne and May study as if it were a surprising result. "In their investigation of honesty in over 8,000 schoolchildren, Hartshorne and May concluded that

While training in virtue might start out for children with context-free rules, such as honesty requiring that you 'always tell the truth', the lessons should not stop there. If they did, then it would not take much experience or practice to figure out how to be honest (and certainly not 10,000 hours). But practical skills are complex and cannot be reduced to mere rules or principles. If a putative virtue is to fit the skill model, then it must demonstrate this kind of complexity. If honesty were to require only that we tell the truth, such that we act dishonestly if and only if we tell a lie, then it would not be so complex as to need lots of experience to be honest. It would be virtually impossible to forget what honesty requires of us, and one would not need any regular practice with honesty to remember what to do. In this case, honesty would not fit a skill model.

Of course, there are many reasons for rejecting the simple views of honesty and telling the truth. First, even with regard to telling the truth, we rarely want someone to tell us everything that they think is true about a subject matter – we do not literally want 'the whole truth'. There is an expectation that when telling us the truth, the person will tell us relevant information. It will not always be obvious which information is relevant and which is not, especially if it involves private or confidential information. A strategy of 'tell everything' is usually either not possible or a great waste of time. Furthermore, one can mislead people by only telling part of the truth. To this we can add to the complexity of trying to specify how much you are required to tell when you are on the witness stand in court, versus when you are representing your company in high stakes business negotiations, versus when you are playing poker, etc. Any plausible account of honesty will be complicated enough to fit the skill model, as it would take a lot of experience to figure out what honesty demands in a variety of situations.[16]

As the skill model makes clear, experience, however, is not sufficient for acquiring expertise. While you have to practice, in order to get better, one needs to engage in a deliberate practice that is structured on improving one's current level of skill. Furthermore, the kinds of strategies used for acting well vary depending on one's level of skill. Novices need to use different strategies than the expert, and the same would be true in the case of virtue. Novices might rely on context-free rules, such as 'switch from

deceptive and honest behavior are not the function of 'unified' traits but are 'specific functions of life situations.'" Doris, John, *Lack of Character* (Cambridge: Cambridge University Press, 2002), 63.

[16] See, for example, Miller, Christian B., "Honesty," in Sinnott-Armstrong, Walter and Miller, Christian B. (eds.), *Moral Psychology Volume 5: Virtue and Character* (Cambridge: MIT Press, 2017), 237–273.

2nd to 3rd gear at 20 m.p.h.', and this can be accommodated into a view of virtues as skills.[17] Hursthouse, for example, claims that there are rules that can be derived from virtues (v-rules as she calls them), such as "Do what is honest," and that these rules are useful for guiding action. Although the v-rules are couched in virtue and vice terms, Hursthouse says it does not follow that simpler context-free rules, like "Never lie," have no use:

> why should a proponent of virtue ethics deny the significance of such mother's-knee rules as 'Don't lie', 'Keep promises', 'Help others'? . . . Virtue ethicists want to emphasize the fact that, if children are to be taught to be honest, they must be taught to love and prize the truth, and that merely teaching them not to lie will not achieve this end. But they need not deny that, to achieve this end, teaching them not to lie is useful, or even indispensable.[18]

In both acquiring a skill and learning virtue, following simple rules can be useful for beginners, but there is a limit to that usefulness.

It takes some experience with practicing a skill to move beyond the use of context-free rules, and since novices by definition lack such experience, they will have to rely on strategies that the expert no longer uses. The non-virtuous person will likewise have to employ different strategies for acting well or avoiding vice. If the novice at virtue did not have to employ different strategies, as Robert Johnson rightly points out, "s/he would already possess the kind of psychological makeup that would make virtuous action second nature. In other words, s/he would not be a novice at all."[19] In both the case of skills and virtues, novices cannot, and should not attempt to, act in exactly the way the expert acts.

The form that deliberate practice takes will vary depending on one's current level of skill. Novices start with following simple rules. As a novice gains experience in a skill, new features of the situation are discovered by, or pointed out to, the novice as relevant. They are then able to follow guidelines, given to them by more experienced practitioners, based on these newly discovered features. Similar practices would be found in the development of virtue, but these practices should not be seen as something external to developing virtue, as Johnson seems to suggest when he claims that, "[o]ne can and should do many things, things other than simply

---

[17] Of course, it is better to change to a higher gear when the engine sounds like it is racing, but it takes experience (which a novice lacks) to recognize the different engine sounds.

[18] Hursthouse, Rosalind, *On Virtue Ethics*. (Oxford: Oxford University Press, 1999), 39.

[19] Johnson, Robert, "Virtue and Right," *Ethics* 113 (2003), 810–834, 821.

developing virtues, given that one's moral perception is imperfect. One is to seek counsel."[20] Feedback is crucial to the development of virtues, and one can gain this both from the counsel of others and from deliberate practice. With regard to the importance of practice and feedback in skill and virtue acquisition, Darcia Narvaez claims "as Aristotle pointed out and modern research confirms, virtuous character takes a lot of immersed *practice* in an environment that provides good, rather than poor, information on performance."[21]

It might be objected, though, that the kind of difficulties that one must practice to overcome are different in virtues and skills. Linda Zagzebski argues that skills are associated with techniques, where techniques are understood to be inherently difficult actions, whereas virtues are not. She claims that "[a]lthough some virtues involve being able to do difficult things, the difficulties involved are due to contrary inclinations (past or present), not to technical difficulties in the actions themselves."[22] The kind of contrary inclinations she has in mind are temptations to do something other than the virtuous act. She borrows this argument from James Wallace, who puts forth several arguments against virtues being skills. His version is as follows:

(1) Courage and patience are capacities to overcome difficulties arising from inclinations contrary to right action.
(2) Inclinations contrary to right action are not technical difficulties, but skills are always capacities to overcome technical difficulties. So courage and patience are not skills.[23]

There are several problems with this line of argument. First, there seems to be the implication in 2. that skills do not involve overcoming contrary inclinations. However, acquiring skills does require overcoming contrary inclinations, especially when Zagzebski cites "just plain laziness" as one of the contrary inclinations that must be overcome in developing virtues. Since achieving expertise is difficult, any inclination towards laziness will be an obstacle that has to be overcome. Second, it does not make sense to

---

[20] Johnson, Robert, "Virtue and Right," *Ethics*, 113 (2003), 810–834, 822.
[21] Narvaez, Darcia, "De neurobiology van ons morel functioneren [The neurobiology of moral formation and moral functioning]" *Pastorale Perspectieven*, 153:4 (2011), 10–18. See also her work on Integrative Ethical Education for putting these ideas to the test: Narvaez, Darcia, "Integrative Ethical Education," in Killen, Melanie and Smetana, Judith (eds.), *Handbook of Moral Development* (Mahwah, NJ: Erlbaum, 2006), 703–733.
[22] Zagzebski, Linda, *Virtues of the Mind* (Cambridge: Cambridge University Press, 1996), 108.
[23] Wallace, James, *Virtues and Vices* (Ithaca, NY: Cornell University Press, 1978), 44.

think of acting virtuously as not involving difficulties other than ones of inclination, as suggested in 1. That would imply that knowing what honesty requires is always simple. But honesty is a particularly difficult virtue to always know what it requires, as discussed above.

Third, even when virtues involve overcoming contrary inclinations, it does not follow that doing so does not involve techniques. Bob Roberts, in responding to Wallace's argument, points out how information of a technical sort may be needed in overcoming inclinations:

> if somebody already has a moral motive, and then finds that bad habits and adverse emotions are getting in the way of acting lovingly, the psychologist has a potential role, and though we would not normally call this role "technical," what the psychologist may supply here is precisely information and training of a "how to" sort. I suggest that when this "how to" knowledge has become assimilated, the person will have gained in the virtue of patience.[24]

Examples of the sort Roberts mentions can also be found in the literature on expertise, for example, "with athletes who have trouble controlling their negative outbursts, Loehr (1991), a sports psychologist at the elite Nick Bolletierri Tennis academy, recommended listing all of their negative responses and finding a positive alternative for each one, such as saying 'let it go' or "come on" (p. 47) when they lose a point."[25] So you cannot clearly separate figuring out how to overcome inclinations from how to solve technical difficulties. Thus, virtues and skills cannot be contrasted merely on the grounds that the difficulties involved in each are entirely distinct.

It might be objected at this point that all the deliberate practice and self-regulating behavior that goes into acquiring expertise is a point of departure from morality, for it might be that one does not need to do such extensive practice to be moral. Narvaez addresses this point in an instructive way, stating:

> As a result of my studies with groups differing in expertise, I believe that moral judgment is a domain that is similar to that of music. Most people

[24] Roberts, Bob, "Will Power and the Virtues," *The Philosophical Review*, 93:2 (1984), 227–247, 239. In fact, the role of social psychology lately in the virtue literature has been to point out some of the bad habits and adverse emotions that interfere with acting morally. I will discuss this more with the 'situationist' critique of virtue in Chapter 5.

[25] . Zimmerman Barry J, "Development and Adaptation of Expertise: The Role of Self-Regulatory Processes and Beliefs," in Ericsson, K. Anders (ed.), *The Cambridge Handbook of Expertise and Expert Performance* (Cambridge: Cambridge University Press, 2006), 705–722, 710. Also, Loehr, James E., *The Mental Game* (New York: Plume, 1991).

have some knowledge of music. For example they can sing songs, having learned from general experience how to carry a tune. Yet general experience does not lead to expertise in music ... Likewise, although one can learn a great deal about moral reasoning in everyday life, in order to reach the highest levels one must undergo deliberative, focused study.[26]

As described in the previous chapter, not only is deliberate practice required for increasing one's level of skill, it is also required to maintain one's current level of skill, even for the expert. The previous objection might then be reformulated, while accepting the claim that virtues require practice to acquire, that while skills might be forgotten if not exercised over time, virtues are more firmly entrenched and are in no danger of being forgotten if a person does not exercise the virtue over time. On this subject, Gilbert Ryle claims that:

> We do not keep up our honesty by giving ourselves regular exercises in it. Nor do we excuse a malicious action by saying that we have recently been short in fair-mindedness and generosity.[27]

According to this line of thought, skills have to be practiced in order to keep expertise, but not so with virtues. If somebody is honest, she does not need to practice at being honest in order to remain so. In this respect, virtue would be unlike a skill, and may represent a departure from the type of practical knowledge that skills represent. There are, however, at least two problems with this line of reasoning. First, at least some skills stay with you for quite a long time even when you have not used them. Even when someone has gone several years without driving a car with a manual transmission, she can pick it up again in mere minutes, as if she had never gone back to driving automatics. Consider also, the popular cliché of "It's like riding a bike" to describe something that is never truly forgotten.

Second, virtues are not as immune to lack of exercise as is suggested. The suggestion that once you have a virtue, you do not need to exercise it, comes from a view of virtues where the knowledge involved is more

---

[26] Narvaez, Darcia, "The Neo-Kohlbergian Tradition and Beyond: Schemas, Expertise and Character," in Carlo, Gustav and Pope-Edwards, Carolyn (eds.), *Nebraska Symposium on Motivation, Vol. 51: Moral Motivation through the Lifespan* (Lincoln, NE: University of Nebraska Press, 2005), 119–163.

[27] Ryle, Gilbert, "On Forgetting the Difference between Right and Wrong," in Melden, A. I. (ed.), *Essays in Moral Philosophy* (Seattle: University of Washington Press, 1958). James Wallace makes a similar argument to Ryle: Wallace, James, *Virtues and Vices* (Ithaca, NY: Cornell University Press, 1978). Bob Roberts offers a similar reply as I do in Roberts, Bob, "Will Power and the Virtues," *The Philosophical Review*, 93:2 (1984), 227–247.

propositional than practical. On this view, once you know that lying is wrong, you do not need any exercises in avoiding it to remember that it is wrong, any more than you need to keep practicing the math of 2 + 2 to make sure it still ends up being 4. An honest person knows not to lie. Even if an honest person were shipwrecked alone on an island for five years, she would supposedly not end up forgetting that it is wrong to lie even though there were no opportunities to lie to anyone (setting aside cases of self-deception).

However, these intuitions seem to stem from equating the possession of a virtue with the possession of knowledge in a form that can be easily put into simple propositional form, i.e. honesty = not lying. But this is the simplistic account of honesty that was rejected earlier. There are situations where not telling the truth is called for, and it represents no failure of honesty to do so. For example, with regard to those who had to lie to the Nazis in order to help save the lives of Jewish refugees, we say that they were courageous, but we do not also think of them as dishonest. You might say that the Nazis did not deserve to know the truth, given what they were planning to do with that information. Beyond that, there is the matter of how much truth to reveal, and in what manner. The social situations can become quite complex (or even contradictory) and navigating your way around the different demands is a skill, and one that can get rusty with disuse. Someone shipwrecked on an island for five years is likely to be quite awkward for a time in anything other than simple social situations. Like other skills, one does not necessarily have to start over learning from scratch, and the initial period of rustiness will fade. Simple tasks like riding a bike may not fade much over time, but complex tasks like riding up and down mountain trails may require regular exercise. It is far from obvious that there is much of a difference here between virtues and skills, and even if there is, it looks to be more of a matter of a difference in degree rather than in kind.

But once you reject this simple picture, and start recognizing different levels of performance, you then have to start asking questions about what levels of performance are going to be expected of people. It might help to think here of a practical skill, for example driving a car. Most people can attain a competent (or mid-way) level of proficiency in driving, such that they can obtain a driver's license and be (for the most part) safe drivers. Only a relatively few people, though, become expert drivers. Obviously, our traffic laws expect people to be able to drive at a competent level, rather than at the level of expertise. But then, what kind of expectations should we have about moral behavior, on an expertise model?

Another way to raise this point is to draw on the idea that 'ought implies can'. That is, it would seem that when we tell someone that they ought to do some act, it implies that this is an act the person can actually perform. Or to put it negatively, it makes little sense to tell people that they ought to do something that they cannot actually do (or are prevented from doing). Non-experts cannot act in the same way that experts do – not only do experts perform better, they also use techniques unavailable to non-experts. The beginner literally cannot do what the expert does, except by sheer luck. So, the appropriate thing for a novice to do differs from the expert, and since they have differing abilities, there are different expectations for each.

If we extend this to ethical expertise, then we are left with a picture of morality where being moral requires that we develop abilities that take effort and experience to acquire.[28] It is not the case that the differing standards means that there is no right answer about what to do, but rather the appropriate thing to do is to some degree relative to what you can do. If a better response in a situation requires that you are sensitive to some specific feature of the situation, and that feature takes a lot of experience to recognize, then it cannot be a response we legitimately expect the novice to make.[29]

We are used to holding differing standards of what novices and experts in a skill can do, but not so in morality, unless we are referring to the difference between children and adults. We recognize that due to differences in mental development, children are not held to the exact same standards as adults. While we do not hold infants to any moral standard, children might be rightly expected to be novices when it comes to morality, and perhaps entering the advanced stages in their teens. Expertise in most skills is rather rare, and given the complex nature of morality, it would not come as a surprise if ethical expertise turns out also to be relatively rare. While we should all be striving for improvement, expertise is likely not something we can all be expected to achieve. While we might legitimately expect all adults to be competent with respect to morality, requiring expertise may be expecting too much.

In any case, we can leave this discussion for now, because it remains an open question what standards we hold people accountable to in their

---

[28] It is important to note that one's moral status is a separate matter and should not be based on one's level of moral skillfulness. Otherwise, we would encounter problems similar to making rationality the basis of moral status, for it leaves out many people and most animals.

[29] Though this ought to also prompt steps to improve one's abilities.

moral behavior. Accounts of virtue ethics using a skill model of virtue can differ on what level of skillfulness is to be morally expected of people. Thus, if someone were to object to the model of ethical expertise being presented here that 'expertise is just too much to expect of a person, thus the model fails', then the response is that this is just a reason not to hold people to expert-level standards, rather than a reason to reject the model itself. After all, just because we hold people to a particular standard, it does not follow that we cannot recognize going above and beyond that standard.[30]

For these reasons, a skill model of virtue is probably best represented by a 'satisficing' or 'non-maximizing' approach to morality, where morality requires not perfect virtue from each of us, but rather that we develop ourselves to be roughly competent with respect to the virtues. As a result, this account preserves the idea of supererogatory actions (or going above 'the call of duty'), since there are higher levels of virtuous performance above the level of competence. In this respect it is similar to the example of getting a driver's license. We need people to be at least competent drivers before we let them on to the road, so that they are not a danger to themselves and others. While we recognize much higher levels of driving performance, we do not think it is necessary to require the highest levels of performance to be permitted to drive. Competence with respect to morality is a reasonable expectation, so that likewise people are not usually a hazard to themselves or others. However, given what goes into ethical expertise, it is too much for morality to require that everyone gains ethical expertise.

Moral Intuition

As with skill acquisition, virtue acquisition should give rise to judgments being made in an intuitive manner. With deliberate practice in general, one can take effortful tasks and make them effortless, thus freeing up attention to deal with more difficult tasks. This is what automaticity refers to, and it can make sense of the common view that virtues are habits.[31]

---

[30] Or for the more cynically minded, an absence of vice may be the real target. Presumably our more immediate moral aims should be preventing the worst kinds of immoral actions from occurring, rather than getting people who are already somewhat competent with respect to virtue to attain higher levels of virtue.

[31] Though as noted in the previous chapter, automaticity should not be equated to leading to fixed responses, for parts of a performance may become automatic (e.g. changing gears) to enable better flexibility and control with a more difficult task (e.g. changing lanes in fast moving traffic).

The idea is that our goals have mental representations, and while we often think consciously about our goals (which can then lead to behavior to accomplish those goals), these goals (and their corresponding goal-directed behavior) can be triggered nonconsciously. Stimuli in one's environment can activate the mental representation of our goals and corresponding behavior without our awareness. Implementation intentions are an example of triggering the goal-directed behavior in this automatic way. Also, if this happens repeatedly, the goal is said to be "chronically accessible" as in easily activated.[32] Importantly, as Nancy Snow notes, "[a]utomaticity researchers are clear that nonconsciously activated goal-directed behaviors are not reflex reactions to stimuli, but are intelligent, flexible responses to unfolding situational cues."[33] Certainly the roles that deliberate practice and self-regulation play in developing automaticity help to explain how the process of habituation can occur in a way that is not merely blind repetition (even though it involves some repetition). Finally, as a result of repeated experience, an association is made between these situational cues and goal-directed behavior. So, this is how behavior can become automatic, without it being mindless or simple rote behavior.

With experience and practice, we should expect that responses to situations will become more intuitive. The talk of intuitions, however, is often met with a fair amount of skepticism. This is especially so when intuitions are discussed in the context of morality. It may remind one of ethical intuitionism, where moral knowledge is arrived at independent of experience, but there is a relevant difference in the concept of intuition in expertise. On the skill model, the intuitive response of an expert is possible only because of the depth of experience the expert has accumulated. Paul Bloomfield helpfully notes that the "sense of 'intuition' here is quite different from the *a priori* intuitions posited by moral intuitions like Sidgwick, Moore, Ross, and Prichard. The relevant intuitions for virtue epistemology and moral epistemology are *a posteriori.* "[34]

---

[32] Lapsley and Narvaez take a similar approach in Lapsley, Daniel K. and Narvaez, Darcia, "A Social-Cognitive Approach to the Moral Personality," in Lapsley, Daniel K and Narvaez, Darcia (eds.) *Moral Development, Self and Identity: Essays in Honor of Augusto Blasi* (Mahwah, NJ: Erlbaum, 2004), 189–212). They put the reference to mental representations of goals in the language of "schemas," claiming that "the moral personality is better understood in terms of the chronic accessibility of moral schemas for construing social events" (202).

[33] Snow, Nancy E., *Virtue as Social Intelligence: An Empirically Grounded Theory* (New York: Routledge, 2010), 43.

[34] Bloomfield, Paul, "Virtue Epistemology and the Epistemology of Virtue," *Philosophy and Phenomenological Research*, 60:1 (2000), 23–43, 39.

However, that it takes experience to acquire moral knowledge, and that this lays the foundation for intuitive responses, are features that are also found in rival accounts of moral intuition. One well-known and controversial account of moral intuition is Haidt's social-intuitionist model.[35] According to Haidt, there are five broad categories of moral intuitions, which are the product of evolutionary history: harm/care, fairness/reciprocity, authority/respect, purity/sanctity, and in-group/out-group. That is to say, we by nature have some concern for these moral distinctions. However, while we may be hard-wired to be responsive to these moral concepts, at the level of evolutionary heritage these are very abstract concepts and underdetermine particular behavior. So, we still have to acquire at some point a specific conception of them, to act on those concerns, and that is the role of culture. Culture gives specific determinations to these innate moral concerns, and can do so in a variety of ways, as is evident by cultural variation in moral standards. In this sense, moral intuitions are part of our intuitive 'cultural capital', as described by Robin Hogarth.[36] So experience growing up in a culture is what provides the knowledge of a particular moral code, which can then be drawn on intuitively to make moral judgments.

Part of the controversial nature of this theory is that it denies that moral principles and reasoning play a role in arriving at moral judgments. For Haidt, moral reason-giving amounts to a form of rationalization for moral judgments arrived at independently of any moral principles or reasoning. For example, one of his famous experiments involves getting people to make a moral judgment about a case of incest. Of course, people have an intuitive response that it is wrong. However, the case is described in such a way that the two use birth control to prevent pregnancy, they enjoy the experience, and they have no regrets though they also agree that it is a one-time experience that they will not tell anyone about. In other words, the reasons people typically give against incest are not present in this case, but participants still view it as wrong. The subjects are 'morally dumbfounded' when confronted by the discrepancies between their judgment and the details of the case. Subjects still try to offer reasons for their judgments, but according to Haidt these attempts are merely 'post-hoc confabulation', since the reasons offered do not actually support their judgment.

---

[35] Haidt, Jonathan, "The Emotional Dog and Its Rational Tail: A Social Intuitionist Approach to Moral Judgment," *Psychological Review*, 108 (2001), 814–834.

[36] Hogarth, Robin M., *Educating Intuition* (Chicago: University of Chicago Press, 2000), 9. But 'cultural capital' is not the only source of intuition, as Hogarth notes, because intuitive judgments can also be based on skill acquisition.

Haidt views moral judgments as the product of automatic processing ('the emotional dog'), and deliberative processing ('the rational tail') is invoked only to try to defend the original intuitive judgment. One of the things that Haidt thinks marks off moral intuitions as different from other intuitions is our resistance to giving them up in the face of contradictory facts. In other words, we usually have little trouble rejecting our initial belief about a subject if we can be given reasons why that judgment is wrong. Usually, we can rely on deliberation to correct for errors that arise from our automatic processes (though this is not to say that automatic processes are more error prone than deliberate ones). But Haidt finds that people are very resistant to revising their moral intuitions, which is why people's use of deliberative processing in the moral case seems to have as its goal to arrive at any possible justification for the original intuitive judgment (i.e. post-hoc confabulation). This is why moral principles and reasoning seem to have no role in generating the initial moral judgments, or even revising them after the fact.[37]

Horgan and Timmons, amongst others, find this picture of moral judgment unappealing, and attempt to argue that moral principles do play a role in moral judgment, even though the judgments are arrived at intuitively. They also argue that given the role moral principles play in forming judgements, that moral reasoning is not generally a matter of confabulation. The view they argue for is morphological rationalism, which amounts to claiming that the content of moral principles is internalized, and as a result can lead to moral judgments being arrived at intuitively (at least in the sense of spontaneous, and not preceded by conscious reasoning). Their view is one that coincides with my skill model of virtue, as they view the possession of moral principles "as a matter of *know how* – a skill that is or has become part of the individual's repertoire for negotiating her social world. When a principle or norm is possessed morphologically, one can say that its manner of operation is *procedural* – in virtue of possessing the principle in this manner, an individual is disposed to form moral judgments that non-accidentally conform to the principle."[38] So they do not see the intuitive nature of moral judgment as evidence that moral judgements are not a product of the internalization of moral principles.

---

[37] Though Haidt at times restricts this to our moral evaluations of other people's actions. See Haidt, Jonathan and Bjorklund, Frederick, "Social Intuitionists Answer Six Questions about Moral Psychology," in Sinnott-Armstrong, Walter (ed.), *Moral Psychology, Vol. 2: The Cognitive Science of Morality: Intuition and Diversity* (Cambridge: MIT Press, 2008), 181–218.

[38] Horgan, Terry and Timmons, Mark, "Morphological Rationalism and the Psychology of Moral Judgment," *Ethical Theory and Moral Practice*, 10 (2007) 279–295, 286.

However, it should be noted that one of the ways they later characterize the morphological possession of a moral principle leads them away from the skill model. They claim that this possession involves not only procedural knowledge, but also disposes you "to present reasons for one's moral judgment if one is prompted to do so," and that you "experience one's reason-giving as fitting smoothly with the moral judgment for which one is giving reasons."[39] However, as pointed out in the last chapter, even experts are often guilty of some confabulation when asked after the fact about what prompted their response, and this is due to the involvement of automatic processes, as we lack full insight into the operations of such processes. So, there are some respects in which they might be overemphasizing the rationalist approach over the intuitionist approach.

Both sides, however, seem to agree that moral judgments could be arrived at in either manner. Haidt does not deny that people can arrive at moral judgments through the use of moral principles and reasoning, but he thinks that is exceptional. Horgan and Timmons do not disagree with Haidt's take on the incest scenario as involving a post-hoc confabulation to defend a judgment arrived at intuitively and independent of moral reasoning, but they see this example of arriving at moral judgments as the exception rather than the rule. In defense of their position, they describe a few cases where it does seem that moral principles underlie a judgment arrived at in an intuitive manner, and where we can expect accurate reasons to be offered. They cite a case from Gilbert Harman regarding coming around a corner and seeing some kids light a cat on fire, where Harman suggests that "you do not need to conclude that what they are doing is wrong; you do not need to figure anything out; you can see that it is wrong."[40] Horgan and Timmons agree, and claim that it would be easy for someone to articulate the reasons behind that judgment, in terms of prohibiting cruelty.

But one can imagine Haidt replying to this by changing the scenario. Say you find out after seeing this incident that the cat was actually unable to feel pain, due to a terminal condition that would cause it to die soon, and that the kids involved agreed this was a one-time event and would not tell anybody about it (and thus presumably contradicting the typical reasons offered in defense of seeing the act as wrong). After having found this out, would you change your mind about the wrongness of their act?

[39] Horgan, Terry and Timmons, Mark, "Morphological Rationalism and the Psychology of Moral Judgment," *Ethical Theory and Moral Practice*, 10 (2007) 279–295, 290.
[40] Harman, Gilbert, *The Nature of Morality* (Oxford: Oxford University Press, 1977), 4.

Probably not, and if not then Horgan and Timmons' case could end up being a case of moral dumbfounding as well.

In any event, we do not need to settle the issue of the frequency of these contrasting approaches.[41] Surely people can arrive at moral judgments in an intuitive manner in more than one way. One is Haidt's focus on intuition as 'cultural capital' in Hogarth's sense, and Hogarth distinguished that from the knowledge gained through skill acquisition that Horgan and Timmons have in mind. What really seems to distinguish Hadit's social-intuitionist model from accounts of intuition built on skill acquisition and expertise is that the intuitions on the social-intuitionist model are acquired before having any real experimental learning or training. To put the point differently, recall that skill acquisition is a process of making previously effortful tasks become effortless (and so one can in turn tackle more complicated tasks). Note that this transition uses deliberate processes to shape automatic responses, and then compare that to Haidt's account where deliberate processes are used only after the fact if a challenge is raised to one's initial intuitive judgment. The expertise model has intuition being trained (though at the same time we know more than we can say, so the automatic response is not limited to merely the conscious thought that went in ahead of time). For Haidt, by contrast, deliberative processes serve only to provide rationalizations for one's intuitive judgment – it is not training before-hand or correcting afterward for the intuitive response. Lapsley and Hill make a similar point when they compare the "front-loaded" automaticity found in the social-intuitionst model, with the expertise model that "locates automaticity on the backend of development. It is the outcome of repeated experience, of instruction, intentional coaching and socialisation."[42]

It is also worth returning to the point, mentioned in the previous chapter, that this repeated experience also helps us to develop mental models of our environment, allowing us to better plan and respond to dynamic contexts. Railton, returning to his work with Seligman on prospection, points out that skilled performers have "greater accuracy, informativeness, and accessibility of the tacit 'forward models'—evaluative landscapes linking circumstances,

---

[41] I tend to be pessimistic and think Haidt is closer to the mark about how most people form moral judgments, but that still allows for moral judgments to be intuitive in the sense of expertise. After all, one of the implications of the skill model is that moral judgments will tend to go astray if they are only grounded in something like cultural capital (which does not involve deliberate practice and an attempt to improve one's level of moral skillfulness).

[42] Lapsley, Daniel and Hill, Patrick, "On Dual Processing and Heuristic Approaches to Moral Cognition," *Journal of Moral Education*, 37:3 (2008), 313–332, 324–325.

actions, and outcomes—they develop and spontaneously follow in training and competition."[43] Furthermore, the use of mental models in prospection provides "a potential mechanism by which individuals can become attuned to their physical and social environment and its demands: a 'good, reliable infrastructure' to explain how skilled individuals and experts can have 'reliably good intuitions.'"[44] In sum, the kind of moral intuition associated with the skill model of virtue differs significantly from the kind of moral intuitions one might have by merely relying on 'cultural capital', and the experience and training is why skill-based intuitions are far more reliable than the intuitions captured by the social-intuitionist model.

While it is important to understand why we should expect reliable intuitive responses to increase with the development of virtue on a skill model of virtue, it is equally important to avoid placing too much emphasis on intuition and automatic processes. As described in the previous chapter, part of the value of automaticity is that it frees up one's attention to focus on more difficult tasks, which is especially important when you are acting in very dynamic contexts (and we should expect this to be at least not uncommon with respect to morality). It is not as if one type of process is inherently superior to another, as superior performances require a combination of both types of processes. So really this discussion should be seen as balancing the tendency to overstate the importance of deliberative reasoning in moral action (which is commonplace in ethical theory), rather than as classifying intuitive responses as inherently better.

Articulation of Moral Knowledge

As covered in Chapter 1, experts should not be expected to necessarily articulate (fully) their reasons for action because of the role of automatic processes in skilled performances, and since goal-directed behavior can be triggered automatically, This is in line with what some virtue ethicists have said about the articulateness (or lack thereof) of the virtuous person. On this, John McDowell claims:

> Of course a kind person need not himself classify the behaviour he sees to be called for, on one of the relevant occasions, as kind. He need not be articulate enough to possess concepts of the particular virtues; and even if he

[43] Railton, Peter, "The Affective Dog and Its Rational Tale: Intuition and Attunement," *Ethics*, 124 (2014), 813–859, 839.
[44] Railton, Peter, "The Affective Dog and Its Rational Tale: Intuition and Attunement," *Ethics*, 124 (2014), 813–859, 839–840.

does, the concepts need not enter his reasons for the actions that manifest those particular virtues. It is enough if he thinks of what he does, when – as we put it – he shows himself to be kind, under some such description as "the thing to do". The description need not differ from that under which he thinks of other actions of his, which we regard as manifesting different virtues; the division into actions that manifest kindness and actions that manifest other virtues can be imposed, not by the agent himself, but by a possibly more articulate, and more theoretically oriented observer.[45]

Part of the reason McDowell puts this in terms of the virtuous person seeing 'the thing to do' without more explicit virtue terms entering the picture is because the virtuous person needs to know what to do 'all-things-considered'. The ethical expert will frequently draw on numerous virtuous skills in arriving at a judgment about what to do and may not be able to articulate which particular virtues played a role.

This leads to some debate between those advancing a skill model of virtue. Because the literature on expertise reveals that expert performance relies on numerous nonconscious processes, there is evidence that experts frequently cannot articulate how they knew to act in a particular situation. A chess master, for example, might say something no more illuminating than 'I saw it was the right move to make.' While experts might be able to articulate some of their mental processes, they cannot necessarily explain why they saw situations in a particular light, or why a particular course of action occurred to them (or why other courses of action did not occur to them). Even when experts are able to articulate an explanation, the explanations can be inconsistent with their observed behavior.

However, for some working with the virtue as skill model, being an expert means being able to give an account of one's actions. Recall that giving an account, according to Annas, means "that the person with a skill be able explicitly to explain and justify her particular decisions and judgements, and to do so in terms of some general grasp of the principles which define that skill."[46] So the question becomes whether or not to view articulation as something necessary for virtue. One aspect that complicates this is that there is some ambiguity about what counts as a sufficient explanation or justification. Presumably, what the chess masters says above is not sufficient. But does a sufficient explanation need to involve discussing all the other possible moves and why they would be ruled out?

[45] McDowell, John, "Virtue and Reason," *The Monist*, 62:3 (1979), 331–350, 332.
[46] Annas, Julia, "Virtue as a Skill," *International Journal of Philosophical Studies*, 3:2 (1995), 227–243, 233.

In addition, if expertise does not go hand-in-hand with the ability to sufficiently give an account of one's actions, how does that affect the virtue as skill thesis? Is it a point of disanalogy but where we should keep the expectation of articulation in virtue? Should we get rid of the articulation requirement altogether?

Part of Annas's motivation in endorsing articulation is to show how skills are relevant for understanding virtue. Annas voices a concern that the lack of articulateness in skills might make the skill model unsuitable for an account of virtue:

> Gardeners can and do have expertise without being able explicitly to articulate it and state the principles on which it rests. Does this not imply that skill is an unsuitable model for virtue? But it is clear by now that what matters for ethics in the skill analogy is the point that virtue shares the intellectual structure of a skill, something accessible only to the critically reflective agent. Thus, examples of skills which do not require this are simply examples of skills which are in this respect not like virtue.[47]

If one argues (as I did in the previous chapter) that skills are best understood as not requiring the intellectual structure that Annas requires, then she could respond that such an account makes skills an unsuitable model for virtue, because it does away with the requirement of being articulate and having a grasp of underlying principles, and that this is undesirable in an account of virtue. The importance of articulation for virtue, and the skill model in general, according to Annas is revealed in the following passage:

> The skill analogy requires that the agent reflect and achieve by reflection a unified grasp of the general principles underlying her patterns of action and decision. And thus the analogy marks a strong contrast with modern versions of virtue ethics which regard virtue as a matter of non-generalizable sensitivity; it brings ancient ethics closer to other modern theories which require that the moral agent reflect on, and try to achieve a theoretically unified basis for, her individual moral judgements.[48]

These intellectual conditions are supposed to show that ancient virtue ethical theories are similar to modern ethical theories, and that she is not advancing a version of virtue ethics that understands virtue as a type of "non-generalizable sensitivity," where one is sensitive to the particular features of situations. Although she does not mention who holds this latter

---

[47] Annas, Julia, *The Morality of Happiness* (Oxford: Oxford University Press, 1993), 73.
[48] Annas, Julia, *The Morality of Happiness* (Oxford: Oxford University Press, 1993), 67–68.

view of virtue, the quote above by McDowell with regard to what it is like to be a kind person would be a likely target. What McDowell appears to be saying is a denial of just the kind of articulate understanding that Annas requires for virtue. She seems to hold that the genuine possession of virtue requires one to be a "more articulate, and more theoretically oriented" person than the person described by McDowell. Annas is arguing for a particular view of virtue, and the intellectual components of her skill model are playing a key role in her argument.

While the concerns she raises about the desirability of articulating moral principles are valid, this can be addressed by keeping in mind that being virtuous is centrally a matter of acting well. There may be many good reasons to want a virtuous person to be able to articulate her reasons for action in terms of general principles, but the skill model rejects the idea that these intellectual requirements are necessary or sufficient for acting virtuously.[49] There are many experts in every field who, while being able to act well within their discipline, are not necessarily good at teaching other people this information. Demands for a greater theoretical understanding will have their source in something more than just our demand that people act well, since on the skill model one can act well without having knowledge of unifying principles. Furthermore, one can accept the limitations on giving a full account of one's knowledge without having to give up the idea that there are principles underlying the skill domain. Bloomfield raises this possibility by pointing out that "what is essential is that a *logos* – a set of basic principles, laws, or rules that governs the 'objects the skills look after' – must underlie any practice that is a skill."[50] As he suggests, experts need to have either an explicit or implicit grasp of these principles, but "there have been plenty of brave people throughout history, without anyone having settled every question about the logos of courage, so more support is found for the thought that skills can be mastered without the expert fully and explicitly knowing the logos of the skill."[51] He provides the helpful example of the speaker of a native language, who knows how to speak well but without necessarily being able to articulate all the rules of grammar for that language.

---

[49] However, I do think that the intellectual requirements that Annas defends do have a place in our overall views about ethics, but I think of it in terms of what a coach or teacher would need to be able to articulate to help someone else perform better, or for use in deciding which moral standards to internalize in the first place.
[50] Bloomfield, Paul, *Moral Reality* (Oxford: Oxford University Press, 2001), 62.
[51] Bloomfield, Paul, *Moral Reality* (Oxford: Oxford University Press, 2001), 63–64.

Speaking a language is a useful example for a skilled competence, as being a competent speaker requires flexibility in coming up with new linguistic statements, rather than being limited to the simple repetition of phrases one already knows. As Peter Railton points out:

> So what is borrowed from the linguistic model is not a template but a picture: open-ended capacities to respond fluently and adeptly to situational or expressive demands cannot be the result of a fixed repertoire of trained responses, so that some essentially generalizable capacities and information structures must be at work; and since an individual with these abilities typically can articulate only a fraction of these generalizable capacities or information structures, they must take the form of a tacit competence, which can be manifest spontaneously in thought and action.[52]

So, while skilled performers can have something to say to explain their actions, we must realize they only have partial introspective access to the processes that underlie their skill, and thus cannot necessarily fully articulate their reasons for action. There are good reasons to avoid denying someone's skillfulness merely on the basis of the person's inarticulateness.

Finally, there is another reason to be concerned about the role of articulation in expertise. Patricia Benner carried out studies of experts in the field of nursing.[53] When studying nurses with a track record of life-saving decisions in emergency situations, she found that often the nurses could not fully articulate how they knew what to do.[54] One of the most serious problems for the nurses is that their judgments are not taken as seriously as doctors because of an assumption that their lack of articulation signaled a lack of knowledge, and so they were accorded less power and status within the hospital.[55] So it matters a great deal that we get an accurate picture of what really goes into acquiring skills and expertise. There are important intuitive and deliberative aspects to both skill acquisition and expert performance. In sum, we should be wary of any approach that would imply that if you cannot fully articulate your reasons for action, then you are not really skilled (or virtuous).[56]

---

[52] Railton, Peter, "The Affective Dog and Its Rational Tale: Intuition and Attunement," *Ethics*, 124 (2014), 813–859, 817.

[53] Benner, Patricia, *From Novice to Expert* (New Jersey: Prentice Hall Health, 2001).

[54] Benner, Patricia, *From Novice to Expert* (New Jersey: Prentice Hall Health, 2001), 32.

[55] Of course, this is also a result of a gendered division in medicine between doctors and nurses. As an example of social influences on skill acquisition, men are encouraged to become doctors while women are encouraged to become nurses, but not vice versa.

[56] This is not an attempt, though, to downplay the importance of articulation and principles in giving justifications for one's actions in moral discourse. It seems that the demands for 'giving an account' are much higher in morality than when compared to non-moral skills. This is partly due to the

Individuating the Moral Virtues

Given this understanding of virtue as a skill, there arises the further question of whether in acquiring virtue we need only to acquire a single skill, or are we aiming instead to acquire a collection of related skills?[57] Some accounts of virtue argue that there is only one virtue, rather than a set of discrete virtues like kindness and honesty. Annas claims that there is just a singular virtue, and it is a skill of living your life well.[58] However, skills require feedback for improvement, so there needs to be some identifiable goal to the exercise of your skill. It is difficult to see how the feedback mechanism would work if virtue is a 'global skill', that is, the skill of living your life as a whole.[59] One problem is that the target in that sense is very broad and vague, which will make it difficult to determine whether you are acting in such a way as to achieve success in living well, and thus receiving proper feedback. The speed at which you receive feedback matters in addition to the frequency and quality of the feedback. Daniel Kahneman, for example, compares learning how to drive a car with learning how to pilot large ships in a harbor.[60] The latter is more difficult to learn in part because of the longer delay between actions and noticeable consequences, which leads to slower feedback on one's attempt to pilot the ship. By comparison, it will be far more difficult to connect up your actions now with how they help to live your life as a whole. Not only will it be difficult to assess the effect of one particular action on how your life

seriousness of the subject matter, partly because there are usually less concrete success conditions for acting well, and since there is less agreement as to who are the ethical experts. If a chess master cannot give much more of an explanation for making certain moves than 'I saw that it was the right move to make,' it does not by itself serve to undermine any claim to expertise so long as the chess master keeps winning games. In morality, there is not such a simple success condition for acting well, and moral disagreement seems to fuel demands for articulate justifications of one's actions. In chess, while we may have reasons for trying to find out if the moves can be understood in terms of rules or principles, in general we do not have broader concerns that make it important for us to play chess or to be able to play it well. On the other hand, it seems that we have very important needs in being able to give an account of what morality requires of us, such as in drafting laws and making social policy, which need to be formulated in explicit rules and principles.

[57] One important respect in which the virtues are individuated broadly is the distinction between moral and epistemic (or intellectual) virtues. Moral virtues have, as their overall goal, living a flourishing life, while the epistemic virtues have epistemic goods like truth, knowledge, understanding, wisdom, and the like as the overarching goals. I will be dealing with the epistemic virtues in Chapter 3.

[58] Annas, Julia, "The Structure of Virtue," in DePaul, Michael and Zagzebski, Linda (eds.), *Intellectual Virtue* (Oxford: Clarendon Press, 2003), 15–33, 26.

[59] Though one solution to this is to argue that even if the goal of virtue is as broad as living well, that in seeing what constitutes living well we will have several more specific ends to aim at.

[60] Kahneman, Daniel, *Thinking, Fast and Slow* (Farrar, Straus and Giroux, 2011), 241.

goes, when so many of your actions will have an effect on your life, but the consequences of such actions could be a long time coming. As Daniel Jacobson points out in a discussion of the virtue as skill thesis, "[t]he plausibility of a skill-based epistemology was earned by arguments focusing on discrete virtues such as courage and kindness."[61] It is with these more discrete virtues that we can get more immediate feedback about how we are doing, as well as figuring out how to structure deliberate practice to improve them.

Morality as a domain is very complex, and so acting well morally is unlikely to boil down to acquiring only a single skill. One way to try to capture both of these perspectives is to point out that while virtue does aim at the overall end of living well, we cannot do this without also thinking in terms of constitutive ends that make up living well (*eudaimonia*). So, we can start out with a commitment to an abstract conception of a flourishing life, and then flesh it out with subgoals that are constitutive of living well, such as being honest, just, kind, etc. These specific virtues are essentially our more proximal subgoals for the superordinate goal of living well. These virtues would give us more concrete ends to aim at relative to just aiming at living well overall, and this would help with knowing what counts as success, how to structure deliberate practice, providing for better feedback, etc.[62] Even the initial constitutive ends could be broken down into further constitutive ends, if needed for better practice and feedback. This meshes well with the framework of a goal hierarchy discussed in the last chapter, where we move from the abstract superordinate goal of living well to more concrete specifications via constitutive subgoals (i.e. the virtues).[63] Also, if we find that acting on a particular conception of a virtue hinders us from living well, then the higher order goal of living well gives us a reason to revise our conception of that virtue. Likewise, if a particular strategy for acting kindly, for example, seems not to hit the target, then the higher order goal of being kind gives us a reason to search for an alternative strategy.

When individuating the virtues this way, there is no guarantee that the skills associated with these constitutive ends will map on to the traditional individual virtues such as honesty, courage, kindness, temperance, etc.[64]

---

[61] Jacobson, Daniel, "Seeing by Feeling: Virtues, Skills, and Moral Perception," *Ethical Theory and Moral Practice*, 8 (2005), 387–409, 401.

[62] Achieving these subgoals, as I will be arguing throughout the book, will require developing skills (e.g. the skill of honesty).

[63] This will also be of relevance to the thesis of the unity of the virtues, which I will cover in Chapter 4.

[64] Another reason why some traditional virtues may not turn out to be virtues on the skill model is that they do not appear to require the training that goes into skill acquisition. It should be noted,

It could turn out that moral skills appear to be more fine-grained than traditional virtue categories. Narvaez, in arguing that expertise is a model for virtue development, claims:

> Through the course of building perceptual skills (sensibilities), motivational skills (focus), reasoning skills (judgment) and action skills (implementation), individuals move towards expertise. There are many kinds of skills necessary for moral or ethical expertise, including procedural and conditional knowledge that can be employed automatically when needed (doing the right thing at the right time in the right way).[65]

She goes on to claim that these four main categories of ethical skills are broken down into 7 more specific skills, each understood in terms of 3 ethical subskills, for a total of 84 separate ethical skills – far more than found on traditional lists of virtues.[66] Is this too many skills to acquire for moral development? There is this danger in getting too fine-grained with respect to the constitutive ends of living well and the associated skills for reaching those ends.

Although Narvaez's approach highlights much of what is important to moral action, the four main processes are all reflected in normal self-regulation. The Christen and Tanner view of five main moral competences was similarly limited when trying to capture the nature of moral skills. Part of what is missing from these accounts of moral skills is the domain specificity of skills. For example, in a discussion of how training one's brain has similarities and dissimilarities to muscle training, Hill and Schneider claim that some kinds of training are general and carry over across different skill domains, but others are too specific to apply to more than one skill:

> The domain general areas might be analogous to cardiovascular training in muscle training (e.g., training endurance transfers across many sports). However, the specific training (e.g., shooting in basketball and hitting in baseball) is unlikely to activate the same areas or representation and do not lead to transfer.[67]

---

though, that traits that fail to be skills can still count as good, even if they are not virtues in the sense of the 'virtue as skill' thesis.

[65] Narvaez, Darcia, "De neurobiology van ons morel functioneren [The neurobiology of moral formation and moral functioning]" *Pastorale Perspectieven*, 153:4 (2011), 10–18.

[66] Narvaez, Darcia and Lapsley, Daniel K., "The Psychological Foundations of Everyday Morality and Moral Expertise," in Lapsley, Daniel K. and Power, F. Clark (eds.) *Character Psychology and Character Education* (Notre Dame: IN: University of Notre Dame Press, 2005), 140–165, 155.

[67] Hill, Nicole M. and Schneider, Walter, "Brain Changes in the Development of Expertise: Neuroanatomical and Neurophysiological Evidence about Skill-Based Adaptations," in Ericsson, K. Anders (ed.), *The Cambridge Handbook of Expertise and Expert Performance* (Cambridge: Cambridge University Press, 2006), 653–682, 675.

So, Narvaez, along with Christen and Tanner, can be understood as focusing on domain general areas of moral agency with their frameworks. But this needs to be distinguished from domain specific forms of moral agency, such as moral skills.

So, are there a few broad virtuous skills, or lots of fine-grained ones instead? This is an area where experimental research may prove insightful, as it could provide evidence that some fine-grained ethical skills are learned together, or 'clustered', such that they would be brought together under a broader virtue term. So while there could be many fine-grained skills, they cluster together with similarly acquired skills. In this respect, there may end up being a limited unity in the possession of some virtuous skills (or subskills). For example, think of the ability of doctors to perform surgery. Surgeons can get specialized in different forms of surgery, such that being good at heart surgery does not make one good at spinal surgery. Nevertheless, there is a large overlap in the skills and knowledge involved in doing either kind of surgery.[68] In the case of courage, perhaps being skilled at courage with respect to physical harm gives you some degree of skill at courage in resisting emotional harm, even though they subdivide out into two different subskills.

This kind of approach is similar to Daniel Russell's view of the cardinality of virtues.[69] He thinks of broad virtues, like generosity, as having related fine-grained virtues. For example, magnificence as a virtue can be understood as making large donations for the public good, which infamously is not a virtue everyone has an opportunity to exercise. However, Russell's point is that magnificence appears to be a special case of generosity – not just in terms of the context, but also that it requires some specialized knowledge. So, in this respect, it is like the surgeon example above. A skill in medicine puts one in a position to specialize in certain types of medical knowledge. Just as it would be odd for someone to declare that she is really good at spinal surgery but does not know much about medicine in general, it would be odd to say one is really good at magnificence but does not know much about generosity. On this Russell points out that "[o]rthodontics is of course a skill, and a skill that requires its own special training and expertise, but it is subordinate to dentistry, not parallel to it; it is a *specialization* of the skill of dentistry."[70] To account for this, Russell

---

[68] Similar thoughts apply to doctors and veterinarians being able to carry over some of their knowledge to working with different species.

[69] Russell, Daniel C., *Practical Intelligence and the Virtues* (New York: Oxford University Press, 2009).

[70] Russell, Daniel C., *Practical Intelligence and the Virtues* (New York: Oxford University Press, 2009), 216.

invokes the concept of a 'conversational shift' in explaining how to individuate virtues – this is where one generalizes one's reasons after repeated reflection on the reasons one has for acting; and that reasons of the same kind converge or cluster during this conversational shift.[71] This kind of idea reflects the hierarchical ordering of goals, discussed in the previous chapter, where you reference higher-order goals to explain the reason for having the lower-order goals.

For Russell, virtues are responsive to different kinds of reasons, and this helps to individuate the virtues. As he notes:

> One of the benefits of likening virtues to practical skills in particular is the emphasis on their flexibility and adaptability, which allows the person with the skill to be creative and innovative. In other words, the practice of any virtue will surely require the constant learning of new competencies by which to succeed in the exercise of that virtue.[72]

For example, one might learn to be competent at driving, while being located in a fairly hot environment. Such a person would have to develop new competences upon moving to a location with lots of snow in order to drive as well in icy conditions. But this would not be the acquisition of a new skill, just an extension of one's existing skill in driving to new contexts. Making these kinds of distinctions, though, is something that is deserving of further empirical research.

A related issue in individuating the skills is whether, for example, overcoming strong inclinations is the focus of a particular moral skill, like temperance, or whether that aspect is found more generally as part of any moral skill, due to its role in self-regulation. We could go the route Lapsley and Narvaez suggest, where reading a situation and being properly motivated are separate skill sets (and presumably portable across contexts that we might associate with particular virtues like honesty or kindness). Or we could maintain that honesty and kindness are themselves separate skills and exercising any one of those skills will require both being able to read situations correctly and being properly motivated (amongst other things) in ways specific to each virtue.

Evidence from the psychological literature on self-control points toward a third way of understanding the role of self-control to the virtues. Duckworth's research on self-control suggests that there are both

[71] Russell, Daniel C., *Practical Intelligence and the Virtues* (New York: Oxford University Press, 2009), 195.

[72] Russell, Daniel C., *Practical Intelligence and the Virtues* (New York: Oxford University Press, 2009), 229.

domain-general and domain-specific aspects to the exercise of self-control on a given occasion.[73] The domain-general aspects are one's level of self-control resources (such as attention and working-memory), and one's general strategies for exercising self-control (such as goal setting and implementation intentions). While these domain-general aspects are predictive of average levels of self-control across individuals, they do not account for the variation we see in what temptations a particular person gives in to. For example, she found that "participants who were especially tempted in the target domain (e.g. work) were not likely to be more tempted in unrelated domains (e.g. food)."[74] Duckworth accounts for this domain-specificity primarily in terms of subjective temptations in certain domains (i.e. the temptation to avoid work, be physically lazy, overeat, abuse alcohol, spend money recklessly, to lose your temper, to give into jealousy, engage in affairs, etc.), and secondarily in terms of the person's construal of how harmful it would be to indulge in that kind of temptation. That is to say, people exhibit consistency within these domains with respect to how likely they are to resist the temptations (e.g. binging on food occurs in a variety of contexts and is stable over time), but the ability to engage self-control in the face of one temptation does not necessarily translate into resisting the temptations of a different domain.

So, for a virtue like temperance, which like self-control is associated with resisting impulses, there are some domain-general features of it. The elements of limited attention and working-memory surely affect the exercise of temperance when it comes to effortful self-control, but they do not fit a model of a skill or a habit (though there are some things you can do to improve them). On the other hand, general strategies such as setting clear goals and developing implementation intentions can involve skill. However, those domain-general features underdetermine the exercise of self-control, as people will find some impulses more tempting (and thus harder to resist) than others. Thus, we could understand temperance on a model of general strategies that apply across domains, along with it having more specific subskills to resist temptations in specific domains of temptation. It

[73] Duckworth, Angela Lee and Tsukayama, Eli, "Domain Specificity in Self-Control," in Miller, Christian B., Furr, R. Michael, Knobel, Angela, and Fleeson, William (eds.), *Character: New Directions from Philosophy, Psychology, and Theology* (New York: Oxford University Press, 2015), 393–411.

[74] Duckworth, Angela Lee and Tsukayama, Eli, "Domain Specificity in Self-Control," in Miller, Christian B., Furr, R. Michael, Knobel, Angela, and Fleeson, William (eds.), *Character: New Directions from Philosophy, Psychology, and Theology* (New York: Oxford University Press, 2015), 393–411, 400.

would be similar to the cardinality approach Russell takes, as the relation between temperance-general and temperance-gluttony would be like that of generosity to magnificence. The subskills of temperance would end up tracking specific domains of temptations. Thus, while you would need self-control to exercise a virtue like honesty, it would not take the form of having a special subskill to exert self-control in the service of honesty. What subskills of temperance you would need to acquire depends then on what temptations you feel most strongly, and this of course would vary amongst people.

It appears that courage will also have domain-general and domain-specific features. Courage requires assessing the value that is at stake in the situation, along with the risk one takes in upholding that value. Here one of the domain-general features will be how well a person can deal with stress and negative affect. Situations requiring courage are going to necessarily involve some risk to the person, which is likely to cause anxiety or stress when considering how to respond to the situation. Evaluations of risk, though, are going to involve a fair amount of subjectivity. Brandstätter et al. provide evidence that "the individual's anticipated negative affect, which depends on his/her affective self-regulation, should be inherently linked to the perception of risk."[75] That is, your perception of risk is going to depend in part on your affective reactions when contemplating the risk you would be taking, and that affective reaction depends on domain-general abilities to regulate negative affect. As they go on to explain, "[i]ndividuals with low self-regulatory abilities to control affect (i.e. state-oriented individuals) have problems to self-generate positive affect in the face of difficulties and downregulate negative affect when exposed to stress."[76] Thus, a person with lower abilities to regulate negative affect is likely to construe courage-relevant situations as being inherently riskier than others, which in turn makes it less likely that the person will do the courageous act.[77] Furthermore, there can be domain-specific features to courage, similar to those of temperance, as people clearly vary in what they find fearful. So, there may be subskills of courage pertaining to physical harm or social embarrassment.

---

[75] Brandstätter, Veronika, Jonas, Kai J., Koletzko, Svenja H., Fischer, Peter, "Self-Regulatory Processes in the Appraisal of Moral Courage Situations," *Social Psychology*, 47:4, (2016), 201–213, 203.

[76] Brandstätter, Veronika, Jonas, Kai J., Koletzko, Svenja H., Fischer, Peter, "Self-Regulatory Processes in the Appraisal of Moral Courage Situations," *Social Psychology*, 47:4, (2016), 201–213, 204.

[77] Another interesting finding of their experiment is that there seem to be separate factors that influence the appraisals of the value at stake from the risk one takes.

As with temperance, one would not need to acquire all the subskills, but rather those pertaining to situations that one encounters with some regularity and that involve a particularly anxiety/stress-provoking element.

This approach to temperance and courage would vindicate to some extent the argument that there are specifically virtues of 'will power'. As mentioned above, Roberts argues that self-regulating behaviors and strategies are fundamental to at least some of the virtues, specifically what he refers to as the virtues of will power.[78] Roberts argues that the virtues of will power (like courage, temperance, and patience) are different from other 'substantive' virtues (like honesty, justice, and kindness), where exhibiting the substantive virtues involves pursuing good ends.[79] He argues that the virtues of will power do not necessarily require this, for someone could seemingly be courageous and patient in carrying out evil deeds. Certainly, having a lot of self-control in resisting impulses would be useful even when one's goals are immoral. The goal of the virtues of will power is a matter of self-control, in terms of your actions aligning with your goals (whatever they may be), rather than specifically the pursuit of morally good goals. While it is controversial to suggest that courage can be exhibited in doing evil deeds, this points to a potential difference between the virtues of will power and the substantive virtues.[80]

Roberts argues that the virtues of will power are essentially skills.[81] His main argument for this is that he thinks such virtues are inherently 'strategic', in the sense that they involve figuring out various techniques for managing one's impulses and emotions. Support for this philosophical approach can be found in Ryle, who argues that "performances in which strength of will is exerted may be performances of almost any sort, intellectual or manual, imaginative or administrative. It is not a single-track disposition."[82] Furthermore, Roberts claims that:

> People can be more or less skilled in the management of their own inclinations, and these skills are an important part of the virtues of will

---

[78] Roberts, Bob, "Will Power and the Virtues," *The Philosophical Review*, 93:2 (1984), 227–247.
[79] Roberts, Bob, "Will Power and the Virtues," *The Philosophical Review*, 93:2 (1984), 227–247.
[80] With courage potentially manifested in the carrying out of evil deeds, it seems like genuine courage (or likewise with patience). Another useful example of a virtue of will power is integrity, because sticking to one's principles seems like it can be genuinely manifested even when one holds clearly corrupt principles. Of course, people can act on corrupt conceptions of substantive virtues like justice, but in such cases we typically claim they are really carrying out acts of injustice.
[81] See also Steutel, Jan, "The Virtues of Will-Power: Self-Control and Deliberation," in Carr, David and Steutel, Jan, (eds), *Virtue Ethics and Moral Education* (London and New York: Routledge, 1999).
[82] Ryle, Gilbert, *The Concept of Mind* (New York: Routledge, 2009), 60.

power. We can be more and less "good at" breaking bad habits and forming new ones, at "deferring gratification," at resisting cravings and impulses; and we can be trained and/or train ourselves in the control of emotions like anxiety, fear, disappointment, anger, and hatred.[83]

Roberts' suggestion here is that some virtues seem to be centrally about managing our own inclinations, so that we do not act in ways contrary to the substantive virtues. In this respect, the moral value of the virtues of will power is derived from the values those virtues support. That is, courage is valuable insofar as it helps us to act honestly or justly when doing so is dangerous. These virtues of will power then play an 'auxiliary' or support- ive role to carrying out the acts of the more 'substantive' virtues.[84] Furthermore, Roberts points in the quote above to some domain-general aspects of will power (like being good at breaking bad habits), and some domain-specific aspects (controlling specific negative emotions).

Vice as a Skill?

Given this understanding of virtues as skills, should we be able to concep- tualize vice in the same way? Being a good liar certainly seems to take skill, but this is not obviously the case with respect to cowardice. As Russell points out, "there is hardly any 'skill' of being prodigal or mean."[85] Furthermore, as Annas notes, people do not seem to aim intentionally at cultivating vice, in the way in which people aim at acquiring virtue.[86] It does not seem as if vice lends itself to being viewed as a skill, but since the virtue as skill model requires us to rethink traditional virtue categories, we might need to do the same with vice.

If vices do not turn out to involve the acquisition of problematic skills, does this undermine the virtue as skill thesis? I do not think so, because there is a fundamental asymmetry with respect to the concept of virtue and vice. Virtues are a complex of cognitive, affective, and self-regulatory abilities. For Aristotle, to act virtuously was to not only act well, but also for the right reason, with the right feeling, in the right way, etc. To hit the target of virtue was like an archer trying to hit a bullseye – there is only one

---

[83] Roberts, Bob, "Will Power and the Virtues," *The Philosophical Review*, 93:2 (1984), 227–247, 238.

[84] This distinction between 'auxiliary' and 'substantive' virtues will reappear in a similar form when I discuss epistemic virtues in the next chapter.

[85] Russell, Daniel C., *Practical Intelligence and the Virtues* (New York: Oxford University Press, 2009), 233.

[86] Annas, Julia, "Virtue, Skill and Vice," *Ethics & Politics*, XVII:2 (2015), 94–106.

way to get it right, and lots of ways to be off target. Virtues focus on all those ingredients that are required for reliably acting well.

By contrast, vice would turn out to be a very narrow category indeed if you had a vice if and only if you reliably acted wrongly, for problematic reasons, with inappropriate feelings, etc. One need not be thrown off target in every possible way in order to qualify as having a vice. Of course, there is also a lot of room between reliably acting well and having vicious habits, such as Aristotle's example of the continent person (who acts well but with conflicted feelings).[87] So vices should turn out to be a motley assortment of habits that can throw you off target.

Conclusion

The features that we find central in expert performance and skill acquisition help to support many aspects associated with descriptions of the virtuous person and the acquisition of virtue. Not only does this show how virtue can be understood as a skill, it also helps to further deepen an understanding of how, for example, the virtuous person can act well in a spontaneous and intuitive way. The next chapter continues the theme of individuating virtues with a discussion of the epistemic virtues, though in the context of an objection that has been raised against a skill model of virtue in both the virtue ethics and the virtue epistemology literature – namely that virtues necessarily involve an element of intrinsic motivation that is not required in skill acquisition.

---

[87] My thanks to an anonymous reviewer for highlighting this.

CHAPTER 3

Motivation in Skill and Virtue

In this chapter, I challenge a long-held objection to understanding virtues as practical skills, and one that comes up in both discussions of virtue ethics and virtue epistemology.[1] The objection is that skills lack a key motivational element found in virtue. This difference is frequently cited as a reason why virtues cannot be understood as skills, despite their other many similarities. In tackling this objection, I will first draw out some connections between goals, values, and motivations. Since levels of motivation are connected to the value we place on a goal, I highlight the ways in which skills can have more than mere instrumental value, and thus can be significant sources of a motivation to perform well.

Nevertheless, there are other ways to argue for a motivational gap between skill and virtue, which I will bring out with a discussion of several cases.[2] The essence of the challenge is that evaluations of skillfulness seem to consider only what a person can do (regardless of what motivates a skillful performance), whereas when evaluating virtue we also have to inquire what a person is motivated to do (to make sure they are motivated in the right way). In response to these cases, I argue that this motivation-based objection fails to undermine the 'virtue as skill' thesis. The motivations of a skilled performer can be evaluated as to whether they express a commitment to achieving the ends of their practice, and in a way that mirrors the motivational commitment we expect from virtue.

---

[1] For examples of the challenge, see Stalnaker, Aaron, "Virtue as Mastery in Early Confucianism," *Journal of Religious Ethics*, 38:3 (2010), 404–428. Aristotle, *Nicomachean Ethics* (Grinnell: The Peripatetic Press, 1984). Watson, Gary, "Two Faces of Responsibility," in *Agency and Answerability* (Oxford: Oxford University Press, 2004). Zagzebski, Linda, *Virtues of the Mind* (Cambridge: Cambridge University Press, 1996).

[2] With kind permission from the Australasian Journal of Philosophy, this chapter draws on my article: Stichter, Matt, "Practical Skills and Practical Wisdom in Virtue", Australasian Journal of Philosophy, 94:3 (2016): 435–448, copyright © Australasian Association of Philosophy, reprinted by permission of Taylor & Francis Ltd, www.tandfonline.com on behalf of Australasian Association of Philosophy.

Furthermore, I explore additional concerns about motivation that arise specifically in the context of virtue epistemology, as it is an issue that divides two main camps within virtue epistemology – virtue reliabilists and virtue responsibilists. Although both groups have drawn on skill analogies, a skill model lends itself more to the reliabilist approach, as evidenced by some of the critiques on skill coming from the responsibilists. I will argue that virtue as skill can accommodate many of the concerns of the responsibilists. As I make my case for this, I will continue the discussion of individuating the virtues from the previous chapter.

Goals, Values, and Motivation

In the self-regulation framework, as discussed in the first chapter, motivation is associated with phases of goal setting, and the strength of one's motivation depends on how the goal is valued.[3] A highly valued goal will provide a lot of motivation to engage in striving to meet that goal, because of the strong anticipated feelings of self-satisfaction or self-censure for success or failure in achieving it. A less valued goal will provide less motivation, and is less likely to be pursued when a situation affords opportunities to pursue multiple mutually exclusive goals, as (all things being equal) we will tend to pursue the more valued goal.

There are reasons why we might believe that skills as goals will tend to be less valued than the value we associate with virtue. Skill acquisition often seems to be a mere means to an end, thus only having instrumental value as a tool in achieving more highly valued goals. Driving, for example, is a skill that people learn today as a means of helping them to achieve more valued goals. It may be a skill that people are quite willing to give up on if self-driving cars become a reality. It does not seem to be usually valued for its own sake, and perhaps skill at driving is then at best an instrumentally useful subgoal. If skills in general are limited to instrumental value, then they will be limited in their value relative to intrinsically valued goals such as virtue.

Aristotle at one point argues along these lines, claiming that there is a distinction between skill and virtue because skills have a separate end that they aim at, like a carpenter building a house, unlike virtue.[4] In his view skills only concern 'making' things with a value that is independent of its production (i.e. instrumental value), while virtues are concerned with

---

[3] Feasibility also affects motivation, but it does not seem to play a role in the reasons why people see a difference between virtues and skills.

[4] Aristotle, *Nicomachean Ethics* (Grinnell: The Peripatetic Press, 1984), 1140b4–8.

'doing', as in activities where the value is in the activity itself (i.e. intrinsic value). However, this is a fairly weak argument, for not all skills are like this. In performance skills (such as acting, dance, music, etc.) there is no separate end or product apart from the performance itself, so his distinction does not hold. The virtue as skill thesis is thus best understood in terms of acquired performance, rather than productive, skills.

However, a similar kind of worry can be expressed about epistemic skills, as skills that help us to acquire true belief might be viewed as having merely instrumental value in producing truth, where truth is what is intrinsically valuable.[5] So skills of inquiry that allow us to solve complicated problems, or generate predictions and explanations, might have only instrumental value in arriving at truth, and thus fall short of the value associated with virtue. A response to this kind of worry, though, can be found in the work of Ernest Sosa, who has argued that in accounting for the special value we place on having knowledge (which is above and beyond the value of having merely true belief), epistemic skills are shown to have more than instrumental value.

Sosa begins with a general account of 'performance normativity', and then applies it specifically to performances of epistemic skills. He claims that there are three questions we can raise about any practice with a characteristic aim:

> Performances with an aim, in any case, admit assessment in respect of our three attainments: accuracy: reaching the aim; adroitness: manifesting skill or competence; and aptness: reaching the aim *through* the adroitness manifest.[6]

Take Sosa's example of an archer trying to hit a bull's-eye. We can ask if the target was hit, and whether the shot manifested the archer's skill. The two can come apart, because a novice can get lucky, and an expert might get unlucky (say from a gust of wind blowing the arrow of course). The goal is not just to hit the target in addition to manifesting one's skill, but rather that the target is hit *because* of the archer's skill, which is what makes it an apt performance. The success an archer has in hitting a target through skill represents an achievement for which the archer deserves credit, which would not be the case if she hit the target merely by luck.[7] Drawing on another skill analogy, Sosa says of a ballerina that what we really value is

---

[5] This would be in addition to whatever instrumental value truth might have in pursuing some of our other goals.

[6] Sosa, Ernest, *A Virtue Epistemology: Apt Belief and Reflective Knowledge*, Vol. 1 (Oxford: Oxford University Press, 2007), 23.

[7] Gilbert Ryle raises similar questions as Sosa does about hitting a bullseye, in his discussion of know-how. See Ryle, Gilbert, *The Concept of Mind* (New York: Routledge, 2009), 33–34.

not just her performance, but that it manifests the ballerina's skill. If the performance was 'produced' in some other way, say by her performing those moves by accident, then we would not value it as much.[8]

Furthermore, he argues that you can extend this 'AAA' account to epistemology, where the fundamental value (or aim) to be realized is truth. The goal is not merely to attain true belief (i.e. hitting the target), but also for true belief to be attained *because* of the exercise of cognitive skills (i.e. epistemic or intellectual virtues). One of the implications of this that Sosa notes is that "epistemic virtues enter constitutively in the attainment of fundamental value, not just instrumentally. Virtues are thus constitutive because the aptness of belief is constituted by its being accurate because competent."[9] If the goal were merely truth, then epistemic skills would be viewed as just instrumental to attaining truth. But if the goal is really aptness, which shows the epistemic skills to be of constitutive value, then it is like the kind of value we associate with virtue. My concern here, though, is not with defending the specifics of Sosa's account of knowledge. While his 'AAA' account of performance normativity was developed within the context of virtue epistemology, it generalizes to any performance with an aim that we try to reach via the exercise of our competences, which shows how skills can have constitutive value, and so are not limited to being of merely instrumental value.

An even stronger case can be made on behalf of the value of skills, though, as skills can also be important sources of intrinsically valuable experiences. Mihalyi Csikszentmihalyi's work on 'flow' shows that a significant source of intrinsically valuable activities, or 'optimal experiences', comes from the exercise of skills. Flow experiences are characterized phenomenologically, in part by an "[i]ntense and focused concentration on what one is doing in the present moment," "[l]oss of reflective self-consciousness (i.e., loss of awareness of oneself as a social actor)," and "[d]istortion of temporal experience (typically, a sense that time has passed faster than normal)."[10] People report that these kind of experiences, where they are fully immersed in an activity, are intrinsically rewarding (and apart from whatever may be the outcome of the activity). Importantly, Csikszentmihalyi notes that "the overwhelming proportion of optimal experiences are reported to occur within

---

[8] Sosa refers to the special value we attach to aptness as "performance-immanent value." Sosa, Ernest, *A Virtue Epistemology: Apt Belief and Reflective Knowledge*, Vol. 1 (Oxford: Oxford University Press, 2007), 88.

[9] Sosa, Ernest, *A Virtue Epistemology: Apt Belief and Reflective Knowledge*, Vol. 1 (Oxford: Oxford University Press, 2007), 88.

[10] Nakamura, Jeanne and Csikszentmihalyi, Mihaly, "The Concept of Flow," in Snyder, C. R., and Lopez, S. J. (eds.), *Oxford Handbook of Positive Psychology* (Oxford University Press, 2009), 89–105, 90.

sequences of activities that are goal-directed and bounded by rules—activities that require the investment of psychic energy, and that could not be done without the appropriate skills."[11]

Why is there this connection between flow and skill? What seems to be rewarding is the tackling of challenges that are appropriate for one's competences, as in being neither too easy (resulting in boredom) nor too difficult (resulting in anxiety). While accomplishing a goal typically results in feelings of self-satisfaction, as discussed in Chapter 1, with flow it is instead the exercise of the skill itself in response to an appropriate challenge that is experienced as rewarding. It is skillfulness that allows one to meet the challenge with the kind of phenomenology described above. Automaticity, for example, clearly contributes to the ability to act effectively without reflective self-consciousness. One interesting implication of this for virtue as skill has been pointed out by Julia Annas. She notes that Aristotle claimed that virtuous activity is supposed to be in some sense 'pleasant', and that this can be understood in terms of flow, as "virtuous activity, as opposed to merely self-controlled activity, is pleasant, not in involving extra feelings but in being unimpeded by contrary impulses, and in harmony with all of the person's thoughts and feelings."[12]

Finally, while some level of skillfulness is necessary to have initial flow experiences, you will have to increase your level of skillfulness to keep on having those kind of experiences. Since the reward comes from balancing one's level of skill against an appropriate challenge, eventually with more experience the same challenge will become easier, perhaps to the point of it being boring. The next more challenging task may require some deliberate practice before you can engage in it with a sense of flow. As Csikszentmihalyi points out, the experience of flow is one of "engaging just-manageable challenges by tackling a series of goals, continuously processing feedback about progress, and adjusting action based on this feedback."[13] Skill enables flow experiences, and the intrinsically rewarding experience of flow provides further motivation to keep improving one's skillfulness. Thus, skills can be important sources of intrinsic value and motivation for self-improvement, as we would also expect with virtue.

---

[11] Csikszentmihalyi, Mihay, *Flow: The Psychology of Optimal Experience* (New York: HarperCollins, 1991), 49.

[12] Annas, Julia, "The Phenomenology of Virtue," *Phenomenology and the Cognitive Sciences*, 7 (2008), 21–34, 30. See also Annas, Julia, *Intelligent Virtue* (Oxford: Oxford University Press, 2011), chapter 5.

[13] Nakamura, Jeanne and Csikszentmihalyi, Mihaly, "The Concept of Flow," in Snyder, C. R., and Lopez, S. J. (eds.), *Oxford Handbook of Positive Psychology* (Oxford University Press, 2009), 89–105, 90.

The Motivation Objection – an Initial Formulation

So far we have seen that skillfulness requires setting goals of high performance for oneself, which motivates striving to improve one's performance.
Being able to maintain a high level of motivation over long periods of time,
and in the face of obstacles and setbacks, is key for skill development,
especially for those on the difficult path to achieving expertise in a skill
domain. Thus, virtues cannot be contrasted with skills merely on the
grounds that virtue requires that you be strongly motivated to act well
while skill does not. Not only does it take a high degree of motivation to
put forth the approximately 10,000 hours of deliberate practice to achieve
expertise, but you still need to be motivated to practice regularly to retain
that expertise. Similar to our expectations for acquiring virtue, achieving
expertise and maintaining it requires being consistently motivated to act
well. Thus, skills cannot be characterized simply as capacities that one
could have regardless of one's overall motivation to act skillfully.

However, Linda Zagzebski suggests that there is a way in which virtues
and skills differ with respect to motivation. While she makes this objection
from the perspective of virtue epistemology, it applies equally to moral
virtues and epistemic virtues. She claims that "virtues and skills have
numerous connections, but virtues are psychically prior to skills. I propose
that this is because the motivational component of a virtue defines it more
than external effectiveness does, whereas it is the reverse in the case of
skills."[14] Here the issue is not that skills lack a motivational component,
but rather that the motivational component is more important for virtue
than it is for skill. Furthermore, Zagzebski sees virtues as being associated
with skills due to this motivational component:

> Since skills *are* connected with actions of a certain specifiable sort, it follows
> that effectiveness in action requires skills, and to the extent that a virtuous
> person is motivated to produce external consequences desirable from the
> point of view of the virtue, s/he would also be motivated to acquire the
> skills that are associated with such effectiveness in action.[15]

Since the motivation spurs the acquisition of skills that make one effective,
motivation is prior to skillfulness. But in that sense, motivation is also
prior in the acquisition of practical skills, since gaining a skill takes

---

[14] Zagzebski, Linda, *Virtues of the Mind* (Cambridge: Cambridge University Press, 1996), 115.
[15] Zagzebski, Linda, *Virtues of the Mind* (Cambridge: Cambridge University Press, 1996), 115.
Although she sees virtues as associated with skills, she resists the claim that virtues can be
understood as skills.

determined and sustained effort that you will not put forward unless you are highly motivated. In either case, you start with goal setting, which then provides motivation to take actions to reach the desired goal. Hence, these observations do not require us to think of virtues and skills as two different things. Both virtue and expertise require being motivated to act well and being effective (or successful) in action.

What then of Zagzebski's claim that the difference between virtues and skills lies in the motivational component defining virtue more than success, in contrast to skills? Perhaps it is the case for virtue, but not similarly for expertise, that the motivation to act well must always be present in order to possess the virtue. This claim is plausible if we are imagining a perfectly virtuous person, in which case we would expect no failures of motivation. Of course, if we are thinking in terms of ideals, we might also expect no failures of motivation in a perfect expert. After all, one achieves expertise in part by actively trying to improve one's performance, and so we might expect the highest level of expertise to be achieved with a constant motivation to act well. But the more important point is that the possession of virtue is typically understood as a matter of degree, and in that respect someone could possess a virtue even with some lapses in motivation. That puts virtue back on a par with expertise, since expertise also admits of degree.

To what else could we attribute the greater emphasis on motivation over effectiveness in the case of virtues? Heather Battaly provides one possible explanation when she distinguishes conceptions of virtue by whether virtue requires good motives, good effects, or both. She claims that "good motives are necessary for virtue because they tell us what we care about, and do so in ways that good actions and hard-wired capacities can't."[16] For example, Tim Schroeder has suggested that we seem to be willing to label people as partially virtuous if they express good motives even if they do not produce good effects, but not vice versa.[17] For example, a business person who treats others fairly only because it seems like a good business practice does not seem like someone we would want to attribute the virtue of fairness. But someone who has good intentions to help others, perhaps being 'kind-hearted', seems to exhibit some degree of kindness, even if that person usually fails in attempts to actually help others.

However, if the business person reliably treats people fairly, that is still something praiseworthy from the perspective of producing good effects.

[16] Battaly, Heather, "A Pluralist Theory of Virtue," in Alfano, Mark (ed.), *Current Controversies in Virtue Theory* (Routledge, 2015), 7–21, 14.
[17] Personal communication.

And while we may find something praiseworthy in the 'kind-hearted' but inept person, it does not seem apt to really attribute virtue to that person, at least insofar as we understand virtue as embodying knowledge and as a term of success. The merely 'kind-hearted' person has internalized a good moral standard, but does not display any success in implementing the standard, and so seems to lack knowledge of how to do so. In which case, while still having praiseworthy motives, the lack of good effects should be a reason to deny the virtue attribution.

Part of the difference between virtues and skills with regard to motivation surely lies in their different subject matter, as skills like chess do not involve matters that stand to seriously benefit or harm people, and so there is not an inherent problem if you are not motivated to play your best. That is, passing up an opportunity to play chess does not reflect badly on your chess playing skills. But with virtues it always seems to matter whether we are motivated to exercise them or not, notwithstanding some virtues where there is a choice of when we exercise them (like generosity).[18] Thus, the shift in emphasis can be accounted for if one views virtues as specifically normative skills, either in the moral or epistemic sense, where the emphasis on motivation derives from the importance of placing a high value on these virtues as goals, along with striving for improvement. That is, levels of motivation are connected to having set a goal for oneself along with how valued that goal is relative to other goals. Again, one neither needs to have playing chess well as a goal, nor needs to strive to improve. But that is not the case with virtue. It is important to note that this does not show that virtues are not skills, but rather that there are some skills we have normative reasons for setting as goals to acquire – namely those related to moral and epistemic goods (i.e. acquiring moral and epistemic virtues).[19]

Further Motivation Objections: Case 1 – Less Than Wholehearted Performances

Despite the arguments in the previous section, one might still object that motivation does not seem to play a role in evaluating skilled performances in quite the same way as it would for virtue. So far the defense of the role of motivation in skill has been on its importance in acquiring and

---

[18] Although morality might make the demand to act well mandatory, this is not the same as claiming that one must in fact be always motivated to act well in order to possess virtue or expertise (and it is this latter claim that was rejected earlier in this chapter).

[19] At least in the case of moral virtues as skills, these would be skills that could not be used for inherently immoral purposes, given that they necessarily aim at morally appropriate ends.

maintaining skillfulness. But with virtue, it also matters that one is motivated to exercise one's virtue whenever it is appropriate. An honest person, for example, is one who is not only motivated to acquire the virtue of honesty, but also one who is reliably motivated to exercise that virtue when honesty is called for (rather than just whenever she feels like being honest). That kind of commitment, however, does not seem to hold true for skill. For example, Gary Watson suggests something along these lines when he claims that:

> Indifference in a performance doesn't count against one's skill, whereas a less than wholehearted effort to save someone's life does impugn my moral character. Talent and skill are fully displayed only in wholehearted perform-ances, whereas the aretaic perspective is also concerned with the "will," that is, with one's purposes, ends, choices, concerns, cares, attachments, and commitments. Not trying can be a failure of virtue but not of skill.[20]

Judgments of skillfulness are based only on "wholehearted performances," and not on the degree to which I am motivated to give such performances. As Watson points out, my failure to achieve the end of a skill does not necessarily count against me being skilled. For example, let's say I am an expert tennis player, but today I am just not motivated to 'give it my all'. That day on the court, I do not perform at the level of expertise. What can you infer about my level of skill from this performance? You cannot infer that I am not an expert, since my performance itself is consistent both with being a merely competent player giving a wholehearted performance and with being an expert giving a half-hearted performance. Of course, without evidence to the contrary, it would be reasonable for you to assume from this performance that I am not an expert. If I want to prove it to you that I am an expert, I have to deliver an expert-level performance. What matters for assessing my actual level of skill is what I can do when I am giving a wholehearted performance. Choosing to give a half-hearted performance does not make me any less of an expert. The same goes for me not even trying at all.[21]

As Watson points out, the same is not true of our assessments of virtue. Half-hearted attempts at kindness, or not even attempting to be honest, indicate some failure to possess those virtues. The choice not to give a

---

[20] Watson, Gary, "Two Faces of Responsibility," in *Agency and Answerability* (Oxford: Oxford University Press, 2004), Appendix.

[21] Of course, one could not become an expert without 'giving it one's all' consistently over many years. But that is compatible with choosing not to on some occasions, though if one chooses not to try hard too frequently, then one would start to lose their expertise.

wholehearted performance with respect to virtue shows that one is not fully virtuous. Furthermore, if you are not convinced that I am fully kind because of a half-hearted attempt at kindness today, then I am unlikely to convince you otherwise with a wholehearted attempt at kindness tomorrow. My lack of commitment to being kind on this particular occasion seems to undermine my claim to being kind in general, whereas my lack of commitment to playing tennis well today does not similarly undermine my claim to being skilled. As Abrol Fairweather remarks, "[t]o have an excellence of character requires a normative commitment to the end one reliably attains, whereas to have a skill simply requires that the end attained is due to a competence involving training, understanding and discipline."[22] Assessments of level of skill depend on what you can do when you give a wholehearted performance, and not directly on the extent to which you are motivated to give such performances. Of course, you will not be able to achieve expertise without being strongly motivated to act well in the face of difficult challenges, and over a long duration of time. But the half-hearted performances will not count as evidence of a lack of skill, in the way such performances would count as evidence of a lack of virtue.

Case 2 – Acting For Some Other End

Given what was said in the previous section on case 1, will our intuitions about virtues and skills then coincide in cases where people are giving wholehearted performances? Not necessarily. Consider, for example, a highly skilled doctor who practices medicine primarily for the sake of wealth rather than for the sake of healing others. Medicine has as its aim healing patients, and presumably most doctors practice medicine for this reason. But doctors also get paid a lot of money, and surely some of them got into the profession in order to get wealthy. Of course, if such doctors want to get wealthy then they need to become experts at healing patients, and so will need to be focused on the welfare of their patients (and especially when they are in the middle of surgery). But it does not appear to count against the surgeon's level of expertise if we found out that she is motivated ultimately by wealth, where improving the welfare of the patient is a means to an end rather than the end itself.

---

[22] Fairweather, Abrol , "Duhem-Quine Virtue Epistemology," *Synthese*, 187 (2012), 673–692, 678. See also Sosa, Ernest, *A Virtue Epistemology: Apt Belief and Reflective Knowledge*, Vol. 1 (Oxford: Oxford University Press, 2007), 73–74.

However, it would count against someone's possession of kindness if we found out that all the putative kind acts were motivated out of some selfish desire, even if the person was reliable in doing kind acts. This marks this concern with acting for specific ends as different from the kind of example Watson was concerned about earlier, where there was a failure to try hard enough (or to try at all). That is, there could be a concern with the ends that motivate the action, even if there is no failure to be motivated to do one's best. This appears to have been one of the reasons Aristotle thought virtues were not skills, despite the numerous analogies he drew between them. He argues that acting virtuously requires having specific ends that motivate the action. Aristotle sets out the following conditions for acting as a virtuous person would:

(1) Doing what is virtuous (doing the act considered honest, brave, moderate, etc.).
(2) The agent who acts has a certain disposition:
  (a) The agent knows what s/he does.
  (b) The agent intends to do what s/he does and intends to do it for its own sake.
  (c) The agent acts with certainty and firmness.[23]

An example of an agent who satisfies only condition (1) is someone who does what is virtuous only by luck. An example of an agent who satisfies only conditions (1) and (2)(a) is someone who does what is virtuous for the sake of some other end, such as honor or money. An example of an agent who satisfies all the conditions except (2)(c) is someone who is in the process of acquiring a virtue but has not yet had the experience necessary to form a virtuous habit. Acting, as a virtuous person would, requires satisfying all of the above criteria.

It is condition (2)(b) that appears to mark an important difference between virtues and skills, for it is not considered a requirement for expertise in a skill. Again, a doctor can achieve expertise in medicine and perform well, even though she does so for the end of wealth rather than the end of promoting the patient's welfare. We need not inquire about whether the doctor is practicing medicine for its own sake in order to assess whether the doctor is an expert. On the other hand, we do need to inquire about the ends being pursued when assessing a putative virtuous act. If it is revealed that the action was motivated by a selfish end, then that undermines the claim that it was a virtuous act.

---

[23] Aristotle, *Nicomachean Ethics* (Grinnell: The Peripatetic Press, 1984), 1105a29–34.

Case 3 – Intentionally Acting Wrongly

This consideration of the ends of action connects to a third example used to illustrate a difference between virtues and skills. The example concerns our differing intuitions about a case where someone intentionally does wrong. Aristotle noted this difference between virtues and skills when he argued that "the man who goes wrong intentionally is better than the man who goes wrong unintentionally, but in the sphere of practical wisdom he is worse, just as he is worse in the sphere of moral goodness."[24] It seems as though doing something wrong would count against one's level of skill, unless we find out that you did wrong intentionally. For example, a chess master might make a wrong move in a game that causes her to lose. Normally this would signal that she is less skilled than her opponent, unless you find out that she intentionally made the wrong move (say because she was throwing the game for the purposes of illegal betting).[25] With respect to skills, if two people make the same mistake, but one did so intentionally and the other did so without knowing how to act better, then the latter looks less skilled than the former.

However, we seem to have the opposite intuitions when it comes to virtue. If someone acts cruelly, we tend to regard it as worse if it was intentionally done than if it was done accidentally. So intentionally acting cruelly counts more against you possessing the virtue of kindness than doing so accidentally. As with the other examples, when it comes to assessing one's level of virtue, it matters that you are motivated in the right way.

Bob Roberts considers this argument, and tries to claim that virtues and skills are actually on a par here. He thinks the intuitions about virtue just described are mistaken.

> It is of course true that an action does not become any the less immoral by being intentional; and so where doing the moral thing (say, being compassionate) requires the exercise of a skill virtue (say, patience), the fact that one's failure of patience was intentional is no moral exculpation. But claiming that the failure to exercise patience was intentional would defend against the accusation of lacking patience.[26]

While you still have done wrong by failing to be compassionate, Roberts is claiming that it does not necessarily signal that you lack the skill of

---

[24] Aristotle, *Nicomachean Ethics* (Grinnell: The Peripatetic Press, 1984), 1140b23–24.

[25] In fact, it might take a high level of skill to pull this off – ending the game in a particular way without it being too obvious.

[26] Roberts, Bob, "Will Power and the Virtues," *The Philosophical Review*, 93:2 (1984), 227–247, 241.

patience, as it may be that you simply choose not to exercise your skill of patience. However, it is not clear why this would be so. If the virtues are concerned with motivation, and one chooses not to exercise patience when patience is required to act morally, then it seems like a failure to actually be patient. The problem is that one is not properly responsive to the reasons to be patient in the situation, and that lack of responsiveness counts against one's level of virtue.

Reply to the Three Cases – Being Responsive to the Distinctive Demands of a Skill

Although these three cases point to an important issue, there is a way to bring our views about skills more in-line with that of virtues. If we switch our evaluations from the performance to the performer, then it looks like we can evaluate the performer in a way that brings in concerns about motivational commitments.[27] To return to the example of less than wholehearted performances, Watson suggests:

> My half-hearted effort on the tennis court would not support a negative evaluation of my proficiencies at that sport. Nevertheless, it might bear negatively on me as a tennis player. One can be "good at" playing tennis without being overall a good tennis player. A good tennis player, overall, possesses not only a high level of skill but, among other things, a commitment to the game, a responsibility to its distinctive demands. (In this way, 'good tennis player' functions rather like 'good human being'.)[28]

A good performer, as distinguished from a good performance, not only displays a "feel for the game" but also a "commitment to the game." As another example of criticizing less than wholehearted performances, we would likely regard a doctor who gives half-hearted attempts at surgery as a bad doctor, even if she can wholeheartedly perform surgery with expertise. Likewise for a doctor in an emergency room who does not treat a patient simply because she does not feel like it. These doctors are not being responsive to the distinctive demands of medicine, and so we could criticize them for their lack of commitment like we would if someone acted half-heartedly with respect to a virtue like kindness. Watson's approach closes the

---

[27] It might help to note that even Aristotle recognized that you can evaluate performances as to whether they were in conformity to virtue, independent of what motivated the performance, as described previously in case 2 (with the difference in conditions 1 and 2b for Aristotle). So it is not as if we cannot separate performance and performer evaluations with respect to virtue.

[28] Watson, Gary, "Two Faces of Responsibility," in *Agency and Answerability* (Oxford: Oxford University Press, 2004), Appendix.

initial gap between judgments of expertise and virtue, as the expert can also be assessed in aretaic terms, where a failure of motivation does count against one being a good performer.

This approach of evaluating performers with regard to their commitment to the end of the skill domain can also help with the cases of acting for some other end and intentionally acting wrongly as well. With regard to performing well but for some other end, consider again the doctor who practices medicine to gain wealth. If such a doctor were more likely to recommend expensive but unnecessary medical procedures, we would likely think that this person was not a good doctor, even though we would not deny her expertise at performing those procedures. Being responsive to the distinctive demands of your practice requires more than just giving wholehearted performances. The case of intentionally acting wrongly, like a chess master throwing a game, can also be handled by this approach. Aristotle is right that there is something better about, for example, the chess master who goes wrong intentionally relative to the chess player who is trying hard but goes wrong unintentionally, in that the former is more skilled than the latter. But the latter is better in the sense of displaying a commitment to the game. The judgments we have with respect to the cases of virtue can be duplicated in the cases of skill if we evaluate the performer and not just the performance.

Being virtuous requires both knowing how to act well and being motivated to do so, and this can be captured on the skill model of virtue.[29] The ends of a practice can be used not only to judge the effectiveness of a performance, but also the commitment of the performer. This approach can also vindicate the emphasis Tanner and Christen place on 'moral commitment', where "moral commitment consists of an implicit or explicit committing of oneself to moral goals that instigates an enduring striving for moral ends."[30] The same kind of commitment can be seen in dedicating oneself to expertise in a skill. In exercising a skill, you are already subject to being evaluated as to whether you have the proper motivations, as in the case of the doctor recommending unnecessary medical procedures. While these three cases capture the importance of being motivated in the right way, this does not require giving up on the skill model altogether,

[29] This is not to deny that we can assess an act as to whether it is virtuous or vicious without knowing the actor's motivations (i.e. doing the right thing but perhaps for the wrong reason).

[30] Tanner, Carmen and Christen, Markus, "Moral Intelligence – A Framework for Understanding Moral Competences," in Christen, Markus, van Schaik, Carel, Fischer, Johannes, and Huppenbauer, Markus (eds.), *Empirically Informed Ethics: Morality between Facts and Norms* (Switzerland: Springer, 2014), 119–136, 128.

which is the conclusion usually drawn from these cases. Thus, we do not need to reach beyond a discussion of skills and expertise to incorporate a concern for the responsiveness to the demands of a practice.

We might, therefore, add another level to Sosa's 'AAA' structure for practices with a characteristic aim, which is otherwise restricted to evaluations of performances. To move our evaluation from performances to the performers, we might then ask of a particular performance whether the person in so acting was responsive to the distinctive demands of the practice. Perhaps what we want is an *assurance* that someone has a normative commitment to the end of a practice, in which case we end up with an 'AAAA' structure for evaluating performers (rather than merely performances). An advantage of this is that it helps to explain why we think there is something of value to those who are committed to good ends (i.e. having good motives), even when they fail in practice to achieve them. The distinction between evaluating the performance and evaluating the performer brings us back to the distinction between good effects and good motives. Both matter, and this kind of mixed view echoes Liezl van Zyl's view that "good effects (or ends) and good motives are independent sources of value."[31] Because they are independent sources of value, they can be evaluated separately in both the cases of virtue and skill.

The incorporation of motivational commitment into an account of expertise is also reflected in the approach Darcia Narvaez takes in arguing that moral behavior should be understood as skilled behavior.[32] The view of expertise that she is working with includes the idea of an expert being committed to the ends of her practice, and in a way that shapes various aspects of the person. As Narvaez goes on to explain:

> Learning the skill means changing oneself to be the kind of person who fully embodies the skill, consciously and intuitively. The skill flavors and modifies one's perceptions, attention, desires, and intuitions, as well as semantic, procedural, and conditional knowledge. The skills are simultaneously process focused and content rich and are refined throughout one's life.[33]

In this sense, expertise does capture the motivational aspects of virtue that gave rise to the putative disanalogy between virtues and skills in the case of

---

[31] Van Zyl, Liezl, "Against Radical Pluralism," in Alfano, Mark (ed.), *Current Controversies in Virtue Theory* (New York: Routledge, 2015), 22–32, 28.

[32] By moral behavior is intended the idea of not only doing the right thing, but also going about it in the right way. That is, one can do the right thing by accident, in which case the moral behavior would not be a product of a skill. My thanks to Christian Miller for pushing this point.

[33] Narvaez, Darcia, "Integrative Ethical Education," in Killen, Melanie and Smetana, Judith (eds.), *Handbook of Moral Development* (Mahwah, NJ: Erlbaum, 2006), 703–733, 722.

half-hearted performances. In sum, the initial concern about their being a crucial motivational difference between virtues and skills is misplaced. Achieving and maintaining expertise requires not only extensive practical know-how, but also a very strong commitment to acting well according to the ends that define the particular skill domain. This shows that the three cases described do not reveal a significant difference between virtues and skills.

Epistemic Skills – Virtue Reliabilism Versus Virtue Responsibilism

There is one further instance of the motivation objection that is raised specifically in the context of virtue epistemology, as it is part of what divides two groups in virtue epistemology – virtue reliabilists and virtue responsibilists.[34] One context in which skills are discussed is the attempt in virtue epistemology to explain the special value we attach to knowledge (beyond the value already present in true belief), by reference to some features of the knower (such as her faculties, skills, or traits), instead of just focusing on properties of the belief itself.[35] For virtue epistemologists, knowledge is an intellectual achievement – a term of success, and one where the success was brought about (to some extent) by your own competences (whether that is understood as abilities, character traits, faculties, skills, etc.). So the special value that we attach to knowledge could be explained by the addition of something for which you deserve credit – the exercise of your intellectual competences. To say that somebody knows something is to give them epistemic credit for having a true belief.[36]

One main divide amongst virtue epistemologists is what specifically the agent needs to contribute to get credit for the true belief. Virtue 'responsibilists' focus on character traits, such as open-mindedness, intellectual humility, conscientiousness, curiosity, etc.[37] Virtue 'reliabilists' focus on abilities and faculties, including memory and perception, which do not necessarily involve the kind of motivations found in character

---

[34] In virtue ethics you do not have this particular division.

[35] Though, this is by no means the only thing that virtue epistemologists focus on in applying virtue concepts to epistemological debates. It just happens to be a central issue in which a skill model of virtue has specific implications.

[36] My goal here is not to defend a full account of knowledge, but rather to highlight the implications of a skill model of virtue for already existing virtue-theoretic accounts of knowledge. So, while I believe it supports a virtue reliabilist position, I do not intend to discuss some of the challenges to mere faculties like vision or memory in the reliabilist account of knowledge.

[37] See Zagzebski, Linda, *Virtues of the Mind* (Cambridge: Cambridge University Press, 1996); and Baehr, Jason, *The Inquiring Mind: On Intellectual Virtues and Virtue Epistemology* (New York: Oxford University Press, 2012).

traits.[38] Where do skills fall in this debate? Skill-based approaches have so far found themselves put into both camps, as they share some aspects with character traits (emphasized by responsibilists) as well as faculties like perception (emphasized by reliabilists).

Skills, and self-regulation more generally, involve intentional agency through goal setting (motivation) and striving (volition). Clearly self-regulation and the exercise of skill qualifies as something that one deserves credit for generally, and the exercise of epistemic skill in arriving at true belief looks worthy as qualifying as knowledge.[39] This is the kind of position Sosa adopts in his virtue reliabilabilism. We can return to his 'AAA' account of performance evaluation (that although being a general account of evaluation was introduced specifically in the context of virtue epistemology), where knowledge is specifically apt belief: Apt = Accurate (true) because of being Adroit (manifesting intellectual competence).

Skills have also been associated with virtue responsibilism. Zagzebski's virtue responsibilism claims that virtues are associated with skills, as skills provide the knowledge of how to reach the aim of virtue (as discussed earlier). However, she denies that virtues are themselves skills, as the relationship is such that having the virtuous motivations is what leads you to then acquire the skills necessary to reach the ends of the virtuous motivation. So it might seem that skills by themselves may not feature the right kind of credit to belong in the responsibilist camp. In summarizing the responsibilists' position, Heather Battaly notes that:

> The rift between Zagzebski's and Sosa's views is exacerbated by their disagreement over whether the virtues are skills ... But, skills are not habits. While skills need not be exercised, habits will not exist unless they are exercised on the appropriate occasions.[40]

However, given that habitual virtuous action can be understood on a model of skills, the skill–habit distinction is hard to maintain.

If the problem is instead that the possession of a skill does not require exercising it on (most) every appropriate occasion, then it is similar to the

---

[38] See Sosa, Ernest, *A Virtue Epistemology: Apt Belief and Reflective Knowledge*, Vol. 1 (Oxford: Oxford University Press, 2007); and Greco, John, Achieving Knowledge: A Virtue-Theoretic Account of Epistemic Normativity (Cambridge: Cambridge University Press, 2010).

[39] Duncan Pritchard argues that expertise "is best thought of in terms of the exercise of epistemic virtues on the agent reliabilist model than in the internalist terms suggested by Zagzebski and others." Pritchard, Duncan, "Virtue Epistemology and the Acquisition of Knowledge," *Philosophical Explorations*, 8:3 (2005), 229–243, 238. While I tend to think this is right, it does depend on the extent to which the internalist/externalist debate mirrors the responsibilist/reliabilist debate.

[40] Battaly, Heather, "What is Virtue Epistemology?" *Proceedings of the Twentieth World Congress of Philosophy*, www.bu.edu/wcp/Papers/Valu/ValuBatt.htm

problem noted in case 1 regarding half-hearted performances. Sosa appears to take this position when he claims that:

> Disinterested, high-minded motivation must be distinguished from intentional, volitional agency. Dispositions to succeed when one tries need not be closely allied with, and much less do they need to be constituted by, a high-minded motivation, one that can bear on the personal worth of the agent, on how fine a person they are. Professionals *are* indeed routinely engaged in intentional, volitional truth-seeking in their work lives, even when they do not disinterestedly, lovingly seek the truth.[41]

The reference to "[d]ispostions to succeed when one tries" clearly separates performance evaluation from performer evaluation.[42] It is for this reason that Zagzebski rejects virtues as skills, since she thinks virtue centrally involves the 'high-minded' kind of motivation that appears absent in skill by itself.

Sosa wants to claim that the kind of intentional agency shown by the professional inquirer is enough to be deserving of credit when it produces true belief, and that no 'high-minded' motivation that reflects on personal worth need also be involved. As Jason Baehr puts it, in outlining his and Zagzebski's positions, intellectual virtues require "*intrinsic epistemic motivation.* We maintain that virtue-manifesting intellectual activity must be motivated at least partly by an intrinsic concern with epistemic goods like truth and knowledge – a concern or desire for these goods *as such* or *considered in their own right*, not merely for the sake of some additional (potentially non-epistemic) good that might result from their acquisition."[43] In this respect, it is similar to the problem noted in case 2 of acting for some other end. This responsibilist concern for intrinsic motivation is supposed to drive a wedge between virtue and skill, as intrinsic concerns need not factor into an explanation of what motivated someone's process of inquiry in the case of skill.

What Baehr seems to want is proper epistemic 'responsiveness' to truth or other epistemic goods like understanding or wisdom. In that sense,

[41] Sosa, Ernest, "Virtue Epistemology: Character versus Competence," in Mark Alfano (ed.), *Current Controversies in Virtue Theory* (New York: Routledge, 2015), 62–73, 71–72.
[42] Sosa also describes the dispositional structure of the competence in terms of skill, shape, and situation ('SSS'). That is, the disposition to succeed requires not only that we have the requisite level of skill, but also that we are in a certain shape (e.g. not drunk or asleep), and that we are in an appropriate situation (e.g. even a skilled archer is unlikely to hit the target if there are strong gusts of wind). Sosa, Ernest, "Virtue Epistemology: Character versus Competence," in Alfano, Mark (ed.), *Current Controversies in Virtue Theory* (New York: Routledge, 2015), 62–74, 74.
[43] Baehr, Jason, "Character Virtues, Epistemic Agency, and Reflective Knowledge," in Alfano, Mark (ed.), *Current Controversies in Virtue Theory* (Routledge, 2015), 74–86, 78.

I think his concerns can be handled in a similar way as the motivational concerns that started off this chapter. If we take into account being responsive to the distinctive demands of a practice, then we can evaluate not just performances but also the performers. This brings us back to what I termed an 'assurance' addition to Sosa's 'AAA' model (thus an 'AAAA' model), as I think that a skill based account has more resources to address responsibilist concerns than what Sosa provides on his own. Here we would be asking for an assurance that the exercise of a skill that led to true belief was also at least partially motivated by an intrinsic concern for the epistemic goods that the inquiry aims at. But it need not be fully or even primarily motivated by such a concern. There are good reasons for this kind of qualification, as the primary motivation for starting an inquiry is often the need to know some specific information in a particular domain (and not a search for truth simpliciter).[44] Thus, even on a skill model of virtue we can inquire about the motivations of the performer vis-à-vis an intrinsic concern for epistemic goods, and recognize an additional source of value (beyond aptness) if the performer also has the 'high-minded' kind of motivation.[45] However, it would be problematic to build in that 'high-minded' kind of motivation as a requirement for knowledge, as skilled performers clearly have knowledge and are not necessarily motivated out of a 'love for truth as such'.

Sosa is willing to count the high-minded epistemic motivation as an intellectual virtue, but says that the exercise of such a virtue only "puts you in a position to know" in contrast to those intellectual virtues whose exercise can constitute knowledge.[46] Putting you in a position to know could be understood to cover both motivating a certain line of inquiry (say by curiosity), or preventing an inquiry from being biased (say by being open-minded). However, for Sosa, "[w]hen the correctness of a belief is due to competence in a way that *constitutes* knowledge, it is not enough that the competence reliably puts one *in a position to know*, in a position where one can now exercise one's knowledge-constitutive competences,

---

[44] This may mark a slight contrast with the moral case. While people have plenty of instrumental reasons to acquire and exercise epistemic skills, it is less common in the moral case to have someone instrumentally concerned with good moral performances (though an exception may be for example a business person trying to treat others fairly as a matter of good business practice). That is not to deny that most people do have moral goals as part of their identity due to socialization, and that basic competence in several moral skills is going to be necessary just to get along in society.

[45] It is worth noting that it is still to the credit of the performer if the performance is apt, even if it is not ultimately motivated in a praiseworthy way.

[46] Hereafter I shorten 'high-minded' or 'personal-worth involving' epistemic motivations to just 'epistemic motivation'.

those whose exercise *does* constitute knowledge."[47] For Sosa the epistemic virtues that are central to epistemology are those whose exercise constitutes knowledge, and epistemic virtues that position you to know are of secondary importance (in other words, 'auxiliary' virtues).[48]

In this respect, we may see a parallel to the distinction drawn in the previous chapter when individuating virtues between 'substantive' virtues (like honesty, kindness, or justice) and the 'auxiliary' virtues of will power (like courage, patience, or temperance). The virtues of will power seem to play a supporting role to the more substantive virtues, as being courageous or patient could be just as helpful in pursuing immoral ends as moral ends. They support the other virtues by preventing us from acting in ways contrary to the other virtues, such as when honesty requires us to speak truth to power when it is dangerous to do so.[49] The 'auxiliary' virtues of will power can also be viewed as putting one in a position to exercise the substantive virtues, in a similar way to how the auxiliary epistemic virtues put one in position to exercise one's knowledge-generating virtues. The distinction between substantive and auxiliary virtues would then be based on whether the virtue in question helps secure the moral or epistemic good (which would be substantive), or whether it puts one in a position to exercise another virtue that secures the good (which would be auxiliary). In this sense, there may be some auxiliary virtues that cross the moral and epistemic lines, like courage or patience, as they can play a supporting role to both moral and epistemic virtues. 'Intellectual courage' may share domain-general features with moral courage, as discussed in the previous chapter, and may differ only in regards to some of its domain-specific features. If so, then there would not be two virtues of courage, as it is usually presented, but rather one auxiliary virtue that has domain-specific features. Thus, the division between substantive and auxiliary virtues in the moral case may lend support to a similar division in the epistemic case.

More generally, we can ask: what difference does responsiveness to the demands internal to a practice make in performance? Presumably a chess player will not play poorly when it could be in her self-interest to throw the

---

[47] Sosa, Ernest, "Virtue Epistemology: Character versus Competence," in Mark Alfano (ed.), *Current Controversies in Virtue Theory* (New York: Routledge, 2015), 62–73, 67.

[48] "The reason for this is that what makes them auxiliary virtues is mostly that their exercise enables us to acquire or sustain the complete competence – the Skill, Shape, and Situation, SSS complete knowledge-constitutive competence – in virtue of whose manifestations we know answers to questions in a given domain." Sosa, Ernest, "Virtue Epistemology: Character versus Competence," in Alfano, Mark (ed.), *Current Controversies in Virtue Theory* (New York: Routledge, 2015), 62–73, 67.

[49] Again, this is not the only function of virtues of will power, as they also have prudential value in helping us to achieve other non-moral goals, such as temperance assisting with staying on a diet.

game; or a business person will be fair even when it does not necessarily pay to be; or a person will remain open-minded even when not a matter of professional inquiry; etc.[50] That is, there could be the achievement of skilled, moral, or epistemic goods on some occasions when it would otherwise be missed.[51] But that responsiveness only presents opportunities to display one's competence at chess, fairness, domain-specific inquiry, etc. Whether someone actually wins the game or treats people fairly or arrives at knowledge (or other cognitive achievement) depends on the successful exercise of their competence. In other words, responsiveness is still a matter of putting someone in a position to exercise their competence.[52]

Baehr in response to Sosa agrees that epistemic motivations can result in putting someone in a position to know. However, he also thinks that the epistemic motivations can be relevant in constituting knowledge:

> Consider, for instance, a case in which a person notices an important visual clue or detail on account of his focused attention or attentive observation. As I am conceiving of the case, it is not as if the person exercises attentiveness and then, only subsequently, sees the relevant detail. Rather, attentiveness is manifested in the act of visual perception itself. It is *in* or *through* focused or attentive looking that the detail is perceived.[53]

Assuming that being attentive to detail is an epistemic motivation, this might be a case where the motivation manifests itself in an act that constitutes knowledge. However, one difficulty with his proposal is whether it is really possible to be attentive in general. Being attentive to detail requires knowing what details are relevant both in a context and for some purpose. As shown in skill acquisition, with greater experience in a domain, one can better filter out the relevant from the irrelevant details. It is why chess masters have greater recall of the details of board positions than less experienced players (and it is not the result of just better memory in general), and also why they do not have a better recall for completely randomized board positions.

[50] It is possible to treat someone fairly without having been motivated intrinsically by fairness. Again, we must keep separate performance from performer evaluations.
[51] Of course that only matters to someone if they value those ends/goods more than what they could give it up for, which brings us back to the relevance of moral and epistemic goals being high on people's value hierarchy.
[52] Of course it will also have the effect of promoting improvement in one's competence, but external motivations can have the same result.
[53] Baehr, Jason, "Character Virtues, Epistemic Agency, and Reflective Knowledge," in Alfano, Mark (ed.), *Current Controversies in Virtue Theory* (New York: Routledge, 2015), 74–86, 81–82.

Furthermore, as in the case described, if one discovers a 'clue', it must be a clue that aids in some inquiry or task performance. People do not just go out and merely 'observe' and see what comes of it. I may value truth for its own sake, but that does not motivate me to go out trying to learn all sorts of new random facts. The goal is not to maximize my stock of true beliefs. Rather, I narrow my focus based on my other interests, such that I seek out truth in specific domains. If a clue is discovered through observation, then there is already a search for information underway. In which case, it is hard to see how the epistemic motivation really functions any different from the attentiveness to detail that can be manifested by a professional who is not disinterestedly seeking the truth.

Baehr at one point argues that the intrinsic epistemic motivation might matter with respect to improving skilled performances. He suggests that we:

> Compare, for instance, two people with the skills required for conducting technical research in some area, but only one of whom has any desire to reach the truth or to achieve understanding in this area. It is plausible to think that, other things being equal, the skills of the latter person will be greater and more refined than those of the person who lacks the relevant desire—that a desire for truth or understanding, which is characteristic of intellectual virtue, will play an enhancing or perfecting role in connection with these skills. The person who lacks such a desire, by contrast, may be disinclined to use her skills when doing so strikes her as tedious or inconvenient, or she may be prone to use them in a sloppy or careless manner.[54]

I will assume in this example that the former person is being paid to be a researcher in an area that they are not fundamentally interested in – such that they have had a reason to acquire the necessary skills of inquiry to acquire knowledge in that domain, but the reason owes to extrinsic motivation (i.e. getting paid). The latter person is presumably someone who has an interest in the research domain in question, and is lucky enough to be getting paid to carry out such research. Is it likely that the latter person has been motivated to develop her skills to a higher level than the former? It depends. I suspect that there are some doctors who are strongly motivated enough by the desire for money or status that they have developed their skills to a higher level than some who are in the profession just to help people. Intrinsic motivation is not necessarily stronger than extrinsic motivation.

---

[54] Baehr, Jason, *The Inquiring Mind: On Intellectual Virtues and Virtue Epistemology* (New York: Oxford University Press, 2012), 31–32.

That being said, I am willing to admit that it is plausible to think that in general an intrinsically motivated person would on average display a higher level of skill development.[55] Is it then a problem that the former person may be sometimes disinclined to use her skills? Well it might be if she is otherwise getting paid to use her skills. If not, it is hard to see how it matters independent of that person having an interest in the research domain in question. Notice in this example that the latter person need not have a desire for truth as such, as all it requires is a domain-specific interest that motivates the inquiry. But Baehr is trying to defend a domain-general desire for truth or understanding, and his example does not suffice for that purpose.

Further questions can be raised about what a domain-general desire for truth consists in. Baehr, as quoted earlier, requires "an intrinsic concern with epistemic goods like truth and knowledge – a concern or desire for these goods *as such* or *considered in their own right*, not merely for the sake of some additional (potentially non-epistemic) good that might result from their acquisition."[56] He thinks of it in terms of not viewing the truth as of merely instrumental value in acquiring some non-epistemic good. But it is not clear whether that is something which could partially motivate an intellectual activity. What motivates a search for knowledge is a desire to know for some purpose of the agent. It is not a love of knowledge per se that motivates a particular inquiry.

The idea of not treating truth as merely instrumental in pursuing other interests is I think best captured along the lines of the Kantian idea of a respect for persons.[57] We are not supposed to treat persons as if they have merely instrumental value in achieving our own ends. But that serves as a constraint on what we can do in striving to achieve our goals.[58] The pursuit of any particular goal need not be *motivated* by a respect for persons, but rather it needs to be *constrained* by a respect for persons. An intrinsic concern for the truth would thus put a similar domain-general

---

[55] Though this is really a claim that would require some empirical verification.

[56] Baehr, Jason, "Character Virtues, Epistemic Agency, and Reflective Knowledge," in Alfano, Mark (ed.), *Current Controversies in Virtue Theory* (New York: Routledge, 2015), 74–86, 78.

[57] This idea came from a conversation with Quassim Cassam regarding indifference to the truth. It may share some affinities with forthcoming work by Kurt Sylvan, "Veritism Unswamped."

[58] It seems like I would show that I do not value truth for its own sake if I willingly deceive or distort the truth for my own ends, but that is different from showing that the intrinsic concern plays a role in constituting knowledge. Maybe my intrinsic concern shows up if I have two routes to achieving my goal, and one respects the truth and the other does not, and I choose the route that respects the truth (and not because it is more feasible but because it coheres with my commitment to honesty). In that sense, a standing goal commitment to truth might play a role, but seemingly one that still merely puts one in a position to know.

constraint on the pursuit of our goals. In which case, it would be a
problem if in the pursuit of a goal someone was willing to ignore the truth
when it furthered their goal, as this would be to treat the truth as purely
instrumental.

So a respect for the truth as not of merely instrumental value does not
require it being a partial motivator for a particular line on inquiry.
Curiosity, rather, seems like a trait that can be a partial motivator of
inquiry.[59] Curiosity, in cybernetic/control theory from Chapter 1, plays
a role in motivating us to set new goals, as we want to learn something
new.[60] Self-inquisitiveness, in particular, could be an especially important
epistemic virtue, even if in the auxiliary sense described above.[61] The
reason for this is its fundamental role in self-regulation broadly. In order
to self-regulate effectively, you need to know a fair amount about yourself –
strengths, weaknesses, preferences, biases, goals, limitations, etc. Recall
here Conant and Ashby's theorem from Chapter 1 that "Every Good
Regulator of a System Must Be a Model of that System." While they
apply it to the need to model one's environment, in goal striving what one
often has to regulate are one's own thoughts, feelings, responses, etc. This
is a reason why self-knowledge is important. It is also important in goal
setting to accurately address questions of desirability (given one's preferences) and feasibility (given one's abilities and limitations).

Self-inquisitiveness can motivate getting this kind of knowledge.[62]
Though, how we go about generating this knowledge is another matter.
Getting this kind of self-knowledge is not straightforward, as not everything about us is open to a simple process of introspection. So self-
inquisitiveness may not only involve monitoring oneself, but also seeking
out feedback from people you know who might have insights into your
own behavior that you lack, or as another example finding out more about
human psychology in general. It can also be a difficult process, as you
might be afraid of some of the things that you might find out about

---

[59] In this respect curiosity may play a unique unifying role with respect to inquiry.

[60] Haase, Claudia Maria, Poulin, Michael, and Heckhausen, Jutta, "Engagement and Disengagement
Across the Life Span: An Analysis of Two-*Process Models of Developmental Regulation," in
Greve, W., Rothermund, K., and Wentura, D. (eds.), *The Adaptive Self: Personal Continuity and
Intentional Self-Development* (New York: Hogrefe, 2005), 117–135.

[61] See, for example, Miscevic, Nenad, "Virtue-Based Epistemology and the Centrality of Truth
(Towards a Strong Virtue Epistemology)," *Acta Analytica*, 22 (2007), 239–266.

[62] It is also likely to still be a targeted line of inquiry. Presumably I do not need to inquire into so
much depth about my preferences such that I need to try every possible ice cream flavor to know
what I really prefer most (despite that likely being an enjoyable line of inquiry). See, for example,
Cassam, Quassim, *Self-Knowledge for Humans* (Oxford: Oxford University Press, 2015).

yourself. Overall, given the centrality of self-knowledge to self-regulation, I think there is a case to be made that self-inquisitiveness is one of the virtues that is constitutive of agency.[63] Granted, it still has this status because of its supportive role in goal striving, be it moral, epistemic, or prudential goals.

So curiosity and self-inquisitiveness by themselves would again only put us in a position to know, as it motivates the performance of other knowledge-generating competences.[64] Baehr seems to admit as much when he claims that "[a] person's inquisitiveness about a given technical subject matter *might* lead her either to develop or to make use of the skills necessary for acquiring an understanding of this subject matter."[65] But this kind of prior motivation is no different from what you see in skill acquisition in general. It is because I find the game of chess interesting, for example, that I am motivated to develop the skills to understand how to play the game well.

Here Baehr might want to invoke another distinction he sees between virtues and skills – namely that virtues bear on the personal worth of a person but skills do not. Baehr offers the following claim as an example of marking the distinction he has in mind: "While so-and-so may be a terrific X (athlete, musician, artist, legislator, attorney, etc.), he sure seems like a rotten *person*."[66] Someone might be a rotten person because they have the vices of dishonesty and cruelty, or might be a good person because they have the virtues of honesty and kindness. However, that requires buying into his account of personal worth, as not all virtue responsibilists rely on such a notion, and I do not think his account is compelling. While he rejects the idea of people being categorically good or bad, he motivates the plausibility of his account with seemingly familiar ways people talk about somebody being a good or bad person simpliciter.[67] While he claims that the "notion of personal worth does not in any way suggest (let alone entail) that some persons are entirely (even mostly) good or bad qua persons" he at the same time argues that personal worth is distinct from human

---

[63] In this respect it avoids a potential regress problem for curiosity: if curiosity is a central motivating virtue, what motivates acquiring it for those who are not curious?

[64] Furthermore, curiosity by itself without a respect for persons could motivate vicious inquiry, like forced human experimentation.

[65] Baehr, Jason, *The Inquiring Mind: On Intellectual Virtues and Virtue Epistemology* (New York: Oxford University Press, 2012), 31. Emphasis mine.

[66] Baehr, Jason, *The Inquiring Mind: On Intellectual Virtues and Virtue Epistemology* (New York: Oxford University Press, 2012), 92.

[67] Baehr, Jason, *The Inquiring Mind: On Intellectual Virtues and Virtue Epistemology* (New York: Oxford University Press, 2012), 92–95.

dignity because it is "widely agreed" that "some persons are "better persons" than others."[68]

Furthermore, even if we do not understand the concept categorically, it is not clear that the idea of personal worth does any important work. If intellectual dishonesty is problematic, and you engage in it, what does it add to also claim that it reflects poorly on your personal worth? That is, there must be reasons not to engage in that kind of behavior that are independent of how it reflects on your personal worth. Finally, I take it that the kind of difference between virtue and skill that Baehr thinks is reflected in the idea of personal worth is such that if you choose to play chess poorly that it does not seem to reflect poorly on your personal worth. This would presumably be because people need not play chess at all, let alone play it well. But if so, then this does not imply that virtues are not skills, as I argued previously, but rather just that not all skills are equally important for people to acquire.[69]

Conclusion

In sum, the initial concern about there being a crucial motivational difference between virtues and skills is misplaced. Achieving and maintaining expertise requires a very strong commitment to acting well according to the ends that define the particular skill domain. Once we take into account this kind of responsiveness, we can evaluate performers for their motivations in a way analogous to virtue, and this shows that the three cases described do not reveal a significant difference between virtues and skills. Furthermore, within the context of virtue epistemology, we can defend virtue as skill from motivation-based criticisms from virtue responsibilists. In so doing, we have further reasons to see a distinction within both moral and epistemic virtues between 'substantive' and 'auxiliary' virtues.

---

[68] Baehr, Jason, *The Inquiring Mind: On Intellectual Virtues and Virtue Epistemology* (New York: Oxford University Press, 2012), 95. I do not doubt that people make these kinds of judgments, but they seem very likely to be influenced by biases, prejudices, stereotypes, etc.

[69] A related debate about skills in virtue epistemology concerns whether the relevant kind of success in epistemology (truth) allows intellectual virtues to be modeled on ethical virtues. Annas, contra Zagzebski, argues that there are different kinds of success, which prevents the intellectual to be modeled on the ethical. See Annas, Julia, "The Structure of Virtue," in DePaul, Michael and Zagzebski, Linda (eds.), *Intellectual Virtue* (Oxford: Clarendon Press, 2003), 15–33. For a reply, see Stichter, Matt, "Virtues as Skills in Virtue Epistemology," *Journal of Philosophical Research*, 38 (2013), 331–346.

However, even though motivation is not an issue that divides virtue and skill, in the next chapter I will argue that there is an important aspect of moral virtue that is not captured by skills and expertise. While one needs to be strongly motivated to act well in order to acquire skills and virtues, the issue of motivation is also linked to a reflection upon the worth of the ends for which one is acting. This kind of reflection brings us to the topic of practical wisdom.

CHAPTER 4

Skills and Practical Wisdom

Despite the arguments in the previous chapter to move judgments about expertise on a par with virtue, there is another important feature of virtue that may not be so easily captured on a skill model.[1] While one needs to be strongly motivated to act well in order to acquire skills and virtues, the issue of motivation is also linked to a consideration of the ends for which one is acting. Moral virtues require being practically wise about what is good and bad for people, and how various practices fit into an overall conception of the good life.[2] In contrast, skills do not require making these kinds of value judgments. The end to be pursued in any particular skill is essentially fixed, as in chess it is winning the game, and even being an expert in a skill (such as chess playing) does not require reflection on how the practice of that skill integrates into a well-lived life. However, while I admit that moral virtues have an aspect not found in other skills, this does not necessarily undermine the skill model of virtue, as it only shows that not all skills are moral virtues.

Although I argue that we do not find practical wisdom in its full form in expertise, it might then be wondered whether we can at least conceptualize practical wisdom as itself a skill. Despite this being a way to further support the skill model of virtue, I claim practical wisdom cannot be understood as itself a skill. The kind of reflection involved with practical wisdom is too broad and varied to be the result of the exercise of a single

---

[1] With kind permission from the *Australasian Journal of Philosophy*, this chapter draws on my article: Stichter, Matt, "Practical Skills and Practical Wisdom in Virtue," *Australasian Journal of Philosophy*, 94:3 (2016), 435–448, copyright © Australasian Association of Philosophy, reprinted by permission of Taylor & Francis Ltd, www.tandfonline.com on behalf of Australasian Association of Philosophy.

[2] Of note is that there is no real analogue for this in the case of the epistemic virtues covered in the last chapter. Truth, knowledge, and understanding – the traditional aims of epistemic virtue – seem to be more concrete than with what it is to live a flourishing life with respect to the moral virtues. Practical wisdom, though, will likely turn out to involve a set of epistemic virtues involved with reflection.

skill. In arguing this, though, I do not deny that practical wisdom has a role to play in arriving at all-things-considered moral judgments. There needs to be some unity to the virtues, so that the virtues do not pull us in conflicting directions, and practical wisdom can bring that unity to the virtues. As such, I defend a fairly minimal conception of the unity of the virtues, whereby possession of one virtue does not necessarily entail possessing other virtues to some degree.

Practical Wisdom and Skills

All virtues are said to require practical wisdom, where practical wisdom concerns what is good and bad for human beings. Practical wisdom, it must be admitted, is a rather unwieldy concept at times, since it often has so many distinct elements associated with it. As I will argue, some of these elements are explicable on a skill model, while one important element is not. To get clearer on what is involved with practical wisdom, it will be helpful to explore first the ways in which expertise already captures some elements of what is traditionally associated with practical wisdom. These elements are well-described in what Rosalind Hursthouse describes as her "mundane" account of practical wisdom, where she focuses on the more general knowledge and capacities necessary to be practically wise.[3] Her account involves reconstructing some of Aristotle's arguments about the different elements in practical wisdom. Points of comparison and contrast come out in Aristotle's distinction between two types of intellectual virtues – *techne* (expertise) and *phronesis* (practical wisdom). One obvious overlap is that both require experience to develop. How is *phronesis* shaped by experience? Hursthouse suggests that:

> It seems plausible to suppose the well-brought-up but inexperienced tend to think about what the virtues require and the vices rule out in terms of rather conventional generalizations or paradigms. It is only with the experience of exceptions—when an admired figure does what you thought only a pusillanimous coward would do and is widely praised, when the action of someone you respect surprises you until she explains why she did it, when you hear accounts of such examples—that you come to the more sophisticated understanding—the discernment—that the *phronimos* has. . . So there is our first bit of help about how to get closer to full virtue—briefly, don't rely unthinkingly on generalizations about, and paradigms of, the virtues

---

[3] Hursthouse, Rosalind, "Practical Wisdom: A Mundane Account," *Proceedings of the Aristotelian Society*, 106 (2006), 285–309.

and vices, take good note of the exceptions when you come across them, and watch out for others.[4]

This bears a striking resemblance to moving through the earliest stages of skill acquisition – starting with simple generalizations, and then being brought to see the exceptions through experience.

Additional parallels to expertise come out when Hursthouse discusses how experience also shapes our capacity to "see" a situation correctly. This perceptual capacity is:

> absolutely requisite for finding out what 'the situation' is in many central cases in which action is called for. It is needed when the situation is right in front of us, in all its detail, and if we fail to perceive, or misperceive, one of the details, as the inexperienced do, we will make the insensitive blunders that the inexperienced, with natural virtue, typically make.[5]

Experience teaches us which factors of a situation are relevant for action, and this is clearly true in the case of expertise. Importantly, reading a situation correctly is not meant to be cast here in strictly moral terms, as this includes picking up on generic details such as what people seem to be thinking or feeling – for example, knowing when somebody is 'putting on a brave face'. In short, one needs to be good at reading other people's reactions correctly, and this takes experience.

Furthermore, this capacity to read a situation correctly is useful for everyone, no matter whether their ends are morally good or bad. Hursthouse notes that "once we recognize the fact that the *phronimos* and some of the wicked may share this perceptual capacity, we should find it unproblematic that there are other sorts of 'non-moral' details that experience will enable the *phronimos* to perceive which the inexperienced fail to perceive, and thereby blunder."[6] Thus, much of the knowledge necessary for correct moral action is itself non-moral, and could also be put to use in the service of immoral ends. For example, a generous person should be able to perceive people's needs, in order to know what kind of help they could most use. However, there are also people who share a similar ability to anticipate people's needs but put that ability to use in taking advantage of

[4] Hursthouse, Rosalind, "Practical Wisdom: A Mundane Account," *Proceedings of the Aristotelian Society*, 106 (2006), 285–309, 292.

[5] Hursthouse, Rosalind, "Practical Wisdom: A Mundane Account," *Proceedings of the Aristotelian Society*, 106 (2006), 285–309, 299.

[6] Hursthouse, Rosalind, "Practical Wisdom: A Mundane Account," *Proceedings of the Aristotelian Society*, 106 (2006), 285–309, 299–300.

people's vulnerabilities.[7] The ability to anticipate needs by itself is not morally valuable. This can be seen more broadly in the self-regulation literature. As Baumeister and Vohs point out:

> self-control can be employed in the service of dastardly or antisocial aims, but by and large it appears to produce mainly positive effects. It seems appropriate to regard self-control as a strength in the same way that intelligence is a strength: It brings mainly benefits and helps people achieve their goals, although it can enable bad people to be more effective at doing bad things.[8]

Recognition of the non-moral details can be the difference between successful action and well-intentioned but unsuccessful action. Hursthouse points out that the kind of case that shows this side of practical wisdom is one where the person with practical wisdom succeeds where a merely well-intentioned person fails. Take a case of rescuing a child from drowning, specifically in a rushing river. The difference would not show if we compared a person willing to jump in to rescue the child from one who is not willing. Rather, the merely well-intentioned person immediately jumps in the water and starts swimming after the child (but cannot keep up with the speed of the current); whereas the practically wise person runs along the river bank in order to get far ahead of the child before jumping in. Hursthouse's point is that the merely well-intentioned person does not know how best to save the child. Both persons share the same goal and the motivation to achieve that goal, but the person with practical wisdom knows best how to go about achieving that goal. In this respect, the overlap between being skilled and being practically wise should be readily apparent, as acquiring skills is a process of acquiring the knowledge of how to achieve a desired goal.

Hursthouse raises our awareness of the more technical aspects to practical wisdom and virtue, which are more familiar to us in the examples of skill. Support for these mundane aspects of moral behavior can be found in the work of Darcia Narvaez and Daniel K. Lapsley, when they argue that an important dimension to those cultivating ethical skills is being "able to more quickly and accurately 'read' a situation and determine what role

---

[7] It also illustrates how there is more to generosity than just a motivational component. Correctly recognizing people's needs is crucial in being generous, as one could err in trying to be generous by focusing on far less important needs, or by underestimating/overestimating what it takes to meet those needs.

[8] Baumeister, Roy F. and Vohs, Kathleen D., "Self-Regulation [Self-Control]" in Peterson, Christopher and Seligman, Martin (eds.), *Character Strengths and Virtues: A Handbook and Classification* (New York: Oxford University Press, 2004), 499–516, 508.

they might play. These experts are also better at generating usable solutions due to a greater understanding of the consequences of possible actions."[9]

At this point, there may be so much overlap that it seems like there is not a *techne-phronesis* distinction per se, but rather that *phronesis* just is *techne* geared towards moral conduct. Aristotle seems to suggest as much when he describes being clever as that "which is such as to be able to put into practice the means to any proposed end in view, and to discover what those means are. Now if the end in view is a noble one, the ability is praiseworthy; but if the end in view is bad, the ability is villainy."[10] Hursthouse raises this concern about the *techne-phronesis* line being blurred, as she notes that practical wisdom may seem to reduce to "expertise in 'technical' deliberation gained from experience, which in the virtuous happens to be directed to the right end."[11] Similarly, Daniel Russell claims that if *phronesis* is just cleverness aimed at good goals, then this would suggest that there is no real difference in the operations of *phronesis* and *techne*.[12] This issue also arises in the Dreyfus account of skill acquisition, since they view ethical expertise as a matter of *techne* applied to human affairs.[13] On this, Bent Flyvbjerg cautions that:

> Some interpretations of Aristotle's intellectual virtues leave doubt as to whether *phronesis* and *techne* are distinct categories, or whether *phronesis* is just a higher form of *techne* or know-how (for such an interpretation and its problematization, see Dreyfus & Dreyfus, 1990 and 1991, pp. 102–107). Aristotle is clear on this point, however. Even if both *phronesis* and *techne* involve skill and judgement, one type of intellectual virtue cannot be reduced to the other; *phronesis* is about value judgement in specific situations.[14]

Flyvbjerg is arguing here that *techne* is a mere expression of instrumental rationality, while practical wisdom involves making value judgments.

<hr/>

[9] Narvaez, Darcia and Lapsley, Daniel, "The Psychological Foundations of Everyday Morality and Moral Expertise," in Lapsley, Daniel K. and Power, F. Clark (eds.), *Character Psychology and Character Education* (Notre Dame: IN: University of Notre Dame Press, 2005), 140–165, 155.

[10] Aristotle, *Nicomachean Ethics* (Grinnell: The Peripatetic Press, 1984), 1144a24–27.

[11] Hursthouse, Rosalind, "Practical Wisdom: A Mundane Account," *Proceedings of the Aristotelian Society*, 106 (2006), 285–309, 305.

[12] Russell, Daniel C., *Practical Intelligence and the Virtues* (New York: Oxford University Press, 2009), 24.

[13] Dreyfus, Hubert and Dreyfus, Stuart, "Towards a Phenomenology of Ethical Expertise," *Human Studies*, 14 (1991), 229–250. Dreyfus Hubert and Dreyfus, Stuart, "What Is Morality: A Phenomenological Account of the Development of Expertise," in Rasmussen, D. (ed.), *Universalism vs. Communitarianism*, (Cambridge, MA: MIT Press, 1990), 237–264.

[14] Flyvbjerg, Bent, "Phronetic Planning Research: Theoretical and Methodological Reflections," *Planning Theory & Practice*, 5:3 (2004), 283–306, 288. Though as I will point out later, while *phronesis* is specific to making value judgments, it is during the stage of goal setting, not goal striving (as might be implied by Flyvbjerg's reference to 'in specific situations').

How are we to understand this supposed difference between cleverness and practical wisdom? Here it will be helpful to return to the distinction between goal setting and goal striving. Cleverness (*techne*) pertains to phases of goal striving – being effective at achieving one's goal (whatever that may be). Hursthouse's worry is that practical wisdom (*phronesis*) is often described as if it is merely cleverness aimed at specifically morally good goals. Hence Russell's concern that in that case there would be no genuine difference in the operation of cleverness and practical wisdom – it would be the same ability but just directed at different kinds of goals.

However, what is unique to practical wisdom is relevant to goal setting, not goal striving. As discussed in Chapter 2 , while virtue does aim at the overall end of living well, we cannot effectively pursue this end without thinking in terms of the constitutive ends that make up living well (*eudaimonia*). The role of practical wisdom is to make value judgments regarding what it is to live well, what constitutive ends make up living well, and what other ends we could pursue consistent with that overall conception of living well.[15] So while there is a lot of overlap between expertise and what is commonly attributed to practical wisdom, such as those elements found in Hursthouse's "mundane" account of practical wisdom, there remains the crucial difference that expertise does not involve making value judgments about the end being pursued.[16] While skill acquisition requires adopting the end of the skill domain, one need not have ever reflected on how the pursuit of this skill connects up with one's conception of living well, but virtue requires that kind of reflection.

With skills, the end being pursued is essentially fixed – in chess, it is winning the game. In medicine, the end is health. Skills involve knowing how to achieve the end of the skill, but this does not involve making value judgments about the end being pursued, say about the worth of playing chess – which is part of *phronesis*. Even if we can evaluate an expert qua performer, being a good performer does not require *phronesis*, since it is still limited to Watson's idea of being responsive to the distinctive demands of the practice. While nobody will be able to acquire expertise

---

[15] This is not meant to be necessarily an exhaustive list of the relevant value judgments. Also, while skillfulness involves some goal setting, for example in setting out goals for deliberate practice, it is not a matter of value judgments but still means–end reasoning (in terms of setting up subgoals for deliberate practice in the service of the fixed goal of the skill domain).

[16] Hursthouse should not be understood as claiming that the mundane aspects are all there is to practical wisdom, as she also believes practical wisdom involves making value judgments. The point here is that those mundane aspects are better understood as part of expertise rather than practical wisdom.

126   The Skillfulness of Virtue

without this responsiveness, it does not also require reflecting on the ends of the practice within an overall conception of living well.[17] For example, say on the way to a tennis match the expert tennis player comes across the scene of an automobile accident, and decides to help the accident victims even though she knows she will miss her match. This involves her making a value judgment about the relative worth of playing tennis versus saving lives, placing that activity within broader concerns of living well, and so draws on *phronesis*. Presumably, though, we would not think that makes her any better or worse qua tennis player. Neither in evaluating a performance nor a performer with reference to the end of the skill do we think being good at either requires having correctly assessed the worth of that end. So that element of *phronesis* is not part of being an expert performer even in the robust sense described by Watson. Virtues, unlike skills, do require value judgments about the ends being pursued in action for their exercise and possession.

Furthermore, this kind of value judgment about the relative worth of playing tennis is not involved when the question before the tennis player is merely whether to give a wholehearted or half-hearted performance on the court today. That is still a matter of being responsive to the distinctive demands of the practice, without making any value judgments about the worth of the practice. To give another example, one might be engaged in the practice of deceptive advertising, intentionally trying to sell people products that do not actually meet their needs. One could try hard to be good at this practice, acquire expertise in it, and remain responsive to the distinctive demands of the practice, without having *phronesis*. If you added *phronesis* as part of the expert level of skill you would then realize that you ought not to be doing it all – that is, you ought not to be responsive to the distinctive demands of the practice of deceptive advertising.

Moral Expertise and Practical Wisdom

Phronesis involves making good judgments about what the proper conception of the good life consists in, but one need not have it to perform well relative to a particular practice, or for that matter, a particular ethical tradition. As discussed in Chapter 2, all that is required is the internalization of some moral standard or other – it does not require specifically having internalized what we might think of as 'right' or 'correct' moral standards. As Bruce Weinstein points out in a discussion of moral expertise:

[17] Another way of putting this, as one reviewer suggested, is in terms of setting the end of the skill within a grasp of the human good.

We need not resolve the metaethical debate about the good life in order to recognize that certain people live better than others according to the rules and virtues of a particular moral tradition. If a singular understanding of the good could definitively be established, of course, then there would be a standard for evaluating performative expertise across traditions.[18]

There are already conceptions of the good life that one may adopt, and which guide one's moral performance, without requiring one to have ever having reflected on whether that is an appropriate conception. In terms of goal setting, presumably most people have 'living well' as a superordinate goal, and the social environment in which you are raised likely furnishes you with one or more conceptions of what it is to live well. In that sense, some of the subordinate goals on that goal hierarchy are already fleshed out (e.g. maybe living well consists in building strong communal ties).

Recall that skill development requires having high standards of performance that one is trying to achieve. We self-regulate on the basis of having internalized some standard of behavior, and that includes moral standards. These internalized moral standards provide motivation to conform to them, on the basis of feeling good about conforming to them, or feeling bad (i.e. guilty) about acts that would violate the standards.[19] Even what we might commonly regard as immoral standards are still standards that could serve as a basis for self-regulation and skill development. Moral expertise as a phenomenon just requires the internalization of some particular moral standards. In this sense, there is nothing mysterious about moral expertise, as most people inherit some set of moral standards growing up and learn to various degrees how to conform to them.

However, consistently applying a particular conception of morality is clearly not sufficient for virtue, as one could be an exemplar with respect to an overall corrupt conception of morality. This is why virtue has to incorporate practical wisdom, so that there is some critical reflection on one's moral standards.[20] Otherwise we could not recommend acquiring virtues, as there would be no constraint on what conception of morality those moral skills would be realizing. So part of the role of practical wisdom must be to figure out which moral standards to internalize.[21]

---

[18] Weinstein, Bruce D., "The Possibility of Ethical Expertise," *Theoretical Medicine*, 15 (1994), 61–75, 71.

[19] Though as will be discussed in the final chapter, the phenomenon of moral disengagement prevents the normal self-sanctioning process.

[20] Even if there is not one singular correct set of moral standards, critical reflection should enable us to separate out better from worse standards.

[21] I say 'part' because practical wisdom also has a role to play in evaluating the ends of various non-moral practices, to see if they are ends worth pursuing given one's conception of living well.

Notice that you do not find a need for this with regard to skills in domains like sports – there is no reason, for example, in football why touchdowns should be worth 6 points instead of 8, why you get 4 downs to go 10 yards rather than 5 downs to go 15 yards, etc. For sports, there just needs to be some agreed upon set of rules that structure the game, and that will determine what counts as a good performance. Furthermore, if one wants to take up a sport, there is no right answer as to which sport one ought to learn. In choosing to learn a sport, you are basically choosing which set of predetermined rules to play by (e.g. the rules of basketball or the rules of football), and that choice is often merely a matter of personal preference or natural talent.

Presumably, however, this is not the story we want to tell when it comes to moral standards – that the rules of morality are ultimately arbitrary, and there are no good reasons why you ought to adopt one set of rules rather than another. We want people to internalize the right standards, or at least better rather than worse standards, and so not just any standard will do.[22] This is of course a central concern in ethical theory. Various forms of consequentialism, deontology, and virtue ethics purport to give us better sets of moral standards to internalize. Those involved with the justification of particular moral standards (over others) are doing something different from what is involved with moral expertise (where some set of standards is already assumed). So to go back to the sports analogy, it is like trying to figure out what the rules of the game ought to be, where there are reasons for favoring some rules over others. Or to reference Sosa's 'AAA' structure for performances, we are trying to figure out what should count as 'accuracy' in moral performance.

However, we must be careful to distinguish the work of practical wisdom from what goes on in ethical theory. Ethicists can give us important insights to consider in determining better and worse standards, but exercising practical wisdom is about reflecting upon and improving one's own moral standards, and ethicists turn out to be no more moral than the average person despite their insights. They come up with considerations that can be relevant to consider for practical wisdom but are not thereby necessarily exercising practical wisdom themselves. Furthermore, in exercising practical wisdom, you have to reflect on the moral standards you specifically have internalized, and that cannot be a matter of merely doing abstract ethical theory.

---

[22] Although I do not intend to take a stand on the meta-ethical issues here, the issue here seems relevant to moral objectivists and those taking a mixed objectivist-relativist stance. It is harder to see why a pure moral relativist would worry about which standards are being internalized.

It is only with practical wisdom in virtue, where there needs to be some acquired competence to figure out which ends are worth pursing, and how various practices fit into an overall conception of the good life, that we cease to find an analogue in skill. However, this should not be seen as an objection to the claim that virtues are skills. The response I am giving here is along the same lines that Linda Zagzebski uses in her response to James Wallace's argument that virtues are not skills because all virtues are valuable, but not all skills are valuable. As Zagzebski points out:

> This argument does not support the conclusion that virtues are not skills, however, but only that the class of virtues is not coextensive with the class of skills. On Wallace's reasoning it might be the case that every virtue is a skill, although not every skill is a virtue.[23]

So, consistent with Zagzebski's response to Wallace, I claim that not every skill is a virtue. For those skills aiming at moral ends, because of the need to also critically reflect on one's moral standards, there is the need for practical wisdom.[24] Since other skills do not require this kind of reflection on the end of the skill domain, they do not need to be guided by practical wisdom.

Is *Phronesis* a Skill?

Since I take the moral virtues to be essentially skillful activity guided by practical wisdom, this then leads us to the question of whether practical wisdom should be understood as itself a skill. Although having expertise does not involve having practical wisdom, it may be the case that the exercise of practical wisdom is itself a skill. Jason Swartwood has recently argued that wisdom is an expert skill.[25] However, much of what he characterizes as wisdom is already captured by expertise.[26] Furthermore, what remains central to practical wisdom, in terms of reflection on what is good and bad for people, does not seem to fit the model of a singular skill, even if the knowledge is gained through experience.

---

[23] Zagzebski, Linda, *Virtues of the Mind* (Cambridge: Cambridge University Press, 1996), 107.

[24] No attempt is made here to determine what criteria should be used to determine which skills count as moral skills. This account is compatible with a variety of criteria for picking out the virtues, though some conceptions of virtues are ruled out if they do not exhibit the complexity found in skills.

[25] Swartwood, Jason, "Wisdom as an Expert Skill," *Ethical Theory and Moral Practice*, 16 (2013), 511–528.

[26] In this respect it is similar to my views about the mundane aspects of wisdom discussed by Hursthouse.

Swartwood characterizes practical wisdom generically as a kind of understanding, specifically understanding how one should act all things considered. Swartwood defines 'understanding' in ways familiar to what goes into expertise:

> Understanding how to conduct oneself in a domain D is (a) an ability to identify (accurately, non-accidentally, and in a wide range of situations in D) what features in a situation require what response in order to achieve the goals of D, and, when there are internal obstacles to carrying out that response, (b) an ability to identify how to overcome those internal obstacles.

As was seen in Chapter 1, expertise involves learning how to act well, and in practice requires a lot of self-regulating abilities. So here we agree at least that knowing how to act well in a domain requires these abilities, and that we should expect acting well in the moral domain to require the same abilities. However, all of this is captured already by expertise, so I would not label this as wisdom. Wisdom in the moral domain requires more than the instrumental reasoning that goes into expertise, and his characterization of 'understanding' misses this distinction between virtues and skills.

However, Swartwood offers a reply to those like myself and Russell who object that practical wisdom differs from expertise in skills because the latter is limited to mere instrumental reasoning. In response to this objection, Swartwood draws on the recognition-primed-decision model (RPD), that I discussed in Chapter 1, to argue that expertise requires reasoning about the goals being pursued:

> A good firefighter doesn't just aim at the goal of putting out fires but at various other goals as well: ensuring firefighter safety, ensuring the safety of citizens, protecting property, and so on. These are the goals that constitute the supreme end of firefighting, which we could say is to combat fires well or effectively. Some of these more specific goals compete with each other: a firefighter will sometimes have to decide, qua firefighter, between securing someone's safety and getting the fire under control. Thus expert decision makers in areas of complex choice and challenging performance (including both firefighting and all-things-considered decisions) will often have to specify which particular goal in a situation constitutes the supreme end of their domain.[27]

This response does show that more of what is associated with practical wisdom can be found in expertise, insofar as it can involve an attempt to balance multiple goals. However, this still does not overcome the

---

[27] Swartwood, Jason, "Wisdom as an Expert Skill," *Ethical Theory and Moral Practice*, 16 (2013), 511–528, 525.

distinction argued for earlier in this chapter between virtues and skills, as he does not show that skills do not have fixed goals, but rather that some professions have multiple fixed goals, which have to be balanced against each other at the time of action.

To return to the action phase model from Chapter 1, firefighters have a superordinate goal of 'combating fires well', and in the goal hierarchy there will be multiple goals that constitute what it is to fight fires well (such as those mentioned by Swartwood – stop the fire from spreading, save innocent lives, prevent property damage, etc.). The challenge posed to firefighters (and of course others working in complex domains) is that these subordinate goals have to be balanced against one another relative to the particular context at the time of action. You are going to have to, at the very least, prioritize which goals to accomplish first or to devote more resources to achieving. This contextual decision to "specify which particular goal in a situation constitutes the supreme end" takes place during the action phase (phase 3), and is a volitional concern about how best to adhere to one's preexisting goal commitments in the situation.[28] It does not involve a re-examination of one's goal commitments, as it is still a question of how best to achieve one's existing goals. In other words, in specifying the particular goal to pursue in a situation qua the practice of firefighting, the firefighter is not wondering 'do firefighters really need to save lives', or 'do I really want to be a firefighter?'[29]

So, this element of contextualizing the goal is not a matter of reflecting on whether the goal is worthy of pursuit. Practical wisdom, by contrast, requires reflection on our values, goals, and practices; not merely on how to balance a few fixed goals in particular situations. Practical wisdom as I am describing it here is a matter of goal setting in the first action phase, as well as the fourth phase of reflection after acting – the two phases concerned with goal commitment and motivation. You are determining what goals to set for yourself, what those goals consist in (such as setting more proximal subgoals that, for example, determine what living well more specifically consists in), and how valued those goals are relative to your other goal commitments. Of course, you will go through a similar process of goal setting with skill acquisition, but with skill acquisition it is fine if your goals are adopted purely on the basis of subjective concerns such as what you find pleasurable to do, or for instrumental reasons such as what

---

[28] This is the kind of 'higher strategic control' discussed by Christensen, Sutton, and Mcilwain in their hierarchical account of control in skilled performances, as mentioned in Chapter 1.

[29] Though they might engage in this kind of reflection after a difficult day on the job.

might help you to earn a living. Even when judging skilled performers, rather than just performances, the question is whether you are being responsive to the demands of the practice. By contrast, with practical wisdom, you need to be asking whether you should be responsive to the demands of specific moral standards and conceptions of the good life.

Furthermore, Swartwood's argument may complicate the way Russell distinguishes practical wisdom from cleverness. Russell claims that practical wisdom is about making indeterminate ends determinant in specific situations, such as "What would be benevolent in this case?"[30] Or in other words, practical wisdom is about specifying the goal (as in 'this is what counts as benevolent'), rather than the details of how to achieve the goal (such as figuring out how one can best go about doing the act that counts as benevolent). This way of putting it sounds very much like what is already going on in the firefighter case – it is one thing to decide that securing someone's safety takes highest priority in the situation, and another to figure out how best to go about securing that person's safety. Russell seems to be suggesting as much when he claims that an exercise of practical wisdom is one that "specifies the hitting of that goal in a way that takes the various goals or 'targets' of the other virtues into account in an overall way," just like the firefighter has to take into account the other goals of controlling the fire and reducing property damage.[31] In addition, when referencing Aristotle, Russell says that "the physician does not deliberate (obviously) about whether her mark is to heal her patient, nor, yet, about what medicines or procedures to use, but first about what constitutes healing in the case at hand."[32] So we see that skills can also involve making judgments about what counts as the determinant end in a specific situation, in the way described by Russell.

But again, this is different from the distinction I am defending here, where what is unique about practical wisdom is that it involves identifying which ends constitute living well, rather than what constitutes achieving those now fixed ends in specific situations. With the latter, you are trying to apply the conceptions of virtue you already have and make them more determinant to the specific circumstances you are acting in now (during goal striving). But with practical wisdom, it is a reflection that takes place

[30] Russell, Daniel C., *Practical Intelligence and the Virtues* (New York: Oxford University Press, 2009), 80.
[31] Russell, Daniel C., *Practical Intelligence and the Virtues* (New York: Oxford University Press, 2009), 329.
[32] Russell, Daniel C., *Practical Intelligence and the Virtues* (New York: Oxford University Press, 2009), 79.

during goal setting (before or after action). As mentioned earlier, while virtue may aim overall at living well, we cannot really pursue this aim without thinking in terms of the constitutive ends that make up living well, which is the unique role for practical wisdom to play. Granted, Russell in his overall account does make a place for getting the right goals and separates this from specifying the goals in particular situations. He notes that there is another sense in which we construct ends besides making indeterminate ends determinant in particular contexts, which is that we can choose to adopt certain ends through reflection on what living well consists in.[33] For him, it is "virtue that makes one's goal the right one," and this is paired with practical wisdom for specifying the goal (in particular situations), and cleverness for how to achieve the goal.[34] So these three components could be understood to map onto my distinctions between the unique elements of practical wisdom in goal setting and reflection, the specification of goals in situations that is also found in expertise, and knowing how to achieve one's specified goal. Since it is typically claimed that virtues are unique in requiring practical wisdom, we need to identify something specific about virtue that makes this demand, and this makes sense only with respect to the first element. This is the sense of practical wisdom that is unique to virtue, and of course virtue requires us to do this well.

Beyond this, there is a further problem with conceptualizing wisdom as the singular skill of getting it right in the moral domain. This runs into the problem that skills require feedback for improvement, and so there needs to be some identifiable goal to the exercise of your skill, as noted in Chapter 2. It might be argued that virtue has an identifiable fixed goal like other skill domains, which would be *eudaimonia* (or living well). However, it is difficult to see how the feedback mechanism would work if wisdom is a skill in the sense of a singular all-things-considered judgment about how to act well morally. The specific problem is that the target of living well in that sense is very broad and vague, which will make it difficult to determine whether you are acting in such a way as to achieve success. So Swartwood is correct in thinking that acting well in the moral domain requires skillfulness, but not as a singular skill and not without an element of evaluating ends not found in expertise.

---

[33] Russell, Daniel C., *Practical Intelligence and the Virtues* (New York: Oxford University Press, 2009), 375.

[34] Russell, Daniel C., *Practical Intelligence and the Virtues* (New York: Oxford University Press, 2009), 329.

Thinking of practical wisdom as involving multiple intellectual skills reflects that there are multiple routes to gaining insight into how to get a handle on questions of value. For example, Valerie Tiberius provides an account of what she calls "wise reflection," which is a form of reflection that helps us solve questions of value in an appropriate way.[35] It is worth pointing out that this kind of reflection is not what you do at the time of action (i.e. goal striving phases), but rather reflection during goal setting. She notes that reflection can, but need not, consist in analyzing the reasons for our actions. One reason to be wary of putting too much emphasis on this kind of analysis is the role of automatic processes, since we often cannot introspect to find out why we acted one way rather than another, and that sometimes we engage in confabulation. Two other methods she recommends for wise reflection are "imagination and perspective taking, whereby we can try to picture what things will be like for us if we choose one way or another or put ourselves in the shoes of other people to see what things are like from their perspective."[36] There may be then, in the end, multiple intellectual skills that we need in order to reflect well on the whole.[37] This is another reason to resist thinking of practical wisdom as a singular skill.

Phronesis and the Unity of the Virtues

It is important to note here that while I have argued that there are problems in conceiving of wisdom as a singular skill, I do agree with Swartwood that part of the role that practical wisdom needs to play in an account of virtue is to help us to arrive at all-things-considered judgments. As Daniel Jacobson points out, you run into a different problem when thinking of the virtues as discrete. He argues that there is the possibility of the virtuous person (i.e. one with all the virtues) falling short of a full account of moral knowledge:

> For moral knowledge requires not merely that the virtuous person sees the demands of kindness, courage, and the like, but that he can see what to do, all things considered – that is, what he has *most* reason to do. If the discrete

[35] Tiberius, Valerie, "In Defense of Reflection," *Philosophical Issues*, 23: Epistemic Agency (2013), 223–243.
[36] Tiberius, Valerie, "In Defense of Reflection," *Philosophical Issues*, 23: Epistemic Agency (2013), 223–243, 233.
[37] This is an area in moral psychology that needs more research, to better understand the mechanisms by which people can effectively and accurately reflect on, and change, conceptions of living well. Likely these conceptions are often strongly rooted in one's self-identity, such that they can be hard to revise. Hopefully in highlighting what is unique to practical wisdom, I have drawn attention to that which requires more research.

virtues can pull in different directions, then moral knowledge requires the ability to arbitrate between them. Only then will we be able to say that the virtuous person knows what to do, on some occasion.[38]

If the virtues are discrete in the sense that there is no unity to the virtues, then individual virtues could pull us in conflicting directions. For example, honesty may require one course of action while kindness requires a different course. In which case, one could have all the virtues and still not know what to do all things considered. This would be a problematic result for virtue theory, since virtues were all you were supposed to need to know how to act well.

If, on the other hand, there was something that unified the discrete virtues, then the virtues would not conflict in such a way as to prevent the virtuous person from reaching a conclusion about what to do all things considered. Since the virtuous person is supposed to know what to do, all things considered, it appears that virtuous ethicists need to defend some version of the unity of the virtues thesis. However, this runs you into a different sort of problem. A controversial claims made about virtue in the virtue ethics literature is that the virtues form a unity, which is often understood as the view that in order to have any one of the virtues you have to have them all.[39] The unity thesis has been strongly criticized, mainly on the grounds that it conflicts with the common sense view that actual people seem to have a mix of virtues and vices. If having one virtue means you have them all, then nobody could have the virtue of kindness while failing to have the virtue of courage. It seems as if, though, most of us know someone like that. It would also appear that nobody has any virtues, since having a single virtue entails having all the virtues, and it is hard to imagine that anyone has achieved that level of moral perfection. But if you deny the unity claim, then you are back to the problem of discrete virtues pulling you in different directions and not being able to figure out what to do.

One attempt to get around this problem is Neera Badhwar's account of the "Limited Unity of the Virtues."[40] She argues that the counter-intuitive part in traditional accounts of the unity of the virtues is that if someone has a virtue, like kindness, then that person will display kindness in every situation in which kindness is called for. But one could make a more

---

[38] Jacobson, Daniel, "Seeing by Feeling: Virtues, Skills, and Moral Perception," *Ethical Theory and Moral Practice*, 8 (2005), 387–409.
[39] Wolf, Susan, "Moral Psychology and the Unity of the Virtues," *Ratio*, 20:2 (2007), 145–167.
[40] Badhwar, Neera K., "The Limited Unity of Virtue," *Noûs*, 30:3 (1996), 306–329.

limited claim that "virtues are *disunited across different domains* (areas of practical concern), but *united within domains.*"[41] That is, someone might display kindness consistently in one domain of practical concern, say the family, without doing so in other domains, like at work. This is what she means by virtues being disunited across different domains, and this claim does not have the counter-intuitive implication that someone who displays kindness will do so in all situations. However, she does claim that to have one virtue in one domain means at least an absence of vice in other domains, ruling out an example of being kind at home but cruel at work (in the sense that if someone was cruel at work, then they should not be thought of as kind even at home). Finally, to still hold on to a unity claim, she argues that in a particular domain, one could not be kind without also displaying the other virtues: "if P is kind towards her friends and colleagues, she must also be generous, just, temperate, and courageous with respect to them."[42] So one should expect that the actual development of virtue may be disunited across different domains, but united within a domain.

A domain for her is one that we can psychologically isolate from other domains, like we often do with family and work, and one that is of normative significance (where presumably we have some different obligations towards family and employers/co-workers). One of the implications of her view is that at least within a domain virtue is unified. This seems to assume, though, that domains are fairly stable notions from the point of view of each virtue. However, Duckworth's work on the domain specificity of traits challenges this assumption:

> What is needed, in our view, is a taxonomy of situations that emerges from *psychologically meaningful*, as opposed to nominally convenient (e.g., work, love, play) domains ... These domains (i.e., groupings of trait-relevant situations) may vary by trait; the organization of situations relevant to altruism (e.g., family, friends, strangers), for instance, may not be the same as that for self-control (e.g., food, sex, work)[43]

Thus, while someone may display kindness at home with family, it will not follow that one will also display temperance at home with family, as temperance will be disunited across a different set of domains – alcohol,

[41] Badhwar, Neera K., "The Limited Unity of Virtue," *Noûs*, 30:3 (1996), 306–329, 307.
[42] Badhwar, Neera K., "The Limited Unity of Virtue," *Noûs*, 30:3 (1996), 306–329, 308.
[43] Duckworth, Angela Lee and Tsukayama, Eli, "Domain Specificity in Self-Control," in Miller, Christian B., Furr, R. Michael, Knobel, Angela, and Fleeson, William (eds.), *Character: New Directions from Philosophy, Psychology, and Theology* (New York: Oxford University Press, 2015), 393–411, 397.

sex, gambling, etc. So, we should not expect that virtue development will be united even within domains.

The 'Minimal' Unity of the Virtues

In one sense, Swartwood was right to think that wisdom needs to be understood as consisting in helping one to make all-things-considered judgments about how to act well. However, wisdom in this sense is too broad to be understood as a skill itself. Instead, we need to conceive of acting well as involving many virtues as skills. But to avoid the problem of conflicting virtues, there still needs to be a role for practical wisdom to play in unifying the virtues.

If practical wisdom involves specifying the constitutive ends of living well (i.e. virtues), then this suggests that there is at least a theoretical unity to the virtues. Consider again the nature of a goal hierarchy, with the superordinate goal of living well breaking down into constitutive subgoals (i.e. the virtues), where those subgoals all take living well as giving them direction. This conclusion is also suggested by Russell's own critique of Badhwar, as well as the approach he takes to individuating virtues (as discussed in Chapter 2).[44] In addition, Russell points out that we need "to distinguish between the natural makeup of the virtues, on the one hand, and phenomena surrounding the development of the virtues in particular virtuous persons, on the other."[45] That is to say, one need not also accept the developmental claim that if someone has one virtue, then that person has them all.

This approach also coincides with Susan Wolf's account of practical wisdom, insofar as she claims practical wisdom can bring unity to the virtues, but without making highly counter-intuitive claims about the possession of virtue.[46] Like most virtue theorists, Wolf thinks having practical wisdom is a matter of having knowledge about what is valuable in life: what is good, bad, beneficial, harmful, important, trivial, etc. This knowledge will be the same for each virtue. That is, this kind of knowledge is shaping your overall conception of living well, and thus also shaping the virtues that are constitutive of living well. This is the common element that unifies the virtues. Wolf defends this unifying claim by pointing out that:

---

[44] See Russell, Daniel C., *Practical Intelligence and the Virtues* (New York: Oxford University Press, 2009), 364–370.

[45] Russell, Daniel C., *Practical Intelligence and the Virtues* (New York: Oxford University Press, 2009), 207.

[46] Wolf, Susan, "Moral Psychology and the Unity of the Virtues," *Ratio*, 20:2 (2007), 145–167.

knowledge of the value of one item is necessarily knowledge of that item's value *relative to* the values of everything else. Knowing the value of physical safety means knowing what's worth fighting for and what's not; knowing the value of money means knowing when it is and when it is not worth spending it or giving it away. This suggests that perfect and complete knowledge of the importance of, say, physical safety, may require knowledge of the importance of wealth, and vice versa. For one may need to know when a certain amount of wealth is worth fighting for, or when giving money to assure another person's physical safety is appropriate.[47]

The basic idea is that acting virtuously requires, among other things, this kind of evaluative knowledge. Practical wisdom involves a reflection on these kinds of evaluative claims that make up our overall conception of living well and what is valuable in life. Furthermore, this kind of evaluative knowledge is gained incrementally with experience (which is why Aristotle claimed that children could not be practically wise).

In addition, Flyvbjerg draws our attention to the fact that there are multiple methods for contributing to the kind of knowledge we ought to consider when reflecting on what it means to live well. He claims that "[m]any people think that *phronesis* is qualitative, but it doesn't have to be. Or they think that *phronesis* is only about narratives and case studies. But *phronesis* is about what is good or bad for people, whatever it takes to know that."[48] So there are a diverse set of domains that can have important implications for knowledge of what is good or bad for people. Flyvbjerg views, for example, the genealogies produced by Foucault (inspired by Nietzsche's own tracing of the influence of power relations on the development of morality) as playing a part in the project of developing *phronesis*. Such work can help us think more broadly about what is desirable or feasible when it comes to reflection on conceptions of living well and the goals we set for ourselves. So multiple disciplines, with different methodologies and skill sets, can contribute to this body of knowledge. In fact, Flyvbjerg's main critique of contemporary social science is that it has the potential to contribute a lot to this body of knowledge, but instead it generally shies away from dealing with questions of value, and so does little to help people understand how they can improve their lives.

Insofar as practical wisdom requires us to reflect on a general body of knowledge, a failure of practical wisdom in understanding what is valuable can be problematic not just for one virtue, but any of them. For example,

[47] Wolf, Susan, "Moral Psychology and the Unity of the Virtues," *Ratio*, 20:2 (2007), 145–167, 150.
[48] Kirkeby, Inge, "Transferable Knowledge: An Interview with Bent Flyvbjerg," *Architectural Research Quarterly*, 15:1 (2011), 9–14, 14.

suppose a person does not see the suffering of others as bad, and thus does not see the relief of the suffering of others as a good to be pursued. When a situation calls for charity, as an opportunity to relieve the suffering of others, this person will not discern that, and so will not act charitably. Likewise, when a situation calls for courage, to face danger in order to keep others from suffering, this person will not discern that, and so will not act courageously. Other virtues can be affected in a similar way, and this shows how there is some form of unity to the virtues that follows from practical wisdom's role.

While the unity thesis is commonly thought to imply that possessing a virtue necessarily means that you have all the other virtues (at least to some extent), that does not follow on her account. Wolf argues that while the core claim that the virtues are unified is plausible, it does not necessarily follow that the possession of one virtue requires possessing any other virtue.[49] According to Wolf, from the claims that all virtues involve knowledge of what is valuable, and the knowledge is a single comprehensive body of knowledge:

> The conclusion that follows is that *virtue is unified*, in the sense that the perfect and complete possession of one virtue requires at least the knowledge that is needed for the possession of every other ... the argument I have presented supports the thesis that to have one virtue, one must have the knowledge required for the possession of the others, but this is not the same as the requirement that one possess the other virtues themselves.[50]

For example, knowing that you should risk your life for something of value does not guarantee the willingness to take such risks. So contrary to other unity views it does not follow that possessing one virtue entails the actual possession of any other virtue, even to a small degree. What follows from these claims is that possessing a virtue entails possessing one necessary, but not sufficient, condition for possessing any other virtue. A person could have the background knowledge of what is valuable that is relevant to possessing both courage and temperance, while reliably acting courageously in challenging those in power during the day, and reliably acting intemperately at the bars at night.

For a further defense of this, we can return to Duckworth's work on self-control where she shows that there are domain-specific aspects to

---

self-control, because of differences between the strengths of various temptations, such that "an individual's impulsive behavior will vary across domains as a function of his or her idiosyncratic, domain-specific, subjective evaluations of temptation and perceived harm."[51] This by itself should give us enough reason to reject the idea that if someone displays a virtue in one domain, that they will necessarily do so in other domains. Again, while there is a unifying element to virtue, it does not entail strong claims about unity in the possession of virtue. The minimal unity is to be found in the content of practical wisdom, rather than in one's possession of the virtues.

Defending the Minimal Unity Thesis

Despite the advantages of the minimal unity thesis, some virtue ethicists will see this view of the unity thesis as having undesirable implications. Rosalind Hursthouse argues against "the possibility that someone might be, for example, courageous but totally lacking in temperance."[52] Her main concern is that this possibility might undermine the status of virtues as morally good traits. For example:

> It is also said that courage, in a desperado, enables him to do far more wicked things than he would have been able to do if he were timid. So it would appear that generosity, honesty, compassion and courage despite being virtues, are sometimes faults. Someone who is generous, honest, compassionate, and courageous might not be a morally good, admirable person – or, if it is still held to be a truism that they are, then morally good people may be led by what makes them morally good to act wrongly! How have we arrived at such an odd conclusion?[53]

Whether you find the possibility of someone being courageous but not morally good "an odd conclusion" will depend upon your views about virtues. In part, an example like this seems to rely on a virtue of 'will power', like courage, rather than a substantive virtue to generate the problem. It is harder to see, for example, how honesty or compassion in a desperado would enable him to do far more wicked things. In which case,

---

[51] Duckworth, Angela Lee and Tsukayama, Eli, "Domain Specificity in Self-Control," in Miller, Christian B., Furr, R. Michael, Knobel, Angela, and Fleeson, William (eds.), *Character: New Directions from Philosophy, Psychology, and Theology* (New York: Oxford University Press, 2015), 393–411, 398.

[52] Hursthouse, Rosalind, *On Virtue Ethics* (Oxford: Oxford University Press, 1999), 154.

[53] Hursthouse, Rosalind, "Virtue Ethics," *The Stanford Encyclopedia of Philosophy*, Fall 2013 Edition, Edward N. Zalta (ed.), URL = <http://plato.stanford.edu/archives/fall2013/entries/ethics-virtue/>.

virtues like courage are still excellences, because they are necessary, even though they are clearly not sufficient, to act well.

Virtues are sensitivities to morally relevant features of the world. Different virtues are attuned to different factors: courage deals with fear and risk, honesty deals with information and truth, kindness deals with the feelings and interests of other people, etc. If you lack any of the virtues (or lack them to the full degree), then you could possibly end up doing wrong because there are some situations in which you would be insensitive to a morally relevant feature of your situation. As Wolf points out, "if one's views about value are seriously mistaken (if, say, one radically overvalues material wealth or undervalues friendship) it will infect the content of one's other values, marring them to some degree."[54] It is likely in most situations that there are several morally relevant features of the situation, for which you would need two or more virtues to pick up on these features and be able to come to an appropriate judgment about what to do all things considered. So, it should not come as a surprise that someone could have a virtue and still act wrongly, since you would need all the virtues to keep from wrongdoing in all situations. While this claim is admittedly weaker than the claim that the possession of any virtue will make you act more appropriately in every situation, the virtues do not require this strong of an endorsement in order to make them worthy of recommendation.

Virtue ethicists need to defend some version of the claim that there is a unity to the virtues, in order to maintain that a person with all the virtues will know what to do, all things considered. Wolf provides an account of practical wisdom that can support a minimal form of unity, since the body of knowledge about what is good and bad that informs each virtue is a unified body of knowledge. This minimal unity thesis is plausible because it does not make claims about the actual possession of virtue that are counter-intuitive, yet it maintains that there is an essential element in each virtue that unifies all the virtues. The minimal unity thesis holds on to the core idea that the knowledge of what is valuable in life serves to unify the discrete virtues. Since practical wisdom is not the only necessary condition for the possession of virtue, someone may possess a virtue without necessarily possessing all the other virtues. This allows practical wisdom to play a unifying role without also having to think of it as a singular skill.

---

[54] Wolf, Susan, "Moral Psychology and the Unity of the Virtues," *Ratio*, 20:2 (2007), 160.

Phronesis – Value and Power

It is also important to note that reflection on our conceptions of the good life, and the value of the activities we are engaged with, cannot be carried out in complete isolation from the social, political, legal, and economic circumstances in which we find ourselves. For example, Darcia Narvaez points out how "it is only in the West that a person is viewed as an individual who can (and should) stand on his own. In the rest of the world, typically, persons are understood only as members of communities."[55] This kind of understanding of the relationship between the individual and the community would affect both our conceptions of living well and of the constitutive virtues.[56]

These contexts play a role in shaping our views about our activities and the good life, and they need to be further questioned from the standpoint of power relations that influence our views. Flyvbjerg argues that "practical wisdom involves not only appreciative judgements in terms of values but also an understanding of the practical political realities of any situation as part of an integrated judgement in terms of power."[57] Although *phronesis* has always been thought of in terms of making value judgments, it has been typical in the virtue literature to think too individualistically about how to answer questions of value, or when answering these questions involves consulting others (whether a putatively wise person or the standards of one's own community) issues of power relations between those asking and answering these questions have typically been ignored.

By power relations, I mean more specifically a concern with power being exercised by one group in order to oppress another group. In raising a concern about power relations, it is not that one is merely asking questions about power alongside the questions about value, but rather that power can shape our own thinking about morality, what is valuable, and what the good life consists in. Nancy Snow provides an excellent

[55] Narvaez, Darcia, "Wisdom as Mature Moral Functioning: Insights from Developmental Psychology and Neurobiology," in Jones, Mark, Lewis, Paul, and Reffitt, Kelly (eds.), *Toward Human Flourishing: Character, Practical Wisdom and Professional Formation* (Macon, GA: Mercer University Press, 2013).

[56] As Narvaez goes on to argue, we would do well to remember Aristotle's insistence that human beings are social animals, and people learn from and are shaped by their social environment. It is problematic to assume too individualistic a perspective on the relationship between an individual and her community. Also, to go back to Wolf's discussion of what is valuable, surely our own thoughts about the relative value of money and wealth are conditioned by power.

[57] Flyvbjerg, Bent "Phronetic Planning Research: Theoretical and Methodological Reflections," *Planning Theory & Practice*, 5:3 (2004), 283–306, 284. Flyvbjerg relies on Foucault for an analysis of power.

example of this in her discussion of how the talk of virtues has been used historically to oppress certain groups:

> Examining the historical record reveals a common flaw: misconceptions of the natures of certain groups – women and African-American slaves – led to mistaken notions of their flourishing and misidentifications of the traits that constitute the virtues of the members of those groups. These mistakes were often not innocent errors, but worked to the advantage of those who made them and to the detriment of women and blacks.[58]

This more robust form of *phronesis* is of critical importance given the social dimensions of any human life. Too often ethicists content themselves with abstract arguments and miss the power relations shaping their discourse. Furthermore, it is worth keeping in mind that the ethicists who debate ideas of virtue and flourishing, both historically and in contemporary times, are themselves subject to biases and prejudices that can negatively influence their arguments, and so we cannot blindly defer to their judgement.

Conclusion

While some aspects traditionally associated with practical wisdom also appear in expertise, such as having practical know-how and a strong commitment to the ends being pursued, what expertise lacks is the need for practical wisdom. It is the element of evaluating the worth of one's ends, in view of what it means to live well, that is crucial to practical wisdom and the possession of virtue. So moral virtue, on the skill model of virtue, amounts to skillful behavior guided by both responsiveness (as discussed in the previous chapter) and practical wisdom. So, while not every skill involves practical wisdom, that still allows conceptualizing virtues as skills. With all the pieces in place for a skill model of virtue, we turn in the next chapter to see how this conception of virtue fares against the main challenge to virtue – that of the 'situationist' critique of virtue.

---

[58] Snow, Nancy E., "Virtue and Oppression," in Alfano, Mark (ed.), *Current Controversies in Virtue Theory* (New York: Routledge, 2015), 49–58, 56.

CHAPTER 5

The Situationist Critique of Virtue

Virtue theory has come under attack in the past few decades because of the results of experiments conducted in social psychology, which have been interpreted as undermining the widespread possession of virtue. This 'situationist' critique claims that it is often a mistake, an 'attribution' error, to think that personality or character traits are guiding our behavior, because situational factors frequently exert a significant influence on our behavior.[1] What has been challenged is specifically the actual possession of 'robust character traits' – where someone with such a trait can be relied on to behave consistently with respect to the trait in question in a variety of situations, even those situations where there are strong influences to act otherwise. Experiments in social psychology have shown that whether people act morally well or poorly is often strongly influenced by irrelevant (and sometimes trivial) factors of a situation. Whether people stop to help someone in need, for example, can be affected by trivial factors like whether one just found a dime (if so, far more likely to help)[2], or whether there's a loud lawnmower nearby (if so, far less likely to help)[3]. Darley and Batson found that people were far less likely to help someone in distress when in a hurry, even when in a hurry to give a talk on the subject of helping.[4] Then there are the more (in)famous experiments like the

---

[1] For an example of the critique as presented in philosophy, see Doris, John, *Lack of Character* (Cambridge: Cambridge University Press, 2002); and Alfano, Mark, *Character as Moral Fiction* (Cambridge: Cambridge University Press, 2013).

[2] Isen, A. and Levin, P., "Effect of Feeling Good on Helping: Cookies and Kindness," *Journal of Personality and Social Psychology*, 21 (1972), 384–388.

[3] Mathews, K. E. and Cannon, L. K., "Environmental Noise Level as a Determinant of Helping Behavior," *Journal of Personality and Social Psychology*, 32 (1975), 571–577.

[4] Darley, J. M., and Batson, C. D., "From Jerusalem to Jericho: A Study of Situational and Dispositional Variables in Helping Behavior," *Journal of Personality and Social Psychology*, 27 (1973), 100–108.

Milgram obedience experiments, or the Stanford prison experiment, where it seems far too easy to elicit cruel behavior out of average people.[5]

One advantage of the skill model of virtue is that it avoids some of the aforementioned problems because it does not view virtue as a personality trait. However, that is not to say that the situationist critique does not affect a skill model of virtue at all. So, in the remainder of the chapter I will proceed along the following lines. First, I discuss how the situationist debate changes with a skill model of virtue. Second, insofar as improvement in skill requires correcting for errors, what I take to be most significant about the social psychology experiments are what they reveal about some of the causes of moral error. My main concern is then how to combat the effects found in those experiments, and fortunately there are resources for this in the literature on skill and self-regulation. In this respect I view the problems revealed by social psychology experiments as providing the targets for moral skill improvement, rather than as impediments to improvement. Third, I discuss one of the major sources of moral wrongdoing that is usually overlooked in the ethics literature, which is moral disengagement. Fourth, I tackle some issues that arise specifically with the situationist challenge to epistemic virtues in virtue epistemology. Finally, I discuss the rarity of virtue, along with some concluding remarks.

Situationism and the Skill Model of Virtue

It is surprising to learn about the influence of situations if you previously believed that most human behavior was the product of robust character traits. Virtue theorists, though, should not be understood as necessarily endorsing such a claim. Granted, virtue theorists tend to assume that virtues are robust character traits, but they also claim that they are traits that are acquired by degree and take a fair amount of time to acquire. So, there need not be any expectation that most human behavior is the product of robust character traits. However, a threat to virtue theory still remains, mainly because the findings make us doubt whether virtue as a robust character trait is even possible for people to acquire. Though to be fair, what goes usually unremarked about the social psychology experiments described above are the people who do not succumb to the situational influences. It would be consistent with the findings that virtue is

---

[5] Milgram, S., *Obedience to Authority* (New York: Harper and Row, 1974). Haney, C., Banks, C. and Zimbardo, P., "A Study of Prisoners and Guards in a Simulated Prison," in *Readings about the Social Animal*, E. Aronson (ed.), Third Edition (San Francisco: Freeman, 1973,)52–67.

expressed in those people. Then what might be surprising is that so few people seem to exhibit behavior in line with the virtues, but again virtue theorists need not commit themselves to a specific view about how wide-spread the possession of virtue is currently. Really the pressure from situationism comes in the form of trying to come up with good evidence to support the idea that virtues as robust character traits are genuinely possible for human beings to acquire, such that it makes sense to recommend that people try to acquire virtue in order to act well. That is, we cannot be content to assume that our conception of virtue is psychologically realizable for humans, which goes back to Flanagan's principle of psychological realism.

Mark Alfano argues that the results of the experiments in social psychology show that we do not consistently respond to moral reasons in situations, given the influence of situational variables.[6] While it has been difficult to find consistency in human behavior when looking at the objective (or nominal) features of situations in which people act, it looks like you can find consistency in behavior when you take into account how people construe situations differently. That is, you have to understand situations in terms of the features that are psychologically salient for the person acting. For example, whether I will act aggressively in a situation depends on whether I construe it as a situation that is threatening to me, and whether I construe it as threatening depends on more than just the objective features of the situation.

However, as Alfano points out, mere consistency will not be enough for accounts of virtue. What we want is not mere consistency according to our own subjective construal of situations, for we might not be construing situations correctly. I may respond consistently to situations that I construe as requiring kindness, but that is compatible both with me construing a situation as requiring kindness when it does not (perhaps not usually a bad thing) and also a situation as not requiring kindness when it does (which is much more worrisome). Virtue requires people to be consistent in responding to the right reasons in situations. The social psychology experiments, however, definitely throw into doubt our ability to be consistently responsive to good reasons, since our behavior is often responsive to morally irrelevant factors. In addition, consistency is not the only aspect of virtue to be cast into doubt by the situationist critique. Alfano also points out that the explanatory and predictive power of virtue

---

[6] Alfano, Mark, "Identifying and Defending the Hard Core of Virtue Ethics," *Journal of Philosophical Research*, 38 (2013), 233–260.

attribution is also undermined to the extent that situational factors do a better job of explaining and predicting behavior.

Importantly, though, the social psychology experiments undermine consistency, explanation, and prediction only on the further assumption that the possession of virtue is widespread. If virtue is not widespread, then the situationist critique loses much of its power, given that in these experiments some smaller percentage of people manage to still act well, and so the experiments do not necessarily undermine the possibility of virtue possession. Though it must be granted that this still falls short of proof that the behavior of this smaller percentage of people is best explained by virtue, or that most other people can still be led to acquire virtue (despite their current lack of it). In other words, if virtue possession looks to be currently widespread, then we know that most people can be led to acquire virtue – a claim that Alfano refers to as 'egalitarianism' with respect to acquiring virtue. However, given the situationist experiments, virtue possession does not look widespread. Virtue theorists can, in response, give up the claim to widespread virtue possession currently, but then they have to make good on the egalitarian claim that most people can still be led to acquire virtue.

Thus, the skill model response to the situationist challenge needs to emphasize two points. First, there are reasons to expect that full virtue possession would not be widespread. Second, despite it not being widespread, we have good reason to think that we can improve our moral competences. As to the first point, on the skill model of virtue, one would expect that virtue would be as rare as expertise. It is fairly difficult to attain the level of an expert in a field, since the process is challenging and requires thousands of hours of dedicated practice. If we can only expect a select few to become experts, then we would expect the same of becoming a virtuous person. Of course, it would still be the case that we could expect a lot of people to have acquired the virtues to some degree, even if that falls short of full virtue.

If virtues represent an expert-level skill, then it implies that full virtue possession is rare, though without implying that it is rare because it is an unattainable ideal. While it might appear to be a drawback that an expertise model of moral development makes the possession of virtue out to be rare, rather than commonplace, it can be seen as an important advantage of the model. Christian Miller argues that the best response to the situationist critique will have to accept that the possession of virtue is rare, claiming that "virtue ethicists can readily agree that experiments in psychology justify the belief that there currently is not widespread possession of the virtues – there was never any expectation otherwise."[7] Furthermore, this is not an ad hoc move with the skill model of virtue, precisely because expertise is rare.

This claim about the rarity of virtue would involve dropping what Alfano refers to elsewhere as the prevalence component of virtue, and this would remove some of the force of the situationist critique.[8] However, there may be a cost to going this route. Alfano argues that the prevalence component is deeply ingrained in our traditional conceptions of virtue. As he points out, "[i]f virtues are what humans need, but the vast majority of people don't have them, one would have thought that our species would have died out long ago."[9] I think the skill model can accommodate this thought, if we distinguish between different levels of skill acquisition. Without some basic competence with respect to many of the virtues, it would be hard for humans as a social species to survive. To use a skill analogy, people need to display some basic competences with driving a car in order to get a drivers' license, to ensure that those on the road are not a constant hazard to themselves and others. You do not need to exhibit expertise, though, to get a license, as it certainly does not take 10,000 hours of training to get a handle on the basics of driving. But that basic competence is compatible with finding people driving poorly in a variety of situations (like in the snow, or while texting). It is also the case that those who have put in a lot more training in driving will have a higher level of skill than the minimum we require to get a license. So, we can view virtue in the same way – there are some basic levels that you need to attain so that you are not a constant danger to yourself and others, while also recognizing that there are higher levels of performance above our min- imum expectations of people. While we might need basic moral compe- tence to survive, higher levels of moral skill development can enable us to live well, and this is consistent with virtue theorists who conceive of virtues as constitutive of living well (and not merely surviving).[10]

---

[7] Miller, Christian, "The Problem of Character," in Van Hooft, Stan (ed.), *The Handbook of Virtue Ethics* (New York: Routledge, 2014) 418–429, 421. Though, when it comes to virtue epistemology, it might be problematic if the standard for knowledge is having developed intellectual skills to the level of expertise. This point is raised by Olin, Lauren and Doris, John M., "Vicious Minds: Virtue Epistemology, Cognition, and Skepticism," *Philosophical Studies*, 168 (2014), 665–692, 676.

[8] Alfano, Mark, "Ramsifying Virtue Theory," in Alfano, Mark (ed.), *Current Controversies in Virtue Theory* (New York: Routledge, 2015), 124–135.

[9] Alfano, Mark, "Ramsifying Virtue Theory," in Alfano, Mark (ed.), *Current Controversies in Virtue Theory* (New York: Routledge, 2015), 124–135, 134.

[10] Virtue in this regard may be necessary, but not sufficient, for living well. Economic, political, and other social factors matter significantly as well.

The response here has some similarities to James Montmarquet's reply to Alfano.[11] Montmarquet offers a different skill analogy – levels of mathematical skill in American students. He argues that the discouraging test results of students' math skills does not show that such skills are unimportant, and I would add that it also does not show that higher levels of skill are beyond our reach. He further worries about any approach that "dumbs down" the virtues so that it turns out we all do have a satisfactory level of virtue (i.e. we would 'test' well for moral development), as a similar approach to dumbing down our conception of mathematical skill might sound more reassuring about students' current levels of skill while still leaving them no better at math than before. The approach I am taking, however, does not involve dumbing down the notion of virtue. It instead involves taking seriously the different levels of moral skill development, and while we should expect of people some basic competence, we can still acknowledge that higher levels of development are both possible and valuable. Furthermore, I suspect that even on this approach that we will still test lower than people usually expect with respect to basic moral competence. Perhaps I am bit too cynical, but I find myself in agreement with Steven Lukes when he points out that the fact that many people are surprised by how low a level of moral competence we actually have, as revealed by the experiments in social psychology, is itself surprising, at least for "anyone paying attention to the state of the world over the last century, and in particular to the litany of atrocities that stretches from the Nazi Holocaust to the Rwandan genocide and current events in Dafur."[12]

Despite the disappointing current levels of moral competence on display, the skill model gives us reasons to think that this situation can be improved. As Daniel Russell points out, "[s]kill is a matter of taking our capacity to be consistent in accordance with *some* standard and turning it into consistency in accordance with the *right* standard for the skill."[13] Skill acquisition is a matter of learning how to become more responsive to reasons, such as learning how to alter your driving behavior in response to certain environmental conditions (e.g. you have a good reason to drive

---

[11] Montmarquet, James, "Ramsify (by All Means) – but Do Not 'Dumb Down' the Moral Virtues," in Alfano, Mark (ed.), *Current Controversies in Virtue Theory* (New York: Routledge, 2015), 136–146.

[12] Lukes, Steven, "Comment: Do People Have Character Traits?" in Mantzavinos, Chrysostomos (ed.), *Philosophy of the Social Sciences: Philosophical Theory and Scientific Practice* (New York: Cambridge University Press, 2009), 291–298, 294–295.

[13] Russell, Daniel C., "From Personality to Character to Virtue," in Alfano, Mark (ed.), *Current Controversies in Virtue Theory* (New York: Routledge, 2015), 92–105, 99.

slower in icy conditions). If we can do this in the case of skill, we should be able to do so in the case of virtue.

Interestingly, Christian Miller, in his response to Russell, notes that there are two ways of understanding this approach.[14] First, perhaps the most natural reading, is what Miller calls the "Analogy Argument," where the argument depends on how analogous virtues are to skills. But that turns out not to be what Russell had in mind. The second approach, which Russell does embrace, is that skill reveals what psychological mechanisms are available for improvement, and so the hope is then that those same mechanisms can be exploited for moral development (where virtue is not a skill but taps into some of the same mechanisms as skills). So, Russell stops short of saying that virtues are skills. By contrast, I am claiming that virtues are a kind of skill (and not merely analogous in some important respects).[15]

However, making good on this claim requires responding to some challenges Miller poses for understanding the relationship between skill and virtue. The first challenge is whether the cultivation of virtue really does resemble skill acquisition, given that the kinds of problems we face in moral improvement may have no analogue with skill. This is the problem of "surprising dispositions," which Miller takes to be the upshot of the situationist critique. Because these dispositions "are (i) widely held, (ii) causally influential in many morally relevant situations, (iii) non-virtuous in their motivational and/or behavioral effects, and (iv) unconscious in their functioning, the Surprising Dispositions are a significant impediment to virtue cultivation."[16] As he notes, it is not obvious that there are similar obstacles to acquiring skills. If not, then the framework of skill acquisition will have little to offer us for insights into how we can improve morally, as the challenges involved in acquiring either are quite different. However, as I will show in the following sections, the surprising dispositions interfere with skillful and other goal-directed behavior, and not just moral behavior.

Even if this first challenge is met, though, Miller argues there is a second challenge awaiting the skill model of virtue. It is not enough just to show

---

[14] Miller, Christian B., "Russell on Acquiring Virtue," in Alfano, Mark (ed.), *Current Controversies in Virtue Theory* (New York: Routledge, 2015), 106–117.

[15] That is not the only relevant difference. Although Russell uses some of the social–cognitive literature in defending his view, he does not draw on any of Bandura's work, nor does he tap into the self-regulation theory. This is important as responding adequately to Miller's challenges will require drawing on both.

[16] Miller, Christian B., "Russell on Acquiring Virtue," in Alfano, Mark (ed.), *Current Controversies in Virtue Theory* (New York: Routledge, 2015), 106–117, 111.

that there are surprising dispositions that impede skill acquisition as we also need to know how we can overcome such dispositions. If it is not clear what strategies can be used to overcome the surprising dispositions in the case of skill, then again that framework will yield no insights into how to overcome them in the moral case. To be sure, if we do not know those strategies at the present time, it does not follow that we will not be able to figure them out later. But a complete lack of strategies will definitely dim our hope that we can improve morally.

Now Russell is aware of some of these challenges, and draws on Robin Hogarth's work on training intuition, specifically that of overcoming stereotyping when hiring.[17] The strategy is one where you get in the habit of scrutinizing your first impressions, to overcome the potential influence of stereotypes. Russell views this as an example of overcoming dispositions that interfere with the exercise of a skill, in hiring, and concludes that in general "the human limitations that frustrate moral behavior are very the same ones that experts must also learn to manage in acquiring a skill."[18] Miller, however, thinks this strategy might prove to be too limited. The problem he sees is that there are so many surprising dispositions, and to learn about them all and how to overcome them in a variety of situations, along with being sure to be mindful when you are in those situations, is asking too much of people. While this is a relevant concern, automaticity can help turn such initially effortful mindfulness into something much more manageable. Though, as Miller recognizes, this may be merely a tantalizing possibility at the moment, if there is not enough experimental evidence to support this strategy. In response, I think that there is some promising experimental evidence to support this and other strategies, as I will detail in the next section.[19]

---

[17] Hogarth, Robin M., *Educating Intuition* (Chicago: University of Chicago Press, 2000).
[18] Russell, Daniel C., "From Personality to Character to Virtue," in Alfano, Mark (ed.), *Current Controversies in Virtue Theory* (New York: Routledge, 2015), 92–105, 103.
[19] Assuming there are strategies that work to overcome surprising dispositions in the moral case, the third and final challenge of Miller is to understand how we might motivate people to actually employ these strategies, given that it seems like it will be hard work. Miller puts the challenge succinctly: "[s]o how do we get people to *care* enough about becoming more virtuous, and derivatively to care about using these strategies as a means to doing so, in a way that is sufficiently strong and long-lasting to see the project through to completion to at least moderate levels of virtue?" Miller, Christian B., "Russell on Acquiring Virtue," in Alfano, Mark (ed.), *Current Controversies in Virtue Theory* (New York: Routledge, 2015), 106–117, 117. Miller recognizes that the expertise literature might hold a clue, as people need to be strongly motivated to overcome all the obstacles and setbacks involved with trying to master a skill, but at the moment it is an area deserving of more research.

Meeting the Situationist Challenge

A first step that might be of use in replying to Miller's challenge to the skill model of virtue can be found in Ernest Sosa's response to situationism. Sosa runs a skill analogy with driving competence in his response to the situationist critique.[20] He argues that even in a case of skill, our competences are affected by a variety of factors. For example, in the case of driving competence, he notes the variety of factors (lighting, weather, distractions, alcohol, navigation, etc.) that can affect our competence at driving. In this, he treats them as if they might be surprising factors that affect our competence, especially given the range of factors, and then wonders if we should adopt a situationist explanation of the driving competence. That is, should we be tempted to think that a robust driving competence is undermined by the presence of these factors, and that situational factors mostly determine differences in driving behavior? Well, it certainly does not seem like anyone is tempted to think that driving competence does not actually exist on the basis of these factors, and thus he thinks it is a mistake to do so in the moral case. While he admits that "any factor that *surprisingly* matters to our driving competence reveals some inadequacy in our prior view of such competence," this only calls for a revision to our account of the competence (rather than denying such competence exists).[21]

Importantly, Sosa recognizes that some may object to the comparison of driving to morality, insofar as he is claiming that the two are improved by similar methods:

> It might be replied that the analogy between driving and moral competence is limited and potentially misleading. You do not improve your moral competence by avoiding situations where it will be severely tested, in strict analogy to how you improve your driving competence by avoiding bridges when it's wet and wintry. Even if you concede some force to this point, the analogy remains effective. For one thing, you need not avoid the bridges so long as you are sufficiently aware of the risk and adjust your behavior accordingly. Through such adjustments, you *thereby* become more competent as a driver. Similarly, one way to improve your moral competence,

[20] Sosa, Ernest, "Situations against Virtues: The Situationist Attack on Virtue Theory," in Mantzavinos, Chrysostomos (ed.), *Philosophy of the Social Sciences: Philosophical Theory and Scientific Practice* (New York: Cambridge University Press, 2009), 274–290.

[21] Sosa, Ernest, "Situations against Virtues: The Situationist Attack on Virtue Theory," in Mantzavinos, Chrysostomos (ed.), *Philosophy of the Social Sciences: Philosophical Theory and Scientific Practice* (New York: Cambridge University Press, 2009), 274–290, 285.

surely, is to become more sensitive to moral danger, and to proceed with corresponding care.[22]

While I think this is the right line of response to Miller's first challenge of recognizing similar obstacles to skill and virtue cultivation, it is still something of a promissory note. As Miller highlights, to find an analogue in skill for surprising dispositions "we would instead need to find cases where there are unconscious psychological dispositions that, when activated, routinely lead to poor performance *of that very skill*."[23] The factors Sosa mentions as impairing driving competence do not seem to be cases of this, as they have more to do with either environmental conditions or internal conditions that it would be fairly easy to recognize (like being distracted). So, Miller's challenges remain to determine how we can overcome the surprising dispositions both in the case of skill and morality.

Fortunately, the self-regulation and skill literature provide a nice starting point for examples of the kind of psychological dispositions Miller has in mind, along with strategies to overcome them. One seemingly irrelevant factor that has a significant impact on our moral decision making is the way a moral issue is framed, but it appears that this framing effect can be resisted if the moral values at stake are protected values. For example, Tversky and Kahneman tested subject's responses to a public health crisis, specifically a disease threatened to kill 600 people.[24] They presented the subjects with two treatment options, where both treatment options had the same predicted outcome in terms of how many people would survive, but one was couched in terms of a 100 percent chance of saving 200 lives and the other in terms of a 33 percent chance of saving 600 lives (and 66 percent chance of saving none). Subjects overwhelmingly preferred the first treatment, even though the treatments had the same predicted outcome. However, the really surprising result was that if the same two treatment options were put instead in terms of chances that people will die (i.e. 400 lives lost), they overwhelmingly preferred the second treatment. It seems as though we react differently to issues when framed in terms of gain (positive) or loss (negative), such that we want to secure a definite gain but we try to avoid a definite loss.

---

[22] Sosa, Ernest, "Situations against Virtues: The Situationist Attack on Virtue Theory," in Mantzavinos, Chrysostomos (ed.), *Philosophy of the Social Sciences: Philosophical Theory and Scientific Practice* (New York: Cambridge University Press, 2009), 274–290, 285.

[23] Miller, Christian B., "Russell on Acquiring Virtue," in Alfano, Mark (ed.), *Current Controversies in Virtue Theory* (New York: Routledge, 2015), 106–117, 112.

[24] Tversky, Amos and Kahneman, Daniel, "The Framing of Decisions and the Psychology of Choice," *Science*, 211:30 (1981), 453–457.

Tanner and Medin studied the effects of framing with a choice between an act and an omission, where the outcomes of either were the same, by manipulating the descriptions of the outcomes in two ways. Take, for example, a situation "where an outbreak of disease threatens to kill 600 people and one option will save 200 people for sure and the other has a one–third chance of saving all 600 and a two-thirds chance of saving no one."[25] The two options could either be described positively as lives saved or negatively as lives lost, in addition to the choice between a certain outcome and a risky outcome. The framing effect shows itself with the tendencies of people to be more risk averse when the outcome is described positively, for it feels like a gain that people want to preserve; yet more risk seeking when the outcome is described negatively, for it appears as a loss and people are willing to gamble to avoid it.

Tanner and Medin were interested in whether protected values would impact the framing effect, where protected values are understood as those that people try to avoid having to compromise. In other words, protected values would be the higher-ordered values in the hierarchical organization of goals, which people try to preserve above all the lower-ordered values. The experiment involved four scenarios dealing with environmental issues, and they gathered information from the subjects as to how much environmental preservation was a protected value.

What they found was that people for whom the environment was not a protected value, they showed the usual framing effect:

> With a positive frame, there was a strong preference for the riskless option. Acts were preferred when associated with certain outcomes (69%), but not when associated with risky outcomes (13%) ... This pattern was reversed under negative framing. Acts were preferred for risky outcomes (69%), but not for certain outcomes (31%).[26]

However, for those for whom the environment was a protected value, there was no framing effect. Those subjects consistently had a preference for the act over the omission, regardless of the positive–negative framing and whether the outcome of the act was certain or risky. Their explanation for the finding is that those with strong protected values felt a moral obligation to take action. As they note, situational factors alone cannot account for their findings, since those with strong protected values maintained a

[25] Tanner, Carmen and Medin, Douglas L., "Protected Values: No Omission Bias and No Framing Effects," *Psychonomic Bulletin & Review*, 11:1 (2004), 185–191, 186.
[26] Tanner, Carmen and Medin, Douglas L., "Protected Values: No Omission Bias and No Framing Effects," *Psychonomic Bulletin & Review*, 11:1 (2004), 185–191, 187.

preference for the option associated with acting, regardless of how the situation was framed. Insofar as we want consistency in people's moral behavior, it looks like one key ingredient in producing that is whether moral values are of high enough order to discourage trade-offs with other values.

The literature on implementation intentions, as a way to self-regulate, offers another way to resist framing effects, but is also applicable to a number of other situational influences. To recall, self-regulation begins with goals, and it matters how the goals are spelled out, as more specific and proximate goals (as compared to vague or distant goals) allow for better planning before acting, and better feedback after acting. Similarly, not all plans of action for implementing those goals are equally effective. We can make plans of action in the moment, responding to our current situation and trying to determine what act would best further our goals. But that approach suffers from two main drawbacks. First, it is often cognitively demanding to figure out how to achieve a goal (especially in the given context), and you may have to decide quickly on what course of action to take in the moment. Second, with this reactive approach you are forced to respond to the current situation, and you may find out that the situation you have gotten yourself into is not conducive to achieving your goals (like trying to quit drinking alcohol but then agreeing to meet up with friends at a bar).

A more effective route to achieving your goals is through the use of implementation intentions, where we pre-commit ourselves to a specific course of action in a particular situation. There are a few generic advantages to having implementation intentions of this kind. First, it gives you direction as to what kind of situations you want to seek out, or avoid, in order to be in the best position to achieve your goal. This is certainly acknowledging the power of situational influences. Second, having decided in advance of how you will respond to a situation allows you to respond automatically, and so frees up your attention to better focus on the task at hand. Interestingly, this kind of automaticity develops even without repetition, in contrast to how automaticity is usually the result of repeated performance.[27] As Weiber et al. note "[b]ecause forming an

---

[27] As Fujita et al. point out, "[w]hat is remarkable about implementation intentions, however, is unlike habits and acquired skills, they do not appear to require repeated practice to automate. Indeed, simply repeating an implementation intention several times ('If I see the number 5 on the computer screen, then I will type in my response particularly fast!') is sufficient in prompting cognitively efficient goal – directed behavior when the context specified by the plan is later encountered." Fujita, Kentaro, Trope, Yaacov, Cunningham, William A., and Liberman, Nira, "What Is Control? A Conceptual Analysis," in Sherman, Jeffrey W., Gawronski, Bertram, and Trope, Yaacov, *Dual-Process Theories of the Social Mind* (New York: The Guilford Press, 2014), 50–65, 55.

implementation intention entails the selection of a critical future situation, the mental representation of this situation becomes highly activated and hence more accessible."[28] This is especially helpful when a goal is not easy to implement because one has habitual responses that steer one away from the goal (for example, being in the habit of ordering dessert when you have recently formed a new goal of losing weight). In essence, forming the implementation intention will trigger an automatic goal-directed response that preempts the prior habituated automatic response.[29] This represents an interesting interplay between deliberative and automatic processes, as you are using a deliberate self-regulatory strategy (i.e. implementation intentions) in advance, which works by later triggering an automatic response.

This is especially relevant to developing methods to combat some of the surprising dispositions, such as framing effects. Gollwitzer studied the effects of using implementation intentions to achieving prosocial goals (like fairness and cooperation) in negotiations, specifically in respect to loss framing. The framing effect in this context is that the outcomes of negotiations depend on whether they are framed in terms of gains or losses. People appear to be more motivated to avoid a loss than to seek a gain, and so if the outcomes are framed in terms of losses then people are less likely to make concessions in negotiations, such that "loss frames lead to comparatively unfair outcomes and hinder the finding of integrative solutions."[30] In other words, while framing in terms of gains leads to fairer outcomes, those who adopt a loss frame typically come out ahead of the other person. This of course just provides incentives to go in with a loss frame at the start. However, they found that this effect could be mitigated if people supplied their goals (e.g. to be fair) with implementation intentions specifying how they would be fair. In the experiment "participants were randomly assigned to play the role of one or the other representative of two neighboring countries (blue nation vs. orange nation) disputing over an island, said to be close to the main land of both countries" and one group had neither goal nor implementation intentions, a second group had

[28] Wieber, Frank, Gollwitzer, Peter M., and Sheeran, Paschal, "Strategic Regulation of Mimicry Effects by Implementation Intentions," *Journal of Experimental Social Psychology*, 53 (2014), 31–39, 32.

[29] Gollwitzer, Peter M., "Implementation Intentions: Strong Effects of Simple Plans," *American Psychologist*, 54:7 (1999), 493–503.

[30] Trötschel, Roman, and Gollwitzer, Peter M., "Implementation Intentions and the Willful Pursuit of Prosocial Goals in Negotiations," *Journal of Experimental Social Psychology*, 43 (2007), 579–598, 580.

the goal to be fair but no implementation intention, and the third group had both the goal and were supplied with the implementation intention that "if I receive a proposal on how to share the island, then I will make a fair counterproposal!".[31] The first group experienced the typical framing effect, the second group partially mitigated the effects of the framing, and the third group managed to fully mitigate the loss frame effects.

A second study in that experiment provided further evidence of the benefits of implementation intentions in terms of reducing the cognitive demands of the situation. Participants in the second study could "increase their joint outcomes by applying the cognitive demanding strategy of logrolling (i.e. increasing negotiation outcomes by trading the less preferred issues for the more preferred)."[32] Those who were furnished with implementation intentions were better able to use the cognitively demanding strategy of 'logrolling', because the implementation intention allowed them to have an automatic initial response, by forging a strong association between the specified situation and response, thus freeing up attention to better utilize the logrolling strategy.

Importantly, the results of these experiments have implications beyond just the context of negotiations, for "negotiations are cognitively very demanding tasks in which a large amount of information has to be processed on-line and the course of events is hard to predict. Thus, negotiations can be understood as the prototype of a complex situation in which the pursuit of desired goals can easily become derailed."[33] Given how easily the pursuit of moral goals can become derailed, as the social psychology literature highlights, the effects of implementation intentions will likely be of use in resisting some of the surprising dispositions.

Another example of the effects of implementation intentions is in regulating the effects of mimicry. As a social species, people tend to mimic the mannerisms and gestures of those they interact with. Typically, we are not even aware that we engage in mimicry on a regular basis, since it is the result of automatic processes. In general, this is beneficial, as mimicry usually promotes social interaction and prosocial behavior. For example,

[31] Trötschel, Roman, and Gollwitzer, Peter M., "Implementation Intentions and the Willful Pursuit of Prosocial Goals in Negotiations," *Journal of Experimental Social Psychology*, 43 (2007), 579–598, 583.
[32] Trötschel, Roman, and Gollwitzer, Peter M., "Implementation Intentions and the Willful Pursuit of Prosocial Goals in Negotiations," *Journal of Experimental Social Psychology*, 43 (2007), 579–598, 585.
[33] Trötschel, Roman, and Gollwitzer, Peter M., "Implementation Intentions and the Willful Pursuit of Prosocial Goals in Negotiations," *Journal of Experimental Social Psychology*, 43 (2007), 579–598, 582.

an empathic response can be triggered via mimicry. Mimicking someone's pained expression can produce a similar affective state in the mimicker. However, they note that this is something that can be exploited by the person mimicking you, as "being mimicked altered students' preferences for a product that was supposedly favored by the mimicking interaction partner; participants became more willing to buy the product, and consumed more of the product when they were asked to taste it."[34] In response to examples like this, Wieber et al. examined the success people had in protecting a goal of saving money when mimicked by someone who later wanted them to spend their money. Participants in the experiment "were randomly assigned to either a mere goal intention condition ('I want to be thrifty with my money! I will save my money for important investments!'), or an implementation intention condition ('I want to be thrifty with my money! And if I am tempted to buy something, then I will tell myself: I will save my money for important investments!')."[35] Similar to the previous findings, those with implementation intentions resisted the effects of the mimicry and saved more money than those with only the goal intention.

In addition, implementation intentions have been shown to reduce prejudicial behavior by inhibiting the effects of stereotypes – such as stereotypes regarding age, gender, homelessness, etc.[36] For example, in an experiment where participants had formed a goal intention to not judge women in a stereotypical way, those who were told to also form the implementation intention "Whenever I see this person, I will ignore her gender!" suppressed the automatic stereotyped response (in contrast to those who only formed the goal intention of not being biased).[37]

However, implementation intentions are not the only way to resist the effects of surprising dispositions. Deliberate practice and skilled training can also be used to resist stereotypes and problematic situational

---

[34] Wieber, Frank, Gollwitzer, Peter M., and Sheeran, Paschal, "Strategic Regulation of Mimicry Effects by Implementation Intentions," *Journal of Experimental Social Psychology*, 53 (2014), 31–39, 35.

[35] Wieber, Frank, Gollwitzer, Peter M., and Sheeran, Paschal, "Strategic Regulation of Mimicry Effects by Implementation Intentions," *Journal of Experimental Social Psychology*, 53 (2014), 31–39, 35.

[36] Moskowitz, Gordon B., Gollwitzer, Peter M., Wasel, Wolfgang, and Schaal, Bernd, "Preconscious Control of Stereotype Activation through Chronic Egalitarian Goals," *Journal of Personality and Social Psychology*, 77:1 (1999), 167–184.

[37] Gollwitzer, Peter M., "Implementation Intentions: Strong Effects of Simple Plans," *American Psychologist*, 54:7 (1999), 493–503, 500. See also Mele and Shepherd, who draw on implementation plans as a way of handling situationist worries about automatic bias, Mele, Alfred R. and Shepherd, Joshua, "Situationism and Agency," *Journal of Practical Ethics*, 1 (2014), 62–83.

influences. Plant et al. studied how to counteract automatic racial bias in a situation that mirrored police encounters with potential criminals. The subjects were shown a picture of a face of someone with either black or white skin, and an object that was either a gun or something with a similar shape to the gun – a camera, cell-phone, or wallet. Subjects had to make an instant reaction as to whether or not to shoot the suspect, based on these two factors. Initial reactions by subjects showed a racial bias – they were more likely to mistake a gun for something harmless when the picture was of a white person, and more likely to mistake something harmless for a gun when the picture was of a black person. Sadly, this is what we see in the many recent real-life examples of police shooting black males who were actually unarmed.

Plant et al. were able to eliminate this biased response after participants went through a program designed to make race a non-diagnostic factor in determining criminal behavior. Importantly, their approach was different from another approach to reducing stereotype bias, where subjects are exposed to examples that reverse the stereotype. Instead, their approach emphasized training the subjects that race was not relevant to determining the presence of a weapon, via practice with a program where statistically the faces were equally likely to be black or white, and each face was equally likely to be paired with a gun or a harmless object. The initial biased response of the subjects was eventually eliminated through extensive practice with the program. Two aspects of their results are worth pointing out. First, it might be supposed that the automatic bias was counteracted by a conscious and deliberate response. However, they found that "training directly influenced the degree of automatic racial bias as opposed to resulting in some degree of controlled, conscious compensation for the bias."[38] Second, this result could have occurred either because the program changed the positive or negative associations someone had with those racial categories, or because people were not thinking in terms of racial categories at all. They found that it was the latter, since "race was non-diagnostic and paying attention to race only impaired performance on the shoot/don't shoot task, extensive exposure to the program encouraged the inhibition of the participants' racial categories."[39] So this gives hope to overcoming some of our automatic biases with deliberate practice.

---

[38] Plant, E. Ashby, Peruche, B. Michelle, and Butz, David A., "Eliminating Automatic Racial Bias: Making Race Non-Diagnostic for Responses to Criminal Suspects," *Journal of Experimental Social Psychology*, 41 (2005), 141–156, 153.

[39] Plant, E. Ashby, Peruche, B. Michelle, and Butz, David A., "Eliminating Automatic Racial Bias: Making Race Non-Diagnostic for Responses to Criminal Suspects," *Journal of Experimental Social Psychology*, 41 (2005), 141–156, 152.

Another situational influence to impact helping behavior is the presence of an unresponsive bystander, but there are ways to train to mitigate this influence. Latané and Darley did a series of experiments that showed that when people are alone and witness an emergency (like someone having a seizure), they show high rates of responding to the emergency.[40] But all it takes is the presence of one unresponsive bystander in the situation, and helping rates decrease dramatically. There are, however, some examples of being able to mitigate the bystander effect with deliberate practice. Cramer et al. found that registered nurses were not subject to the bystander effect when it came to an emergency situation in which they were skilled in responding. The experiment involved a group of registered nurses who were part of nursing program, and a group of students who were part of a general education program. Half of each group were working alone in a room when they heard a person fall off a ladder in an adjoining room, and the other half were working with a partner in the room when the same event occurred. When each subject was initially led to their room they passed by a person working on a ladder, but the sound of that person falling off the ladder was produced by a pre-recorded tape. Cramer et al. found that when alone, both groups of students responded to the emergency with the same frequency (about 75 percent). When with a bystander, the general education students rate of helping dropped by half, thus showing the bystander effect. However, the registered nurses helped just as often when with a bystander as when alone. Cramer et al. attributed the difference to the greater competence of the nurses:

> As expected, high-competent subjects reported that when the emergency occurred they felt more confident about their ability to help the workman, and more sure about what steps to take to help than their low-competent counterparts. Even among the subjects who helped, high-competent subjects compared to low-competent ones reported feeling more confident about their abilities, and about what steps to take to help. Thus, minimization of the bystander effect appears to have been mediated, in part, by the nurses' skill at emergency responding.[41]

So, some practice with helping in an emergency situation has an influence on self-efficacy beliefs and minimizing the bystander effect. It seems we

---

[40] Latané, Bibb, and Darley, John M., *The Unresponsive Bystander: Why Doesn't He Help?* (New York: Appleton-Century-Crofts, 1970).

[41] Cramer, Robert Ervin, McMaster, M. Rosalie, Bartell, Patricia A., and Dragna, Margurite, "Subject Competence and Minimization of the Bystander Effect," *Journal of Applied Social Psychology*, 18:13 (1988), 1133–1148, 1142.

underestimate just how uncertain people are about how to respond to emergency situations without some training.

Further support for this can be found with Brandstätter and Jonas's work on moral courage training.[42] They have been involved with training programs aimed at increasing people's abilities to intervene in situations of intolerance, discrimination and violence within their community. The problem they address is that while people typically express attitudes that they and others should intervene to stop displays of intolerance and discrimination, it rarely translates into actual behavior. Brandstätter and Jonas describe the work being done by a couple of moral courage training programs taking place in Germany and Switzerland.[43] The programs "aim to strengthen an individual's assertiveness and self-efficacy, on the one hand, while preparing the ground for establishing behavioral routines, on the other hand, as core competencies for bystander intervention."[44]

The programs use the work of Latané and Darley to help identify the different psychological mechanisms that can impede intervention, in order to formulate a training program to help counter those mechanisms. The training has three main components. The first is to increase the knowledge base of the participants, including both potential problems brought out in the work of Latané and Darley on bystander intervention, as well as general strategies for self-regulation as discussed by Gollwitzer. Of special note is that:

> participants learn about what to do and what to refrain from doing in diverse situations of neighborhood violence (e.g., put the victim at the center of your intervention; never touch the perpetrator; never intervene directly in a fist fight; make an emergency call). Notably, participants are informed about the emergency services in their community, which is an important issue in combating neighborhood violence, since bystanders

---

[42] Brandstätter, Veronika and Jonas, Kai J., "Moral Courage Training Programs as a Means of Overcoming Societal Crises," in Jonas, Kai J. and Morton, Thomas A. (eds.), *Restoring Civil Societies: The Psychology of Intervention and Engagement Following Crisis* (West Sussex, UK: John Wiley & Sons), 265–283.

[43] Brandstätter, Veronika, "Kleine Schritte statt Heldentaten. Ein Training zur F€orderung von Zivilcourage gegen Fremdenfeindlichkeit" [Small Steps instead of Heroic Deeds. A Training to Increase Moral Courage against Xenophobia] in Jonas, Kai J., Boos, M., and Brandst€atter, V. (eds.), *Zivilcourage trainieren! Theorie und Praxis* [Training Moral Courage: Theory and Practice] (G€ottingen: Hogrefe, 2007), 263–322.

[44] Brandstätter, Veronika and Jonas, Kai J., "Moral Courage Training Programs as a Means of Overcoming Societal Crises," in Jonas, Kai J. and Morton, Thomas A. (eds.), *Restoring Civil Societies: The Psychology of Intervention and Engagement Following Crisis* (West Sussex, UK: John Wiley & Sons), 265–283, 273.

often remain passive simply because they lack the knowledge of how to activate the emergency system.

What is important about this is that it reinforces the point mentioned above that lack of knowledge, and connected to that low self-efficacy beliefs, about how to handle emergency situations is a significant part of the problem. I imagine that some of the tips they give about what to do or not do in a situation of violence are likely to be new to you, the reader, as well. Without some training, how could you be expected to know all these things?

The second component is the use of role-playing and mental simulations to simulate situations of harassment and violence, so people can try out different ways to respond to such situations. Of interest here is that "participants practice useful de-escalating behavioral strategies in different role-playing situations (e.g. inviting the insulted victim to leave the situation; speaking up in a non-aggressive way; seeking collaborators; confusing the perpetrator by doing something unexpected). Mental simulation is highly effective not only in promoting high goal commitment but also in supporting successful goal achievement."[45] Role-playing the tactics gives a chance to practice them and get feedback on what might be the most effective response, and how best to carry it out. The use of mental simulation is also an important part of developing skillfulness more broadly. The third component is for the participants to form some specific goal and implementation intentions that are relevant to their personal situations, in the manner documented by Gollwitzer.[46]

This is a great example of deliberate practice aimed at overcoming a specific moral weakness. There is also some evidence of their effectiveness, though of course it is harder to gauge as we cannot simply place the participants in dangerous situations to see what happens. But participants in the training had much stronger self-efficacy beliefs about their abilities to intervene even months after the program, and we know the importance of those beliefs from the prior discussion of overcoming the bystander effect. Memory tests also showed that they had a high retention of the information provided in the training, which Brandstätter and Jonas note "is important in that the greater mental presence of the concept of moral

[45] Brandstätter, Veronika and Jonas, Kai J., "Moral Courage Training Programs as a Means of Overcoming Societal Crises," in Jonas, Kai J. and Morton, Thomas A. (eds.), *Restoring Civil Societies: The Psychology of Intervention and Engagement Following Crisis* (West Sussex, UK: John Wiley & Sons), 265–283, 277.

[46] See also Fossheim, Hallvard J., "Virtue Ethics and Everyday Strategies," *Association Revue Internationale de Philosophie*, 267 (2014), 65–82.

courage is an important prerequisite for strengthening the corresponding behavior."[47] The training has helped make the concept of moral courage more accessible, thus it should make the participants more likely to see situations through this perspective. After seeing such a program laid out, it certainly seems difficult to expect untrained people to reliably act well in such situations. In which case, it is no surprise that people are generally not intervening when they should, as they do not have the skills and corresponding self-efficacy beliefs they would need to reliably respond well.

Finally, the automaticity that comes with deliberate practice and skill development can also have positive indirect effects, like in overcoming the effect of mood on helping behavior.[48] Isen et al. found that you could induce a good mood in someone with a small gift, and that those in a good mood helped more often when presented with an opportunity soon after receiving the gift.[49] As Alfano notes, it seems like the evidence from several experiments of this kind point to an elevated mood making one more open to new experiences and opportunities, rather than narrowly promoting just helping behavior.[50] A bad mood, by contrast, makes us more closed off to new experiences or opportunities. Forgas et al. studied the effects of positive moods on customer service behavior by employees in a department store.[51] Coinciding with the aforementioned studies, they found that positive moods did have an effect on the customer service behavior of short-term (i.e. less experienced) employees, as the positive mood led to more helpful behaviors than when the salesperson was in a neutral or negative mood. However, positive moods showed no effect on the behavior of the longer-term (i.e. more experienced) employees, who had similar levels of helping behavior regardless of their mood. What accounts for the difference between the two groups? Forgas et al. draw upon the Affect Infusion Model:

---

[47] Brandstätter, Veronika and Jonas, Kai J., "Moral Courage Training Programs as a Means of Overcoming Societal Crises," in Jonas, Kai J. and Morton, Thomas A. (eds.), *Restoring Civil Societies: The Psychology of Intervention and Engagement Following Crisis* (West Sussex, UK: John Wiley & Sons), 265–283, 278.

[48] For more on moods and helping behavior, see Miller, Christian, *Moral Character: An Empirical Theory* (Oxford: Oxford University Press, 2013).

[49] Isen, A., Clark, M., and Schwartz, M., "Duration of the Effect of Good Mood on Helping: 'Footprints on the Sands of Time'," *Journal of Personality and Social Psychology*, 34 (1976), 385–393.

[50] Alfano, Mark, *Character as Moral Fiction* (Cambridge: Cambridge University Press, 2013), 46–48.

[51] Forgas, Joseph P., Dunn, Elizabeth, and Granland, Stacey, "Are You Being Served ...? An Unobtrusive Experiment of Affective Influences on Helping in a Department Store," *European Journal of Social Psychology*, 38 (2008), 333–342. This, and the studies by Cramer et al. and Forgas et al. above, were brought to my attention in a talk by Matthew Taylor ("Situationism and the Problem of Moral Improvement," APA Pacific Division Meeting, San Francisco, 2016).

The AIM specifically predicts that constructive processing is a necessary prerequisite for affect infusion to occur. When people can employ a routine, direct access process to produce a response, no constructive thinking is required and so affect priming is unlikely to influence the response. In our case, highly experienced employees are more likely to possess a rich repertoire of well-rehearsed responses to customer requests and so they need not engage in constructive, memory-based processing in deciding how to respond.

The difference relates to the effect mood has on our dual-processing system. The "constructive" process is deliberate processing, whereas the "direct access" process refers to automatic processing. It appears that deliberate processing will take the affective information into account as a potentially relevant factor, even though it is not relevant, but that automatic processing bypasses this. Thus, more experienced employees, due to their increased level of skill, are able to handle most customer questions with automaticity, and thus avoid being influenced by mood (even though they were not being trained specifically to avoid this influence). Not only is it an interesting effect of skilled training, but it is a nice example of a bias introduced by deliberative processing that can be avoided by automatic processes.

This is, of course, not an exhaustive list of concerns raised by situationism, nor possible strategies for responding to them. But it should suffice to show that there are plenty of resources for the skill model of virtue in responding to situationism, and for helping people to improve their skillfulness in virtue. However, my line of response might introduce a further worry, which is that it would take too much training to cover all the situational influences that can influence us negatively.[52] This is a fair worry, but I think a few points will mitigate against this worry. To start, we should focus on the problems of greatest concern from the standpoint of morality, and the dispositions that contribute to them. In other words, focus on the dispositions that lead to situations like in the Milgram experiment, as the level of potential harm there was significant. Worrying about whether people are polite enough to pick up someone's dropped papers, which is hardly much of a moral concern even if it falls under the broad umbrella of 'helping behavior', because of trivial influences like finding a dime or coming out of a bathroom, seem to me to be making much ado about nothing. Focusing on the most potentially damaging dispositions should alleviate the worry that we have to be informed about every possible surprising disposition. In addition, it helps that some

[52] My thanks to an anonymous reader for pushing this worry.

important strategies for changing behavior, like the use of implementation intentions, are applicable to a variety of problematic dispositions.

Even after narrowing the scope of our concern for the purposes of moral training, it might appear that we still have an awful lot of training left to do. This seems right to me, though I think what would help alleviate this problem is better moral training throughout our lives. For example, the bystander effect is a common enough occurrence to worry about, especially since in some situations it can have serious, even life-threatening, impacts on people. A good time to be learning about this effect and how to resist it, though, is during our teenage (or earlier) years in school. The reason for this is that bullying is a pervasive problem in schools, and such behavior frequently occurs with bystanders who do not intervene to help. Thornberg and Jungert studied the bystander effect in bullying situations, and found that a significant factor that was positively associated with those who intervened to help was self-efficacy beliefs.[53] That is, those adolescents who had strong beliefs about their ability to successfully intervene were more motivated to actually help, and this is a similar finding to that of Brandstätter and Jonas's work on moral courage training. Those who lacked such beliefs did not see intervention as feasible, even if they knew it was the right thing to do, and so did not strive to intervene. I suspect attempts at moral training stop too often at having mere goal intentions or appropriate attitudes and miss the kind of training that would be needed to actually realize such intentions. It would be a great benefit for adolescents to get this kind of training in school, to curb the pervasive harm of bullying, and likely there are other kinds of moral training we should be receiving long before we reach adulthood.

Moral Disengagement and the Situationist Challenge

There is another factor that was significant in Thornberg and Jungert's study on bullying, though for it being positively associated with pro-bullying behavior instead, and that is moral disengagement. While some of our moral weaknesses are now well known thanks to the situationist debate, moral disengagement has received relatively little discussion, especially given how powerful it is at enabling immoral behavior. One notable exception is a discussion by Merritt, Doris, and Harman in their summary

---

[53] Thornberg, Robert and Jungert, Tomas, "Bystander Behavior in Bullying Situations: Basic Moral Sensitivity, Moral Disengagement and Defender Self-Efficacy," *Journal of Adolescence*, 36:3 (2013), 475–483.

of character and the situationist debate, as they mention a similar phenomenon (though they call it by a different name). But before I discuss
their view, and what I think goes wrong with it, I will provide an overview
of moral disengagement as it is found in the psychology literature.

To understand the phenomenon of moral disengagement, we return to
self-regulation. Goal setting and striving does take on an added dimension
when the goals in question are moral. It is important of course to have
appropriate moral standards, and much of ethical theory and practical ethics
is devoted to figuring these out.[54] However, this is clearly not sufficient,
because of the phenomenon of moral disengagement, which refers to the
various psychological processes by which we convince ourselves that some
action that we have taken, or will take, does not violate our personal moral
standards, even when it blatantly does so.[55] Albert Bandura is well-known
for his work on moral disengagement, where he shows that whether internalized moral standards can effectively guide someone's conduct depends in
large part on the activation of self-regulatory mechanisms. When we feel that
we are keeping to our moral standards, our actions can provide us with a
positive self-evaluation. On the other hand, insofar as we feel that an action
violates our moral standards, this will trigger self-sanctions – either helping
to deter the action ahead of time, or triggering feelings of guilt about it after
the fact (and hopefully a different course of action in the future). These
positive or negative self-evaluations are what provide the motivation to
engage in future acts of self-regulation. Moral disengagement interrupts this
process, by reframing our action in such a way that it no longer appears to
violate our standards, and hence no self-sanctions are triggered in response.
The problem is not that our standards are changing, but rather there is a
failure to see a conflict between those standards and our actions that would
otherwise trigger the self-sanctioning process.

So, internalizing moral standards can help guide our conduct, but
only if we also sanction ourselves on the basis of those standards.[56]

---

[54] As mentioned in an earlier chapter, by 'moral standards' I do not intend to set up a contrast with
'immoral standards'. Rather, I mean to refer to those standards by which we make evaluative
judgments with respect to moral actions.

[55] See Bandura, Albert, "Moral Disengagement in the Perpetration of Inhumanities," *Personality and
Social Psychology Review*, 3 (1999)[Special Issue on Evil and Violence] 193–209. Also, Bandura,
Albert "Selective Moral Disengagement in the Exercise of Moral Agency," *Journal of Moral
Education*, 31:2 (2002), 101–119. For a related concept, see Tenbrunsel, Ann E. and Messick,
David M., "Ethical Fading: The Role of Self-Deception in Unethical Behavior," *Social Justice
Research*, 17:2 (2004), 223–236.

[56] This is the case regardless of the appropriateness of the standards, as any internalized standards will
only help to guide conduct if people are willing to sanction themselves, like in feeling a guilty

Unfortunately, there are many ways to evade this self-sanctioning process. For example, Nazi officials in concentration camps often claimed they were not responsible for the atrocities committed because they were just following orders, implying that if anyone is responsible for violating moral standards it is those giving the orders. However, we need not rely only on such dramatic examples to witness moral disengagement, for the same tactic of displacing responsibility occurs frequently in immoral behavior perpetrated by corporations, where employees who engage in harmful conduct defend themselves by stating that they were just doing what they were told to do by the corporate executives.[57]

Importantly, moral disengagement is different from having inappropriate moral standards, since the disengagement is relative to one's own moral standards (however appropriate or corrupt they may be). Of course, it is not sufficient to just be morally engaged, as one needs to be engaged with appropriate moral standards. But this other half of moral behavior, preventing disengagement, is a relatively neglected topic in contemporary ethics, which is especially surprising given that widespread moral wrongdoing often involves moral disengagement. Furthermore, moral disengagement is not the same as *akrasia* or weakness of will, which is a more widely discussed phenomena. In that case, you view some course of action as right, but cannot bring yourself to do it, and as such you acknowledge having done the wrong thing. Here the failure would be one of self-control when you recognize the conflict. By contrast, moral disengagement prevents you from acknowledging that there is a conflict, for you do not view your behavior as a violation of your moral standards.[58]

What follows are six of the most significant processes by which people become disengaged from their moral standards, though I will be grouping them a little differently from Bandura.[59]

1. Moral Justification: While the use of moral reasoning is often extolled as the best means for determining what is morally right, what goes less noticed is the use of moral reasoning as a means to cover up immoral

conscience, for violating the standards. If one does not feel bad for having violated a held standard, as a result of disengagement, then that standard will not end up helping to guide conduct.

[57] This seems fairly widespread in business. See for example, Moore, Celia, "Moral Disengagement in Processes of Organizational Corruption," *Journal of Business Ethics*, 80, (2008), 129–139; and Detert, James R., Trevino, Linda Klebe, and Sweitzer, Vicki L., "Moral Disengagement in Ethical Decision Making: A Study of Antecedents and Outcomes," *Journal of Applied Psychology*, 93 (2008), 374–391.

[58] For brevity's sake, I will often refer to moral disengagement as just 'disengagement'.

[59] In Bandura, 1999, he groups the first three together, and the last three together. I favor a slightly different categorization, though nothing crucial hinges on this.

behavior. Bandura aptly cites Voltaire's quote that "[t]hose who can make you believe absurdities can make you commit atrocities." Lots of ideologies, especially nationalistic and religious, have been used throughout history to make people believe that immoral conduct is actually morally justified. It is a way of convincing people that no moral standards have been violated, rendering the action essentially harmless.[60] Admittedly, if the behavior really is immoral, then no adequate justification can truly be given for it. But reasoning only needs to be persuasive, not true, to influence people's behavior. Thus, engaging in moral debate does not necessarily reflect a desire to discover or encourage appropriate moral behavior.

2. Advantageous Comparison: Advantageous comparison is a way of acknowledging that harm is being done, but nevertheless making it acceptable by comparison to the alternatives. This makes it related to moral justification, for as Bandura notes, advantageous comparison draws heavily on utilitarian reasoning, since the utilitarian approach can allow for harmful conduct if it produces more overall utility than the alternatives. For example, the United States attempted to defend its bombing of Hiroshima and Nagasaki on the grounds that as bad as that was, it would be worse in terms of human casualties if the war continued. Of course, such calculations are open to numerous problems of bias and uncertainty, but part of how it works is to scare people into submission with the prediction that something much worse might happen otherwise.[61]

With regard to these first two forms of disengagement, Bandura points out what they have in common:

> Investing harmful conduct with high moral purpose not only eliminates self-censure. It engages self-approval in the service of destructive exploits. What was once morally condemnable, becomes a source of self-valuation. Functionaries work hard to become proficient at them and take pride in their destructive accomplishments.[62]

---

[60] 'Harm' should be broadly construed as to include whatever a moral theory deems unfavorable, such as deontologists viewing it as bad when someone's autonomy is violated, rather than construing it narrowly as an application of consequentialism specifically.

[61] Granted, indirect utilitarians will not endorse doing utility calculations as a decision procedure, if the adoption of that procedure actually turns out to lead to worse consequences in the long-run. However, even that indirect assessment of the utility produced by alternative decision procedures is still subject to problems of bias and uncertainty. In the end, the point is not what implications this might have for utilitarianism specifically, but rather to note that this is an easily abused form of reasoning that is nevertheless commonly used and accepted.

[62] Bandura, Albert, "Moral Disengagement in the Perpetration of Inhumanities," *Personality and Social Psychology Review*, 3:3 (1999), 193–209 196.

It is interesting to note that a lot of work usually needs to be done to bypass internal moral sanctions, and that the most powerful way to do this is by moral discourse. Thus, training people to engage in more complex moral reasoning could sometimes result in the opposite of the desired effect.

This is reminiscent of some of Rousseau's critiques of reason and philosophical discourse, in which he argues that it is not uncommon for us to have an initial sympathetic or empathetic reaction to the distress of another but then for us to rationalize not acting on that reaction:

> It is reason that engenders self-respect, and reflection that confirms it: it is reason which turns man's mind back upon itself, and divides him from everything that could disturb or afflict him. It is philosophy that isolates him, and bids him say, at sight of the misfortunes of others: "Perish if you will, I am secure." Nothing but such general evils as threaten the whole community can disturb the tranquil sleep of the philosopher, or tear him from his bed. A murder may with impunity be committed under his window; he has only to put his hands to his ears and argue a little with himself, to prevent nature, which is shocked within him, from identifying itself with the unfortunate sufferer.[63]

It is worth highlighting that these first two forms of moral disengagement rely on deliberate forms of cognitive processing, which shows that the problem is not merely with automatic processes leading us astray. While deliberative process can be used to correct for errors in automatic processes, they can also be used to short-circuit the self-sanctioning process.

The next two disengagement practices, by contrast, serve instead to minimize one's awareness of harm, without necessarily engaging self-approval.

3. Euphemistic Labeling: Euphemistic labeling is a matter of substituting a word or phrase that connotes harmful or immoral behavior with another word or phrase that does not. Examples abound: the killing of innocent civilians in times of war is referred to instead as 'collateral damage', the killing of criminals is referred to as 'capital punishment', firing employees in corporations is referred to as 'career alternative enhancement' etc. Language is thus sanitized of its potential to indicate harm or immorality, and thus avoids any engagement of self-sanction, by using terms that abstract away from the problematic implications.

---

[63] Rousseau, Jean-Jacques, *Origin of Inequality*, GDH Cole (trans), (London: Cosmo Classics, 2005), 52–53.

4. Disregard or Distortion of Consequences: Related to some extent to the earlier form of weighing consequences in the attempt to find an advantageous comparison, is the distortion or complete disregard of the harmful consequences of one's actions. However, this refers more specifically to the non-discursive ways in which harms are ignored. For example, it is well documented that people are more responsive to suffering that is visible and immediate, than suffering that occurs remotely or much later in time. Bureaucracies with hierarchical chains of command, like in government and business, can serve to remove people to some extent from any harmful consequences that they play a role in producing, given their remoteness to the effects produced in the end. Thus, these two mechanisms introduce moral 'blind spots', where we are aware of our behavior, but blinded to the moral implications of it.

The final two forms of moral disengagement by contrast allow harm to be acknowledged but keep self-sanctions from triggering by either removing one's own agency in the production of harm, or by denying the moral status of those being harmed.

5. Displacement or Diffusion of Responsibility: Related to the point above regarding collective action, much wrongdoing is the product of many people acting in concert, and as such responsibility for one's own role in the wrongdoing may be displaced or diffused to others. This is the example used previously of those who try to deny responsibility for violating moral standards by displacing responsibility on those giving the orders. Another classic example of this is the Milgram experiment on obedience, where people were willing to give harmful shocks to others so long as the person running the experiment took responsibility for what happened. Responsibility, though, is not always completely displaced on to another. Sometimes it can be diffused amongst a group through a division of labor. As Bandura notes: "[w]hen everyone is responsible, no one really feels responsible. Social organizations go to great lengths to devise mechanisms for obscuring responsibility for decisions that will affect others adversely."[64] If you do not feel you are responsible for some harmful action, then your own self-sanctions will be bypassed, and can often also result in criticizing those upon whom you have displaced responsibility.

6. Dehumanization: Finally, one can become disengaged by taking a certain perspective on the recipients of the harmful conduct. By viewing the victims as less than fully human, and therefore less entitled to moral

---

[64] Bandura, Albert, "Moral Disengagement in the Perpetration of Inhumanities," *Personality and Social Psychology Review*, 3:3 (1999), 198.

protection, one can evade triggering the self-sanctioning process. Wartime propaganda, for example, often portrays the enemy with bestial qualities, to make them out to be less than fully human. More commonly than that, though, "[b]ureaucratization, automation, urbanization and high geographical mobility lead people to relate to each other in anonymous, impersonal ways. In addition, social practices that divide people into in-group and out-group members produce human estrangement that fosters dehumanization."[65] It is a way of viewing victims as outside the moral community, such that it does not matter what happens to them. This becomes especially problematic if one also places blame on the victims for what happened to them.

Finally, it is important to point out that disengagement will likely be gradual, such that it might not even be noticed by the people it is happening to. If a small violation of one's standards repeatedly fails to trigger self-sanction, then that makes it easier to take a slightly greater violation and still avoid self-sanctions.[66] This can make it much harder to detect, since some of the steps towards disengagement will seem innocuous. It is essentially a process of disengagement through habituation. One of the reasons why it is worth focusing on habitual moral disengagement as a vice is that it threatens adherence to any of our moral standards. By contrast, someone with a bad habit of lying will certainly struggle with honesty, but this does not necessarily create problems for other virtues such as being kind.[67]

While the phenomenon of moral disengagement has received surprisingly little attention in ethics, Merritt, Doris, and Harman in their discussion of the situationist debate do make mention of a phenomenon where people seem to genuinely endorse certain norms while acting in a way that violates those norms, which they suggest labeling as "moral dissociation."[68] However, there is no need to coin a new term for this, as the phenomenon has already been identified as moral disengagement. Strangely, their article makes no mention of Bandura's work on this, or

---

[65] Bandura, Albert, "Moral Disengagement in the Perpetration of Inhumanities," *Personality and Social Psychology Review*, 3:3 (1999), 200.

[66] Bandura, Albert, "Moral Disengagement in the Perpetration of Inhumanities," *Personality and Social Psychology Review*, 3:3 (1999), 203.

[67] Granted, we can imagine some possible situations in which the presence of one vice interferes with the exercise of another virtue (such as when kindness requires telling a hard truth), but that is not the case in every situation, and so it does not so directly interfere with the exercise of any virtue when compared to disengagement.

[68] Merritt, Maria W., Doris, John M., and Harman, Gilbert, "Character," in Doris, John Michael (ed.), *The Moral Psychology Handbook* (Oxford: Oxford University Press, 2010), 355–401, 363.

any of the other moral disengagement literature, despite this phenomenon being the object of their attention throughout most of their article. This definitely hinders their repeated attempts to explain the phenomenon. First, they turn their attention to an article by Sabini and Silver that purports to explain all instances of this phenomenon as based in a fear of embarrassment.[69] Sabini and Silver also make no reference to any of the literature on moral disengagement. I think Merritt et al. are right to critique this attempt to find a one-size-fits-all explanation of this phenomenon, and not just because some of the experiments cannot be explained this way (like in the dime and lawnmower examples), but also because the mechanisms of moral disengagement do not necessarily have anything to do with embarrassment.

But Merritt et al. do not fare much better in their own approach when they try to explain it in terms of a misdirection of one's attention (i.e. away from the relevant factors and on to something irrelevant instead). This approach misses the way that internalized moral standards help to keep us in check, since it does not pick up on the different mechanisms for inducing moral disengagement (denying harm is caused at all, denying one's role in the production of harm, justifying the harm as overall justified, or treating those harmed as if they deserved it). Moral disengagement theory already provides an explanation of the phenomenon they are interested in.

Merritt et al. also focus on the role automatic processing plays in getting us to violate our moral standards without our awareness. They put this in terms of 'incongruency', where incongruency "involves a relation between (1) automatic processes likely to influence a subject's behavior on normatively significant occasions of action, and (2) normative commitments of the subject, such that (3) if the subject knew about (1), he or she would reject (1) in light of (2)."[70] They claim this will be a problem for "the model of virtuous practical rationality – i.e. practical wisdom – as the harmonious interrelation of reflective deliberation and habitual sensibilities," since there is frequently a disconnection between the two.[71] So insofar as situational

---

[69] Sabini, John and Silver, Maury, "Lack of Character? Situationism Critiqued," *Ethics*, 115:3 (2005), 535–562.

[70] Merritt, Maria W., Doris, John M., and Harman, Gilbert, "Character," in John Michael Doris (ed.), *The Moral Psychology Handbook* (Oxford: Oxford University Press, 2010), 355–401, 375. As they note on pages 376–377, automaticity does not cause incongruency, though it does open the door to it.

[71] Merritt, Maria W., Doris, John M., and Harman, Gilbert, "Character," in John Michael Doris (ed.), *The Moral Psychology Handbook* (Oxford: Oxford University Press, 2010), 355–401, 375.

influences affect us through automatic processing, it undermines the ideal of virtue where virtue involves seeing what you have most reason to do in the situation. However, they do claim that if you can use deliberate reasoning to counteract those situational influences, then there is still a role for practical reason to play in an account of virtue. Hopefully, all the examples of deliberate intervention discussed above make good on this possibility. On the other hand, their analysis also suffers from placing the weight of the problems on automatic processes, which neglects the ways in which deliberative processes are engaged in some of the most powerful forms of moral disengagement, such as with moral justification and advantageous comparison.

It is also worth pointing out that a greater focus on the phenomenon of moral disengagement will have some further implications for the current 'situationist' critique of virtue ethics. Some of the social psychology experiments seem to focus more on matters of etiquette than morality, like in stopping to help someone pick up something the experimenter dropped. On the other hand, with regard to the experiments focused on moral behavior, it is certainly disconcerting to learn that ambient smells and sounds can exert any level of influence over whether we act kindly or not.[72] But an awful lot of ink has been spilled on this topic relative to the influence many of these kind of situational variables have on fairly trivial forms of moral behavior (e.g. those that border on etiquette), like stopping to help someone pick up some dropped papers. The kind of experiments that are most worrisome are those like the Milgram experiment, where situational factors influence people to do very harmful things. However, notice that once we are focused on this kind of situation, we are now dealing with situations that can be explained by the mechanisms of moral disengagement.

So, one important lesson of the situationist critique is that you cannot expect people to exhibit good behavior across a variety of situations if people are not actively resisting moral disengagement. As Bandura notes, "[s]elective activation and disengagement of personal control permits different types of conduct by persons with the same moral standards under different circumstances."[73] After all, if we are starting with people who are unaware they have certain weaknesses, and have taken no steps to try to

---

[72] Though, utilitarianism aside, it is common to view examples of kindness, like being more charitable, as 'imperfect' duties – that is, things we should do sometimes but for which we are not obligated to do all the time. Hence, the really worrisome situational factors would be those that lead us to violate moral obligations that are required of us most of the time – like not hurting others.

[73] Bandura, Albert, "Moral Disengagement in the Perpetration of Inhumanities," *Personality and Social Psychology Review*, 3:3 (1999), 193–209 194.

prevent themselves from acting on those weaknesses, is it any surprise that they end up acting on those weaknesses? However, we should not be overly pessimistic about this result, as by itself it does not tell us anything about the extent to which we can correct for those weaknesses. Virtue theory would thus be well served by paying more attention to how one can resist moral disengagement, especially since disengagement usually happens as a result of being habituated in a particular way.

How can moral disengagement be resisted? Helpfully Bandura notes that there is some hope, for "[p]roactive moral action is regulated in large part by resolute *engagement* of the mechanisms of moral agency. In the exercise of proactive morality, people act in the name of humane principles when social circumstances dictate expedient, transgressive, and detrimental conduct."[74] Some examples of how people can remain engaged include:

- Avoid using good social ends to justify harmful means
- Being willing at times to put the interests of others ahead of one's own
- Always accepting responsibility for one's actions
- Being empathetic to the sufferings of others[75]
- Focus on what we have in common as humans, rather than our differences
- In collective action, increase accountability, by engaging for example in participative goal setting[76]

Another example, which Paul Bloomfield helpfully discusses in the context of virtue ethics, is Judith Herman's discussion of a group of Vietnam veterans who employed a variety of specific strategies to avoid becoming dehumanized during the war, and thus managed to avoid committing atrocities or developing post-traumatic stress disorder (PTSD) as a

---

[74] Bandura, Albert, "Moral Disengagement in the Perpetration of Inhumanities," *Personality and Social Psychology Review*, 3:3 (1999), 193–209, 203.

[75] For evidence that those who are more empathetic are less likely to morally disengage, since it is more difficult for them to ignore harm to others or to dehumanize them, see Detert, James R., Trevino, Linda Klebe, and Sweitzer, Vicki L., "Moral Disengagement in Ethical Decision Making: A Study of Antecedents and Outcomes," *Journal of Applied Psychology*, 93 (2008), 374–391.

[76] In general, if you participate in setting the goals, it will be harder for you to displace the responsibility for the outcomes of pursuing those goals on other people. Adam Barsky discusses an interesting example of this in the work of Ludwig and Geller. They found that participative goal setting decreased injurious accidents among pizza delivery drivers, by promoting the goal of coming to a complete stop at intersections. Interestingly, this had the side effect of increased safety belt and turn signal use, which also helped to decrease injuries. Barsky, Adam, "Investigating the Effects of Moral Disengagement and Participation on Unethical Work Behavior," *Journal of Business Ethics*, 104 (2011), 59–75. Ludwig, Timothy D. and Geller, E. Scott, "Assigned versus Participatory Goal Setting and Response Generalization," *Journal of Applied Psychology*, 82 (1997), 253–261.

result.[77] For example, she points out that "[t]hey showed a high degree of responsibility for the protection of others as well as themselves, avoiding unnecessary risks and on occasion challenging orders that they believed to be ill-advised."[78] So there are proactive strategies one can take to remain engaged, and with practice these strategies become habits.

Finally, these strategies for resistance, however, should not be conceived as occurring only at the level of the individual. After all, disengagement is mainly fostered by social, political, and economic structures. For example, much of corporate culture includes mechanisms that foster disengagement. Should we change the corporate culture, or try to make employees more resistant to disengagement? While we can pursue both, likely it will be more effective in the long run to change the corporate culture (especially given turnover in employees). This connects to the idea that striving for moral behavior requires a supportive social environment (or at least one that does not actively foster inappropriate moral standards or moral disengagement). This supports Aristotle's view that people flourish in communities, and you need supportive communities to help develop virtue. Furthermore, this should be a reminder that communities bear some degree of responsibility for how their members turn out, and that power dynamics will need to be taken into consideration. As Bandura aptly concludes: "[r]egardless of whether inhumane practices are institutional, organizational or individual, it should be made difficult for people to remove humanity from their conduct."[79] This point is well-recognized in political philosophy and theory, for example in Hannah Arendt's concept of the "banality of evil," insofar as she pointed out that atrocities can be perpetuated by seemingly ordinary people (basically acting in a morally disengaged way), rather than evil only being carried out by 'monstrous' or especially 'vicious' individuals.[80] She also showed how both governmental and economic structures fostered climates of moral disengagement. Thus, dealing with the problem of moral disengagement will also be a task for political philosophers and theorists, working alongside ethicists and moral psychologists. Importantly, our recommendations for how people behave morally will need to reflect how people become morally disengaged, and what strategies are available for countering it.

---

[77] Bloomfield, Paul, *The Virtues of Happiness* (Oxford: Oxford University Press, 2014), 192–193.

[78] Herman, Judith, *Trauma and Recovery* (New York: Basic Books, 1997), 59.

[79] Bandura, Albert, "Moral Disengagement in the Perpetration of Inhumanities," *Personality and Social Psychology Review* 3:3 (1999), 193–209, 207–208.

[80] See Arendt, Hannah, *Eichmann in Jerusalem: A Report on the Banality of Evil* (New York: Viking, 1963).

Situationism and the Skill Model of Epistemic Virtue

The situationist critique has also been extended from doubts about the possession of moral virtues to similar concerns about the possession of intellectual virtues. Alfano has pushed this critique, though he focused mainly on virtue responsibilism, rather than virtue reliabilism.[81] Given the strong connections drawn between virtue reliabilism and skill, such as with Sosa's 'AAA' account of performance normativity, my focus in this section will be instead with a recent paper by Lauren Olin and John Doris, who extend Alfano's critique to encompass virtue reliabilism as well. Furthermore, while the automaticity of mental processes in general is one of the sources of the situationist concerns, such as the 'incongruency' discussed above by Merritt et al., Olin and Doris discuss the situationist critique specifically with respect to expertise and virtue epistemology.[82] As they note, the situationist critique is more directly targeted in virtue epistemology at virtue responsibilism, which focuses on the kind of domain-global cross-situationally consistent character traits that are most challenged by the social psychology experiments. However, they attempt to broaden the situationist critique to include virtue reliabilism by undermining some claims to reliability in our cognitive processes. They go on to discuss how one might account for some of the unreliability by arguing that it is mainly unreliability in ordinary cognitive processes, and that intellectual virtues should be understood as the result of training such that expertise is a good model for intellectual virtue.

Having said that, they then attempt to undermine reliability even in the domain of expertise. While they initially introduce skepticism of experts when experts are picked out merely in terms of social recognition, they thankfully realize that this was never a good way of identifying experts in the first place. They move on to discuss insights like the approximate 10,000 hours of practice that go into developing expertise, and even mention the concept of deliberate practice. Then they try to sow doubts here, claiming that:

> the record on expertise remains mixed. For example, physicians don't always get better at diagnosing heart sounds as a result of years in practice;

---

[81] See Alfano, Mark, "Expanding the Situationist Challenge to Responsibilist Virtue Epistemology," *The Philosophical Quarterly*, 62 (2012), 223–249. For a reply, see King, Nathan, "Responsibilist Virtue Epistemology: A Reply to the Situationist Challenge," *The Philosophical Quarterly*, 64 (2014), 243–253.

[82] Olin, Lauren and Doris, John M., "Vicious Minds: Virtue Epistemology, Cognition, and Skepticism," *Philosophical Studies*, 168 (2014), 665–692.

on the contrary, their performance can decrease gradually with the accumulation of experience (Choudhry et al. 2005; Ericsson et al. 2007, cf. Ericsson 2008).[83]

This, however, paints a misleading picture of the record on expertise, and reflects a misunderstanding of the literature and the role of deliberate practice. The sources they cite point to groups of doctors that do not keep up with training and recertification despite the constant advances in medicine. Ericsson's diagnosis is that while the doctors are logging many hours, they are not engaging in deliberate practice to improve their performance. Given that the field of medicine is advancing, but these doctors are relying on techniques a few decades old or perhaps on information that is now known to be inaccurate, we can account for their decline in performance. As the studies in aging and expertise also point out, as discussed in Chapter 1, deliberate practice is required to maintain one's level of performance. If the doctors are not doing that, then it is to be expected that their performance degrades.

But even if we are not skeptical about expertise, Olin and Doris think that the reliance on the expertise literature opens up a different kind of skepticism – a skepticism about whether most people have knowledge, given that most of us might at best possess expertise only in a couple of domains. They claim that this "will not quite be skepticism, since there will be some knowledge, possessed by those fortunate, talented, and diligent enough to become experts. But it will be something closely approaching skepticism, since there will be a lot less knowledge than the non-skeptic supposed."[84]

However, for this argument to work, one has to assume that it takes expertise to have knowledge within a domain, and that is not remotely true of skill. While they might be thinking that if knowledge requires virtue, and virtue is understood on a skill model such that the equivalent of expertise might be required for virtue, this ignores that virtue and skill have always been understood as a matter of degree. Skill acquisition is a process

---

[83] Olin, Lauren and Doris, John M., "Vicious Minds: Virtue Epistemology, Cognition, and Skepticism," *Philosophical Studies*, 168 (2014), 665–692, 676. Choudhry, N. K., Fletcher, R. H., and Soumerai, S. B., "Systematic Review: The Relationship between Clinical Experience and Quality of Health Care," *Annals of Internal Medicine*, 142 (2005), 260–273. Ericsson, K. Anders, Whyte, J., and Ward, P., "Expert Performance in Nursing: Reviewing Research on Expertise in Nursing within the Framework of the Expert-Performance Approach," *ANS Advances in Nursing Science*, 30 (2007), E58–E71. Ericsson, K. Anders, "Deliberate Practice and Acquisition of Expert Performance: A General Overview," *Academic Emergency Medicine*, 15 (2008), 988–994.

[84] Olin, Lauren and Doris, John M., "Vicious Minds: Virtue Epistemology, Cognition, and Skepticism," *Philosophical Studies*, 168 (2014), 665–692, 676.

of improvement in knowing how to act well within a domain. Knowledge involved with accomplishing simple tasks requires only a low level of skill, easily obtained by people with limited experience. But, of course, to know how to tackle more difficult tasks, or know the answers to more complicated questions, within the domain requires more experience and deliberate practice. So, what is implied by this view is not as Olin and Doris suggest that knowledge will only be had by experts, but rather that one's level of skillfulness will be a constraint on how much one can know within a domain.[85] But that will not lead to widespread skepticism about the possession of knowledge.

At this point Olin and Doris seem to suggest that the domain-specific aspect to skill and expertise is itself a problem. While virtue reliabilism might evade some of the force of the situationist critique by focusing on domain-specific, rather than domain-general, virtues, the worry is then that "there's something disappointing about the contemplated decomposition of virtue. Talk of virtues compels at least in part because virtue – be it epistemic or moral – promises progress on unusual problems, in difficult conditions."[86] While the diminished cross-situational reliability might sound disappointing, I suspect that is due to either an overly idealistic conception of virtue or an underappreciation of improvement in skill. Virtue is often discussed as something that once you acquire it, then it can guide you appropriately in whatever situation you face (and hence the claims to cross-situational consistency). But unusual problems or difficult conditions must pose challenges that it will take some experience and practice to figure out how to deal with, else they would not be unusual or difficult. So, virtue cannot be so idealized that it no longer requires experience with these kinds of situations to know how best to handle them. This brings us back to skill acquisition, because improvement in skill can be a matter of being more reliable in familiar conditions

---

[85] Pritchard makes a similar point in discussing what kind of epistemic processes we should recommend people employ, as "it may be that the relevant process is one that the agent cannot master straight away, perhaps because it requires special training or abilities. In such cases, it may be that the optimum process in terms of reliability for this agent at this time is very different to the optimum process simpliciter." Pritchard, Duncan, "Virtue Epistemology and the Acquisition of Knowledge," *Philosophical Explorations*, 8:3 (2005), 229–243, 231. As an example, in his discussion of expertise in medicine, Pritchard claims that "it is not immediately obvious that one should teach the more subtle rules followed by experts to medical students, since only the experts have the wealth of background knowledge available to them that can allow them to utilise these rules effectively. Indeed, the 'cautious' rules already followed by many final-year medical students in this regard may be better rules to follow to begin with." (237)

[86] Olin, Lauren and Doris, John M., "Vicious Minds: Virtue Epistemology, Cognition, and Skepticism," *Philosophical Studies*, 168 (2014), 665–692, 679.

(e.g. driving with greater safety), extending your current level of perform-ance to a difficult condition (e.g. driving as safe in icy conditions as dry conditions), or tackling a more difficult task (e.g. driving while also navigating to a new location). The kind of progress Olin and Doris are talking about is possible, but you still have to work for it. Full epistemic responsibility, like with moral responsibility, will require training both our automatic and deliberative process.[87]

The Rarity of Virtue Revisited

There are ways to overcome the effects of situational influences and surprising dispositions, through self-regulatory strategies, deliberate prac-tice, and skilled training. I take these examples to point to a further reason why we might expect virtue to be rare, at least currently. Given that people do not tend to think of moral virtue development in terms of skill acquisition, people presumably have not been doing the kinds of activities that they would need to engage in to improve their skillfulness in virtue.[88] It seems that frequently people think of virtue training in terms of merely internalizing the right standards. However, the work on implementation intentions shows that much more work needs to be done to effectively implement those standards. It requires you to consider the potential obstacles in your way, and to develop plans ahead of time for how to respond. Specific kinds of skilled training may also be required to effect-ively implement one's goals.

Even then, in the moral case, moral disengagement can disrupt the self-sanctioning process that keeps us in line, even with deeply held moral standards. To the extent that people do not tend to think of moral development in terms of these self-regulation strategies or in terms of skill acquisition (but rather just following a set of internalized 'do not do' rules), people presumably have not been doing the kinds of activities that they would need to engage in to achieve better moral performance. That is, because it has not been well-known what steps are required to overcome the more troublesome obstacles to appropriate moral behavior, people have not usually been taking those steps. So, is it really any surprise that we frequently test low for moral competence?

---

[87] Much more can be said about the epistemic challenge, and the ways to train for epistemic virtue, but such a discussion is beyond the scope of this book.

[88] People may tend to associate virtue and vice with more exceptional deeds, rather than with more mundane day-to-day activities, which would also account for this. My thanks to a reviewer for pointing this out.

While that means that we can expect virtue to be rarer than we might have initially suspected, it also means that the situation can be remedied (at least to some extent) once people learn what steps they need to take to further the development of their virtues. Relatedly, there is evidence in the case of skill acquisition that if parents think that skill is mostly a matter of natural talent, where you either have it or you do not, they are less likely to provide support for skill development, in comparison to those who believe that skill development is more of a matter of practice.[89] One could imagine that a similar situation may occur with virtue development, insofar as parents think of character traits as mostly a matter of natural tempera-ment.[90] So an advantage of viewing moral behavior as a form of expertise is that "moral behavior is pried from the rigidity of personality temperament and put into the realm of learnable behavior. It appears more like behavior in other domains like football or chess, as a set of skills that can be learned."[91] A better account of moral development should thus lead to improvements in moral education and development.[92]

Conclusion

It is of course beyond the scope of this chapter to give a comprehensive overview of all the situational influences and surprising dispositions that might interfere with moral behavior, or of all the strategies involving self-regulation and deliberate practice to resist their effects. But hopefully this limited overview suggests that the skill model of virtue provides many resources to come to grips with the implications of the situationist literature. Beyond that, I think the skill approach gives a different twist to the situationist critique. Instead of viewing situational influences and surprising

---

[89] Jourden, Forest J., Bandura, Albert, and Banfield, Jason T., "The Impact of Conceptions of Ability on Self-Regulatory Factors and Motor Skill," *Journal of Sport & Exercise Psychology*, 8 (1991), 213–226.

[90] I will be exploring this in depth in a grant project on "Understanding Virtue and Virtue Development in the Context of Heritability Information" (with Matthew Vess, Rebecca Brooker, & Jenae Nederhiser), as part of the research initiative on "Genetics and Human Agency."

[91] Darcia Narvaez, "The Neo-Kohlbergian Tradition and Beyond: Schemas, Expertise and Character," in Carlo, Gustav and Pope-Edwards, Carolyn (eds.), *Nebraska Symposium on Motivation, Vol. 51: Moral Motivation through the Lifespan* (Lincoln, NE: University of Nebraska Press, 2005), 119–163, 141.

[92] My goal here is modest, as what I have discussed so far is just the beginning of a program for moral improvement. I do not have the space here to be comprehensive with respect to all the situational factors that may influence us, or all the possible remedies for those factors. But hopefully I have indicated both that remedies are possible, and that the self-regulation and skill acquisition literature should be further canvassed for more solutions.

dispositions as barriers to moral development and acquiring virtue, the skill model of virtue can view the overcoming of these influences and dispositions as representing moral development and the development of virtue. That is, improvements in skill come about through awareness of our errors and limitations, along with deliberate practice and strategies targeted at fixing those errors and expanding our abilities. Without that process, one remains at a fixed level of skill development. In that sense, the situationist literature is helpful in bringing out shortcomings we were not fully aware we had, so that we can begin the process of strategizing how to overcome those shortcomings and increase our skillfulness in virtue.

It is my hope that this book has provided good reasons why virtue should be conceptualized as a skill, but I should note that while I have explored some of the implications of the virtue as skill thesis, by no means do I take myself to have explored them all. In developing this account of virtue as skill, I have argued that it requires us to rethink traditional conceptions of the virtues as well as how the virtues are acquired. In which case, this new framework can provide possibilities for new lines of research in both philosophy and psychology.

References

Achtziger, A. and Gollwitzer, Peter M., "Motivation and Volition in the Course of Action," in Heckhausen, J. and Heckhausen, H. (eds.), *Motivation and Action* (New York: Cambridge University Press, 2007), 202–226.

Alfano, Mark, "Ramsifying Virtue Theory," in Mark Alfano (ed.), *Current Controversies in Virtue Theory* (New York: Routledge, 2015), 124–135.

Character as Moral Fiction (Cambridge: Cambridge University Press, 2013).

"Identifying and Defending the Hard Core of Virtue Ethics," *Journal of Philosophical Research*, 38 (2013), 233–260.

"Expanding the Situationist Challenge to Responsibilist Virtue Epistemology," *The Philosophical Quarterly*, 62 (2012), 223–249.

Angier, Tom, *Techne in Aristotle's Ethics: Crafting the Moral Life* (New York: Continuum, 2010).

Annas, Julia, "Virtue, Skill and Vice," *Ethics & Politics*, XVII:2 (2015), 94–106.

Intelligent Virtue (Oxford: Oxford University Press, 2011).

"The Phenomenology of Virtue," *Phenomenology and the Cognitive Sciences*, 7 (2008), 21–34.

"Virtue Ethics," in Copp, David (ed.), *The Oxford Handbook of Ethical Theory* (Oxford: Oxford University Press, 2006), 515–536.

"The Structure of Virtue," in DePaul, Michael and Zagzebski, Linda (eds.), *Intellectual Virtue* (Oxford: Clarendon Press, 2003), 15–33.

"Virtue as a Skill," *International Journal of Philosophical Studies*, 3:2 (1995), 227–243.

The Morality of Happiness (Oxford: Oxford University Press, 1993).

Arendt, Hannah, *Eichmann in Jerusalem: A Report on the Banality of Evil* (New York: Viking, 1963).

Aristotle, *Nicomachean Ethics* (Grinnell: The Peripatetic Press, 1984).

Badhwar, Neera K., "The Limited Unity of Virtue," *Noûs*, 30:3 (1996), 306–329.

Baehr, Jason, "Character Virtues, Epistemic Agency, and Reflective Knowledge," in Alfano, Mark (ed.), *Current Controversies in Virtue Theory* (New York: Routledge, 2015), 74–86.

The Inquiring Mind: On Intellectual Virtues and Virtue Epistemology (New York: Oxford University Press, 2012).

Bandura, Albert, "Selective Moral Disengagement in the Exercise of Moral Agency," *Journal of Moral Education*, 31:2 (2002), 101–119.

"Moral Disengagement in the Perpetration of Inhumanities," *Personality and Social Psychology Review*, 3:3 (1999), 193–209.

"Social Cognitive Theory of Personality," in Pervin, Lawrence A. and John, Oliver P. (eds.), *Handbook of Personality: Theory and Research* (New York: The Guilford Press, 1999), 154–196.

"Self-Regulation of Motivation through Anticipatory and Self-Reactive Mechanisms," in Dienstbier, R. A. (ed.), *Perspectives on Motivation: Nebraska Symposium on Motivation,* Vol. 38 (Lincoln: University of Nebraska Press, 1991), 69–164.

"Self-Regulation of Motivation and Action through Internal Standards and Goal Systems," in Pervin, Lawrence A. (ed.), *Goal Concepts in Personality and Social Psychology* (London: Lawrence Erlbaum Associates, 1989), 19–85.

Bargh, John, "The Four Horsemen of Automaticity: Awareness, Intention, Efficiency, and Control in Social Cognition," in Wyer, R. S. and Srull, T. K. (eds.), *Handbook of Social Cognition*, Vol. 1 (Hillsdale, NJ: Erlbaum, 1994), 1–40.

Barsky, Adam, "Investigating the Effects of Moral Disengagement and Participation on Unethical Work Behavior," *Journal of Business Ethics*, 104 (2011), 59–75.

Battaly, Heather, "A Pluralist Theory of Virtue," in Alfano, Mark (ed.), *Current Controversies in Virtue Theory* (New York: Routledge, 2015), 7–21.

"What Is Virtue Epistemology?," *Proceedings of the Twentieth World Congress of Philosophy* (2000) www.bu.edu/wcp/Papers/Valu/ValuBatt.htm

"Epistemic Self-Indulgence," *Metaphilosophy*, 41 (2010), 214–234.

Baumeister, Roy F. and Vohs, Kathleen D., "Self-Regulation [Self-Control]," in Peterson, Christopher and Seligman, Martin (eds.), *Character Strengths and Virtues: A Handbook and Classification* (New York: Oxford University Press, 2004), 499–516.

Baumeister, Roy F., Vohs, Kathleen D., and Tice, Dianne M., "The Strength Model of Self-Control," *Current Directions in Psychological Science*, 16:6 (2007), 351–355.

Benner, Patricia, *From Novice to Expert* (New Jersey: Prentice Hall Health, 2001).

Bloom, Benjamin, *Developing Talent in Young People* (New York: Ballantine Books, 1985).

Bloomfield, Paul, *The Virtues of Happiness* (Oxford: Oxford University Press, 2014).

Moral Reality (Oxford: Oxford University Press, 2001).

"Virtue Epistemology and the Epistemology of Virtue," *Philosophy and Phenomenological Research*, 60:1 (2000), 23–43.

Brandstätter, Veronika and Jonas, Kai J., "Moral Courage Training Programs as a Means of Overcoming Societal Crises," in Jonas, Kai J. and Morton, Thomas A. (eds.), *Restoring Civil Societies: The Psychology of Intervention and Engagement Following Crisis* (Hoboken, NJ: John Wiley & Sons, 2012), 265–283.

Brandstätter, Veronika, Jonas, Kai J., Koletzko, Svenja H., and Fischer, Peter, "Self-Regulatory Processes in the Appraisal of Moral Courage Situations," *Social Psychology* , 47:4 (2016), 201–213.

Buchanan, Bruce G., Davis, Randall, and Feigenbaum, Edward A., "Expert Systems: A Perspective from Computer Science," in Ericsson, K. Anders (ed.), *The Cambridge Handbook of Expertise and Expert Performance* (Cambridge: Cambridge University Press, 2006), 705–722.

Büttner, Oliver B., Wieber, Frank, Schulz, Anna Maria, Bayer, Ute C., Florack, Arnd, and Gollwitzer, Peter M., "Visual Attention and Goal Pursuit: Deliberative and Implemental Mindsets Affect Breadth of Attention," *Personality and Social Psychology Bulletin*, 40:10 (2014), 1248–1259.

Cantor, Nancy, "From Thought to Behavior: 'Having' and 'Doing' in the Study of Personality and Cognition," *American Psychologist*, 45:6 (1990), 735–750.

Carver, Charles S. and Scheier, Michael F., "Self-Regulatory Perspectives on Personality," in Millon, Theodore and Lerner, Melvin J. (eds.), *Handbook of Psychology, Vol. 5: Personality and Social Psychology* (Hobokon, NJ: John Wiley & Sons, Inc., 2003), 185–208.

Cassam, Quassim, *Self-Knowledge for Humans* (Oxford: Oxford University Press, 2015).

Chi, Michelene T. H., "Two Approaches to the Study of Experts' Characteristics," in Ericsson, K. Anders (ed.), *The Cambridge Handbook of Expertise and Expert Performance* (Cambridge: Cambridge University Press, 2006), 21–30.

Christen, Markus and Alfano, Mark, "Outlining the Field: A Research Program for Empirically Informed Ethics," in Christen, Markus, van Schaik, Carel, Fischer, Johannes, and Huppenbauer, Markus (eds.), *Empirically Informed Ethics: Morality between Facts and Norms* (Springer, 2014), 3–28.

Christensen, Wayne, Sutton, John, and Mcilwain, Doris J. F., "Cognition in Skilled Action: Meshed Control and the Varieties of Skill Experience," *Mind & Language*, 31:1 (2016), 37–66, 49.

Choudhry, N. K., Fletcher, R. H., and Soumerai, S. B., "Systematic Review: The Relationship between Clinical Experience and Quality of Health Care," *Annals of Internal Medicine*, 142 (2005), 260–273.

Cianciolo, Anna T., Matthew, Cynthia, Sternberg, Robert J., and Wagner, Richard K., "Tacit Knowledge, Practical Intelligence, and Expertise," in Ericsson, K. Anders (ed.), *The Cambridge Handbook of Expertise and Expert Performance* (Cambridge: Cambridge University Press, 2006), 613–632.

Conant, Roger C. and Ashby, W. Ross, "Every Good Regulator of a System Must Be a Model of that System," *International Journal of Systems Science*, 1:2 (1970), 89–97.

Cramer, Robert Ervin, McMaster, M. Rosalie, Bartell, Patricia A., and Dragna, Margurite, "Subject Competence and Minimization of the Bystander Effect," *Journal of Applied Social Psychology*, 18:13 (1988), 1133–1148.

Csikszentmihalyi, Mihay, *Flow: The Psychology of Optimal Experience* (New York: HarperCollins, 1991).

Csikszentmihalyi, Mihaly, Rathunde, Kevin, and Whalen, Samuel, *Talented Teenagers: The Roots of Success and Failure* (New York: Cambridge University Press, 1993).

Darley, J. M. and Batson, C. D., "From Jerusalem to Jericho: A Study of Situational and Dispositional Variables in Helping Behavior," *Journal of Personality and Social Psychology*, 27 (1973), 100–108.

Detert, James R., Trevino, Linda Klebe, and Sweitzer, Vicki L, "Moral Disengagement in Ethical Decision Making: A Study of Antecedents and Outcomes," *Journal of Applied Psychology*, 93 (2008), 374–391.

DeYoung, Colin G., "Cybernetic Big Five Theory," *Journal of Research in Personality*, 56 (2015), 33–58.

DeYoung, Colin G. and Weisberg, Yanna J., "Cybernetic Approaches to Personality and Social Behavior," in M. Snyder and K. Deaux (eds.), *Oxford Handbook of Personality and Social Psychology*, Second Edition, in press (New York: Oxford University Press).

Diedrichsen, Jorn, Shadmehr, Reza, and Ivry, Richard B., "The Coordination of Movement: Optimal Feedback Control and Beyond," *Trends in Cognitive Sciences* 14 (2009), 31–39.

Doris, John, *Lack of Character* (Cambridge: Cambridge University Press, 2002).

Dreyfus, Hubert, "Overcoming the Myth of the Mental: How Philosophers Can Profit from the Phenomenology of Everyday Expertise," *Proceedings and Addresses of the American Philosophical Association*, 79:2 (2005), 47–65.

"Could Anything Be More Intelligible than Everyday Intelligibility? Reinterpreting Division I of Being and Time in the light of Division II," in Faulconer, James E. and Wrathall, Mark A. (eds.), *Appropriating Heidegger* (Cambridge: Cambridge University Press, 2000).

What Computers Still Can't Do: A Critique of Artificial Reason (Cambridge: MIT Press, 1992).

Dreyfus, Hubert and Dreyfus, Stuart, "The Ethical Implications of the Five-Stage Skill-Acquisition Model," *Bulletin of Science, Technology & Society*, 24:3 (2004), 251–264.

"Sustaining Non-Rationalized Practices: Body-Mind, Power, and Situational Ethics."Interview conducted by Bent Flyvbjerg, *Praxis International*, 11 (1991), 93–113.

"Towards a Phenomenology of Ethical Expertise," *Human Studies*, 14 (1991), 229–250.

"What Is Morality: A Phenomenological Account of the Development of Expertise," in Rasmussen, D. (ed.), *Universalism vs. Communitarianism*, (Cambridge, MA: MIT Press, 1990), 237–264.

Mind Over Machine: The Power of Human Intuition and Expertise in the Era of the Computer (Oxford: Basil Blackwell, 1986).

Duckworth, Angela Lee, Grant, Heidi, Loew, Benjamin, Oettingen, Gabriele and Gollwitzer, Peter M., "Self-Regulation Strategies Improve Self-Discipline in Adolescents: Benefits of Mental Contrasting and Implementation Intentions," *Educational Psychology*, 31:1 (2010), 17–26.

Duckworth, Angela and Gross, James J., "Self-Control and Grit: Related but Separable Determinants of Success," *Current Directions in Psychological Science*, 23:5 (2014), 319–325.

Duckworth, Angela Lee and Tsukayama, Eli, "Domain Specificity in Self-Control", in Miller, Christian B., Furr, R. Michael, Knobel, Angela, and Fleeson, William (eds.) *Character: New Directions from Philosophy, Psychology, and Theology* (New York: Oxford University Press, 2015), 393–411.

Endsley, Mica, "Expertise and Situation Awareness," in Ericsson, K. Anders (ed.), *The Cambridge Handbook of Expertise and Expert Performance* (Cambridge: Cambridge University Press, 2006), 633–651.

Ericsson, K. Anders, "Deliberate Practice and Acquisition of Expert Performance: A General Overview," *Academic Emergency Medicine*, 15 (2008), 988–994.

"An Introduction to *Cambridge Handbook of Expertise and Expert Performance*: Its Development, Organization, and Content," in Ericsson, K. Anders (ed.), *The Cambridge Handbook of Expertise and Expert Performance* (Cambridge: Cambridge University Press, 2006), 3–20.

"Protocol Analysis and Expert Thought: Concurrent Verbalizations of Thinking during Experts' Performance on Representative Tasks," in Ericsson, K. Anders (ed.), *The Cambridge Handbook of Expertise and Expert Performance* (Cambridge: Cambridge University Press, 2006), 223–241.

"The Influence of Experience and Deliberate Practice on the Development of Superior Expert Performance," in Ericsson, K. Anders (ed.), *The Cambridge Handbook of Expertise and Expert Performance* (Cambridge: Cambridge University Press, 2006), 683–704.

The Road to Excellence (Lawrence Erlbaum, 1996).

Ericsson, K. Anders, Whyte, J., and Ward, P., "Expert Performance in Nursing: Reviewing Research on Expertise in Nursing Within the Framework of the Expert-Performance Approach," *ANS Advances in Nursing Science*, 30 (2007), E58–E71.

Evans, Jonathan and Stanovich, Keith, "Dual-Process Theories of Higher Cognition: Advancing the Debate," *Perspectives on Psychological Science*, 8:3 (2013), 223–241.

Fairweather, Abrol, "Duhem-Quine Virtue Epistemology," *Synthese*, 187 (2012), 673–692.

Feltovich, Paul J. and Barrows, H. S., "Issues of Generality in Medical Problem Solving," in Schmidt, Henck G. and de Volder, Maurice L. (eds.), *Tutorials in Problem-Based Learning* (Maaastricht, the Netherlands: Van Gorcum, 1984), 128–142.

Feltovich, Paul J., Prietula, Michael J., and Ericsson, K. Anders, "Studies of Expertise from Psychological Perspectives," in Ericsson, K. Anders (ed.), *The Cambridge Handbook of Expertise and Expert Performance* (Cambridge: Cambridge University Press, 2006), 41–68.

Fishbach, Ayelet and Converse, Benjamin A., "Identifying and Battling Temptation," in Vohs, Kathleen D. and Baumeister, Roy F. (eds.), *Handbook of Self-Regulation: Research, Theory, and Applications*, Second Edition (New York: The Guilford Press), 244–260.

Flyvbjerg, Bent, "Phronetic Planning Research: Theoretical and Methodological Reflections," *Planning Theory & Practice*, 5:3 (2004), 283–306.

Making Social Science Matter: Why Social Inquiry Fails and How It Can Succeed Again (Cambridge: Cambridge University Press, 2001).

Forgas, Joseph P., Dunn, Elizabeth, and Granland, Stacey, "Are You Being Served . . .? An Unobtrusive Experiment of Affective Influences on Helping in a Department Store," *European Journal of Social Psychology*, 38 (2008), 333–342.

Fossheim, Hallvard J., "Virtue Ethics and Everyday Strategies," *Association Revue Internationale de Philosophie*, 267 (2014), 65–82.

Fridland, Ellen, "Knowing How: Problems and Considerations," *European Journal of Philosophy*, 23:3 (2015), 703–727.

"They've Lost Control: Reflections on Skill," *Synthese*, 191 (2014), 2729–2750.

"Skill Learning and Conceptual Thought: Making a Way through the Wilderness," in Bashour, B. and Muller, H. (eds.), *Philosophical Naturalism and Its Implications* (New York: Routledge, 2014).

"Problems with Intellectualism," *Philosophical Studies*, 165:3 (2013), 879–891.

Fujita, Kentaro, Trope, Yaacov, Cunningham, William A., and Liberman, Nira, "What Is Control? A Conceptual Analysis," in Sherman, Jeffrey W., Gawronski, Bertram, and Trope, Yaacov, *Dual-Process Theories of the Social Mind* (New York: The Guilford Press, 2014), 50–65.

Gollwitzer, Peter M., "Implementation Intentions: Strong Effects of Simple Plans," *American Psychologist*, 54:7 (1999), 493–503.

"Action Phases and Mind-Sets," in Higgins, E. Tory and Sorrentino, Richard M. (eds.), *Motivation and Cognition: Foundations of Social Behavior*, Vol. 2 (New York: The Guilford Press, 1990), 53–92.

Greco, John, *Achieving Knowledge: A Virtue-Theoretic Account of Epistemic Normativity* (New York: Cambridge University Press, 2010).

Haase, Claudia Maria, Poulin, Michael, and Heckhausen, Jutta, "Engagement and Disengagement Across the Life Span: An Analysis of Two-Process Models of Developmental Regulation," in Greve, W., Rothermund, K., and Wentura, D. (eds.), *The Adaptive Self: Personal Continuity and Intentional Self-Development* (New York: Hogrefe, 2005), 117–135.

Haidt, Jonathan, "The Emotional Dog and Its Rational Tail: A Social Intuitionist Approach to Moral Judgment," *Psychological Review*, 108 (2001), 814–834.

Haidt, Jonathan and Bjorklund, Frederick, "Social Intuitionists Answer Six Questions about Moral Psychology," in Walter Sinnott-Armstrong (ed.), *Moral Psychology, Vol. 2: The Cognitive Science of Morality: Intuition and Diversity* (Cambridge MA: MIT Press, 2008), 181–218.

Haney, C., C. Banks, and P. Zimbardo, 1973, "A Study of Prisoners and Guards in a Simulated Prison," in *Readings about the Social Animal*, Aronson, E. (ed.), Third Edition (San Francisco: Freeman), 52–67.

Harman, Gilbert, "Moral Philosophy Meets Social Psychology: Virtue Ethics and the Fundamental Attribution Error," *Proceedings of the Aristotelian Society*, 99 (1999), 315–331.

The Nature of Morality (Oxford: Oxford University Press, 1977).

Hashem, Ahmad, Chi, Michelene T. H., and Friedman, Charles P., "Medical Errors as a Result of Specialization," *Journal of Biomedical Informatics*, 36 (2003), 61–69.

Heckhausen, Jutta, "The Motivation–Volition Divide and Its Resolution in Action-Phase Models of Developmental Regulation," *Research in Human Development*, 4:3–4 (2007), 163–180.

Herman, Judith, *Trauma and Recovery* (New York: Basic Books, 1997).

Hill, Nicole M. and Schneider, Walter, "Brain Changes in the Development of Expertise: Neuroanatomical and Neurophysiological Evidence about Skill-Based Adaptations," in Ericsson, K. Anders (ed.), *The Cambridge Handbook of Expertise and Expert Performance* (Cambridge: Cambridge University Press, 2006), 653–682.

Hogarth, Robin M., *Educating Intuition* (Chicago: University of Chicago Press, 2000).

Horgan, Terry and Timmons, Mark, "Morphological Rationalism and the Psychology of Moral Judgment," *Ethical Theory and Moral Practice*, 10 (2007) 279–295.

Horn, John and Masunaga, Hiromi, "A Merging Theory of Expertise and Intelligence," in Ericsson, K. Anders (ed.), *The Cambridge Handbook of Expertise and Expert Performance* (Cambridge: Cambridge University Press, 2006), 587–612.

Hunt, Earl, "Expertise, Talent, and Social Encouragement," in Ericsson, K. Anders (ed.), *The Cambridge Handbook of Expertise and Expert Performance* (Cambridge: Cambridge University Press, 2006), 31–38.

Hursthouse, Rosalind, "Virtue Ethics," *The Stanford Encyclopedia of Philosophy*, Fall 2013 Edition, Edward N. Zalta (ed.), http://plato.stanford.edu/archives/fall2013/entries/ethics-virtue/.

"Practical Wisdom: A Mundane Account," *Proceedings of the Aristotelian Society*, 106 (2006), 285–309.

On Virtue Ethics (Oxford: Oxford University Press, 1999).

Hutchinson, D.S., "Doctrines of the Mean and the Debate Concerning Skills in Fourth-Century Medicine, Rhetoric, and Ethics," *Apeiron*, 21 (1988), 17–52.

Inzlicht, Michael, Berkman, Elliot, and Elkins-Brown, Nathaniel, "The Neuroscience of 'Ego Depletion': How the Brain Can Help Us Understand why Self-control Seems Limited," in Harmon-Jones, Eddie and Inzlicht, Michael (eds.), *Social Neuroscience: Biological Approaches to Social Psychology* (New York: Routledge, 2016), 101–123.

Isen, A., Clark, M., and Schwartz, M., "Duration of the Effect of Good Mood on Helping: 'Footprints on the Sands of Time'," *Journal of Personality and Social Psychology*, 34 (1976), 385–393.

Isen, A. and P. Levin, "Effect of Feeling Good on Helping: Cookies and Kindness," *Journal of Personality and Social Psychology*, 21 (1972), 384–388.

Jacobson, Daniel, "Seeing by Feeling: Virtues, Skills, and Moral Perception," *Ethical Theory and Moral Practice*, 8 (2005), 387–409.

Jansson, Anders, "Goal Achievement and Mental Models in Everyday Decision Making," in Juslin, Peter and Montgomery, Henry (eds.), *Judgment and Decision Making: Neo-Brunswikian and Process-Tracing Approaches* (London: Lawrence Erlbaum Associates, 1999), 23–43.

Johnson, Robert, "Virtue and Right," *Ethics*, 113 (2003), 810–834.

Jourden, Forest J., Bandura, Albert, and Banfield, Jason T., "The Impact of Conceptions of Ability on Self-Regulatory Factors and Motor Skill," *Journal of Sport & Exercise Psychology*, 8 (1991), 213–226.

Kahneman, Daniel, *Thinking, Fast and Slow* (New York: Farrar, Straus and Giroux, 2011).

Kahneman, Daniel and Klein, Gary, "Conditions for Intuitive Expertise: A Failure to Disagree," *American Psychologist*, 64:6 (2009), 515–526.

Keren, Gideon and Schul, Yaccov, "Two Is Not Always Better than One: A Critical Evaluation of Two-System Theories," *Perspectives on Psychological Science*, 4 (2009), 533–550.

King, Nathan, "Responsibilist Virtue Epistemology: A Reply to the Situationist Challenge," *The Philosophical Quarterly*, 64 (2014), 243–253.

Kirkeby, Inge, "Transferable Knowledge: An Interview with Bent Flyvbjerg," *Architectural Research Quarterly*, 15:1 (2011), 9–14.

Klein, Gary A. and Hoffman, Robert R., "Seeing the Invisible: Perceptual-Cognitive Aspects of Expertise," in Rabinowitz, Mitchell (ed.), *Cognitive Science Foundations of Instruction* (Hillsdale, NJ: Erlbaum, 1993).

Krampe, Ralf and Charness, Neil, "Aging and Expertise," in Ericsson, K. Anders (ed.), *The Cambridge Handbook of Expertise and Expert Performance* (Cambridge: Cambridge University Press, 2006), 723–742.

LaBarge, Scott, "Socrates and Moral Expertise," in Rasmussen, Lisa. M. (ed.), *Ethics Expertise: History, Contemporary Perspectives, and Applications* (The Netherlands: Springer, 2005), 15–38.

Lapsley, Daniel and Hill, Patrick, "On Dual Processing and Heuristic Approaches to Moral Cognition," *Journal of Moral Education*, 37:3 (2008), 313–332.

Lapsley, Daniel and Narvaez, Darcia, "A Social-Cognitive Approach to the Moral Personality," in Lapsley, Daniel K. and Narvaez, Darcia (eds.), *Moral Development, Self and Identity: Essays in Honor of Augusto Blasi* (Mahwah, NJ: Erlbaum, 2004), 189–212.

Latané, Bibb and Darley, John M., *The Unresponsive Bystander: Why Doesn't He Help?* (New York: Appleton-Century-Crofts, 1970,).

Loehr, James E., *The Mental Game* (New York: Plume, 1991).

Ludwig, Timothy D. and Geller, E. Scott, "Assigned versus Participatory Goal Setting and Response Generalization," *Journal of Applied Psychology*, 82 (1997), 253–261.

Lukes, Steven, "Comment: Do People Have Character Traits?," in Mantzavinos, Chrysostomos (ed.), *Philosophy of the Social Sciences: Philosophical Theory and Scientific Practice* (New York: Cambridge University Press, 2009), 291–298.

Mathews, K. E. and Cannon, L. K., "Environmental Noise Level as a Determinant of Helping Behavior," *Journal of Personality and Social Psychology*, 32 (1975), 571–577.

McDowell, John, "Virtue and Reason," *The Monist*, 62:3 (1979), 331–350.

Mele, Alfred R. and Shepherd, Joshua, "Situationism and Agency," *Journal of Practical Ethics*, 1 (2014), 62–83.

Merritt, Maria W., Doris, John M., and Harman, Gilbert, "Character," in John Michael Doris (ed.), *The Moral Psychology Handbook* (Oxford University Press, 2010), 355–401.

Milgram, Stanley, *Obedience to Authority* (New York: Harper and Row, 1974)

Miller, Christian, "Character and Situationism: New Directions," *Ethical Theory and Moral Practice*, 20:3 (2017), 459–471.

Miller, Christian B., "Honesty," in Sinnott-Armstrong, Walter and Miller, Christian B. (eds.), *Moral Psychology, Vol. 5: Virtue and Character* (Cambridge: MIT Press, 2017), 237–273.

"Russell on Acquiring Virtue," in Alfano, Mark (ed.), *Current Controversies in Virtue Theory* (New York: Routledge, 2015), 106–117.

Character and Moral Psychology (New York: Oxford University Press, 2014).

"The Problem of Character," in Van Hooft, Stan (ed.), *The Handbook of Virtue Ethics* (New York: Routledge, 2014), 418–429.

Moral Character: An Empirical Theory (Oxford: Oxford University Press, 2013).

Miscevic, Nenad. "Virtue-Based Epistemology and the Centrality of Truth (Towards a Strong Virtue Epistemology)," *Acta Analytica*, 22 (2007), 239–266.

Mischel, W. and Y. Shoda. "A Cognitive-Affective System Theory of Personality: Reconceptualizing Situations, Dispositions, Dynamics, and Invariance in Personality Structure," *Psychological Review*, 102 (1995), 246–268.

Montmarquet, James, "Ramsify (by All Means) – but Do Not 'Dumb Down' the Moral Virtues," in Mark Alfano (ed.), *Current Controversies in Virtue Theory* (New York: Routledge, 2015), 136–146.

Moore, Celia, "Moral Disengagement in Processes of Organizational Corruption," *Journal of Business Ethics*, 80 (2008), 129–139.

Moskowitz, Gordon B., "The Implicit Volition Model: The Unconscious Nature of Goal Pursuit," in Sherman, Jeffrey W., Gawronski, Bertram, and Trope, Yaacov, *Dual-Process Theories of the Social Mind* (New York: The Guilford Press, 2014), 400–422.

Moskowitz, Gordon B., Gollwitzer, Peter M., Wasel, Wolfgang, and Schaal, Bernd, "Preconscious Control of Stereotype Activation through Chronic Egalitarian Goals," *Journal of Personality and Social Psychology*, 77: 1 (1999), 167–184.

Nakamura, Jeanne and Csikszentmihalyi, Mihaly, "The Concept of Flow," in Snyder, C. R. and Lopez, S. J. (eds.), *Oxford Handbook of Positive Psychology* (New York: Oxford University Press, 2009), 89–105.

Narvaez, Darcia, "Wisdom as Mature Moral Functioning: Insights from Developmental Psychology and Neurobiology," in Jones, Mark, Lewis, Paul, and Reffitt, Kelly (eds.), *Toward Human Flourishing: Character, Practical Wisdom and Professional Formation* (Macon, GA: Mercer University Press, 2013).

"De neurobiology van ons morel functioneren [The neurobiology of moral formation and moral functioning]" *Pastorale Perspectieven*, 153:4 (2011), 10–18.

"Integrative Ethical Education," in Killen, Melanie and Smetana, Judith (eds.), *Handbook of Moral Development* (Mahwah, NJ: Erlbaum, 2006), 703–733.

"The Neo-Kohlbergian Tradition and Beyond: Schemas, Expertise and Character," in Carlo, Gustav and Pope-Edwards, Carolyn (eds.), *Nebraska Symposium on Motivation, Vol. 51: Moral Motivation through the Lifespan* (Lincoln, NE: University of Nebraska Press, 2005), 119–163.

Narvaez, Darcia, Gleason, Tracy and Mitchell, Christyan, "Moral Virtue and Practical Wisdom: Theme Comprehension in Children, Youth and Adults," *Journal of Genetic Psychology*, 171:4 (2010), 1–26.

Narvaez, Darcia and Lapsley, Daniel, "The Psychological Foundations of Everyday Morality and Moral Expertise," in Lapsley, Daniel K. and Power, F. Clark (eds.) *Character Psychology and Character Education* (Notre Dame: IN: University of Notre Dame Press, 2005), 140–165.

Olin, Lauren and Doris, John M., "Vicious Minds: Virtue Epistemology, Cognition, and Skepticism," *Philosophical Studies*, 168 (2014), 665–692.

Parry, Richard, "*Episteme* and *Techne*," *The Stanford Encyclopedia of Philosophy* (Fall 2014 Edition), Edward N. Zalta (ed.), http://plato.stanford .edu/archives/fall2014/entries/episteme-techne.

Plant, E. Ashby, Peruche, B. Michelle, and Butz, David A., "Eliminating Automatic Racial Bias: Making Race Non-Diagnostic for Responses to Criminal Suspects," *Journal of Experimental Social Psychology*, 41 (2005), 141–156.

Pritchard, Duncan, "Virtue Epistemology and the Acquisition of Knowledge," *Philosophical Explorations*, 8:3 (2005), 229–243.

Railton, Peter, "Social Skill and Empathetic Modelling," Presented at Virtue and Skill Workshop, Centre for the Study of Mind in Nature, University of Oslo, Norway (June 1–2, 2015).

"The Affective Dog and Its Rational Tale: Intuition and Attunement," *Ethics*, 124 (2014), 813–859.

Roberts, Bob, "Will Power and the Virtues," *The Philosophical Review*, 93:2 (1984), 227–247.

Ross, Karol, Shafer, Jennifer, and Klein, Gary, "Professional Judgments and "Naturalistic Decision Making," in Ericsson, K. Anders (ed.), *The Cambridge Handbook of Expertise and Expert Performance* (Cambridge: Cambridge University Press, 2006), 403–419.

Rouse, William B. and Morris, Nancy M, "On Looking into the Black Box: Prospects and Limits in the Search for Mental Models" (No. DTIC #AD-A159080). (Atlanta, GA: Center for Man-Machine Systems Research, Georgia Institute of Technology, 1985).

Rousseau, Jean-Jacques, *Origin of Inequality*, GDH Cole (trans), (London: Cosmo Classics, 2005).

Russell, Daniel C., "From Personality to Character to Virtue," in Mark Alfano (ed.), *Current Controversies in Virtue Theory* (New York: Routledge, 2015), 92–105.

    Practical Intelligence and the Virtues (New York: Oxford University Press, 2009).

Ryle, Gilbert, *The Concept of Mind*, (New York: Routledge, 2009).

    "On Forgetting the Difference between Right and Wrong," in Melden, A. I. (ed.), *Essays in Moral Philosophy* (Seattle: University of Washington Press, 1958).

Sabini, John and Silver, Maury, "Lack of Character? Situationism Critiqued," *Ethics*, 115: 3 (2005), 535–562.

Seligman, Martin E. P., Railton, Peter, Baumeister, Roy F., and Sripada, Chandra, "Navigating into the Future or Driven by the Past," *Perspectives on Psychological Science*, 8:2 (2013), 119–141.

Snow, Nancy E., "Virtue and Oppression," in Mark Alfano (ed.), *Current Controversies in Virtue Theory* (New York: Routledge, 2015), 49–58.

    Virtue as Social Intelligence: An Empirically Grounded Theory (New York: Routledge, 2010).

    "Habitual Virtuous Actions and Automaticity," *Ethical Theory and Moral Practice*, 9 (2006), 545–561.

Sosa, Ernest, "Virtue Epistemology: Character versus Competence," in Mark Alfano (ed.), *Current Controversies in Virtue Theory* (Routledge, 2015), 62–74.

    "Situations against Virtues: The Situationist Attack on Virtue Theory," in Mantzavinos, Chrysostomos (ed.), *Philosophy of the Social Sciences: Philosophical Theory and Scientific Practice* (New York: Cambridge University Press, 2009), 274–290.

    A Virtue Epistemology: Apt Belief and Reflective Knowledge, Vol. 1 (Oxford: Oxford University Press, 2007).

Stalnaker, Aaron, "Virtue as Mastery in Early Confucianism," *Journal of Religious Ethics* 38:3 (2010), 404–428.

Stanley, Jason, *Know How* (Oxford: Oxford University Press, 2011).

Stanley, Jason and Williamson, Timothy, "Knowing How," *Journal of Philosophy*, 98:8 (2001), 414–444.

Steutel, Jan, "The Virtues of Will-Power: Self-Control and Deliberation," in Carr, David and Steutel, Jan (eds.), *Virtue Ethics and Moral Education* (London and New York, Routledge, 1999).

Stichter, Matt, "Practical Skills and Practical Wisdom in Virtue," *Australasian Journal of Philosophy,* 94:3 (2016): 435–448.

    "Philosophical and Psychological Accounts of Expertise and Experts," *Humana. Mente – Journal of Philosophical Studies*, 28: Experts and Expertise. Interdisciplinary Issues (2015).

    "Virtues as Skills in Virtue Epistemology," *Journal of Philosophical Research*, 38 (2013), 331–346.

"Virtues, Skills, and Right Action," *Ethical Theory and Moral Practice*, 14 (2011): 73–86.

"Ethical Expertise," *Ethical Theory and Moral Practice*, 10 (2007), 183–194.

"The Skill Model of Virtue," *Philosophy in the Contemporary World*, 14 (2007): 39–49.

Swartwood, Jason, "Wisdom as an Expert Skill," *Ethical Theory and Moral Practice*, 16 (2013), 511–528.

Sylvan, Kurt, "Veritism Unswamped," *Mind*, fzwo70, https://doi.org/10.1093/mind/fzwo7. Published 28 July 2017.

Tanner, Carmen and Christen, Markus, "Moral Intelligence – A Framework for Understanding Moral Competences," in Christen, Markus, van Schaik, Carel, Fischer, Johannes, and Huppenbauer, Markus (eds.), *Empirically Informed Ethics: Morality between Facts and Norms* (Switzerland: Springer, 2014), 119–136.

Tanner, Carmen and Medin, Douglas L., "Protected Values: No Omission Bias and No framing Effects," *Psychonomic Bulletin & Review*, 11:1 (2004), 185–191.

Tanney, Julia, "Rethinking Ryle: A Critical Discussion of the Concept of Mind," in Gilbert Ryle, *The Concept of Mind*, (New York: Routledge, 2009), xxviii.

Tenbrunsel, Ann E., and Messick, David M., "Ethical Fading: The Role of Self-Deception in Unethical Behavior," *Social Justice Research*, 17:2 (2004), 223–236.

Thornberg, Robert and Jungert, Tomas, "Bystander Behavior in Bullying Situations: Basic Moral Sensitivity, Moral Disengagement and Defender Self-Efficacy," *Journal of Adolescence*, 36:3 (2013), 475–483.

Tiberius, Valerie, "In Defense of Reflection," *Philosophical Issues*, 23: Epistemic Agency (2013), 223–243.

Tiberius, Valerie and Swartwood, Jason, "Wisdom Revisited: A Case Study in Normative Theorizing," *Philosophical Explorations*, 14:3 (2011), 277–295.

Trope, Yaacov and Liberman, Nira, "Construal-Level Theory of Psychological Distance," *Psychological Review*, 117:2 (2010), 440–463.

Trötschel, Roman and Gollwitzer, Peter M., "Implementation Intentions and the Willful Pursuit of Prosocial Goals in Negotiations," *Journal of Experimental Social Psychology*, 43 (2007), 579–598.

Tversky, Amos and Kahneman, Daniel, "The Framing of Decisions and the Psychology of Choice," *Science*, 211:30 (1981), 453–457.

Van Zyl, Liezl, "Against Radical Pluralism," in Mark Alfano (ed.), *Current Controversies in Virtue Theory* (New York: Routledge, 2015), 22–32.

Voss, James F. and Wiley, Jennifer, "Expertise in History," in Ericsson, K. Anders (ed.), *The Cambridge Handbook of Expertise and Expert Performance* (Cambridge: Cambridge University Press, 2006), 569–586.

Wallace, James, *Virtues and Vices* (Ithaca, NY: Cornell University Press, 1978).

Watson, Gary, "Two Faces of Responsibility," in *Agency and Answerability: Selected Essays* (Oxford: Oxford University Press, 2004).

Webb, Thomas L. and Sheeran, Paschal, "Does Changing Behavioral Intentions Engender Behavior Change? A Meta-Analysis of the Experimental Evidence," *Psychological Bulletin*, 132: 2 (2006), 249–268.

Weinstein, Bruce D., "The Possibility of Ethical Expertise," *Theoretical Medicine* 15 (1994), 61–75.

Whitehead, Alfred North, *An Introduction to Mathematics* (New York: Henry Holt and Company, 1911).

Wieber, Frank, Gollwitzer, Peter M., and Sheeran, Paschal, "Strategic Regulation of Mimicry Effects by Implementation Intentions," *Journal of Experimental Social Psychology*, 53 (2014), 31–39.

Wilson, T. D., Lisle, D. J., Schooler, J. W., Hodges, S. D., Klaaren, K. J., and LaFleur, S. J., "Introspecting about Reasons Can Reduce Post-Choice Satisfaction," *Personality and Social Psychology Bulletin,* 19 (1993), 331–359.

Wilson, T. D. and Schooler, J. W., "Thinking Too Much: Introspection Can Reduce the Quality of Preferences and Decision," *Journal of Personality and Social Psychology*, 60 (1991), 181–192.

Wolf, Susan, "Moral Psychology and the Unity of the Virtues," *Ratio*, 20:2 (2007), 145–167.

Wu, Wayne, "Mental Action and the Threat of Automaticity," in Clark, Andy, Kiverstein, Julian and Vierkant, Tillman (eds.), *Decomposing the Will* (Oxford: Oxford University Press, 2013), 244–261.

Yarrow, Kielan, Brown, Peter and Krakauer, John W., "Inside the Brain of an Elite Athlete: the Neural Processes that Support High Achievement in Sports," *Nature Reviews Neuroscience*, 10:8 (2009), 585–596.

Zagzebski, Linda, *Virtues of the Mind* (Cambridge: Cambridge University Press, 1996).

Zimmerman, Barry J., "Development and Adaptation of Expertise: The Role of Self-Regulatory Processes and Beliefs," in Ericsson, K. Anders (ed.), *The Cambridge Handbook of Expertise and Expert Performance* (Cambridge: Cambridge University Press, 2006), 705–722.

  "Attaining Self-Regulation: A Social Cognitive Perspective," in Boekaerts, Monique, Pintrich, Paul R., and Zeidner, Moshe (eds.), *Handbook of Self-Regulation* (San Diego: Academic Press, 2000), 13–39.

Zsambok, Caroline E., "Naturalistic Decision Making – Where Are We Now?," in Zsambok, Caroline E. and Klein, Gary (eds.), *Naturalistic Decision Making* (New Jersey: Erlbaum, 1997), 17–28.

Index

CPSIA information can be obtained
at www.ICGtesting.com
Printed in the USA
LVHW022339110123
736950LV00004B/487

9 781108 459389